D0897609

HOW NEW YORK
BECAME AMERICAN,
1890–1924

THE JOHNS HOPKINS UNIVERSITY PRESS   BALTIMORE

HOW
NEW YORK
BECAME
AMERICAN,
1890–1924

Angela M. Blake

9 8 7 6 5 4 3 2 1

The Johns Hopkins University Press
2715 North Charles Street
Baltimore, Maryland 21218-4363
www.press.jhu.edu

Library of Congress Cataloging-in-Publication Data
Blake, Angela M.
    How New York became American, 1890–1924 / Angela M. Blake.
        p.   cm.
    Includes bibliographical references and index.
    ISBN 0-8018-8293-1 (hardcover : alk. paper)
    1. New York (N.Y.—History—1898–1951. 2. New York (N.Y.)—
History—1865–1898. 3. New York (N.Y.)—Public opinion. 4. National
characteristics, American. 5. Public opinion—United States. 6. New
York (N.Y.)—Economic conditions. 7. City and town life—New York
(State)—New York—History. 8. City planning—New York (State)—New
York—History. 9. Tourism—New York (State)—New York—History.
10. Architecture—New York (State)—New York—History. I. Title.
F128.5.B59 2006
974.7′1—dc22   2005018073

A catalog record for this book is available from the British Library.

CONTENTS

ILLUSTRATIONS

ACKNOWLEDGMENTS

With a project of such long duration—originally my doctoral dissertation and then a book—the individuals and institutions to whom I owe thanks are legion. In the first instance I wish to acknowledge the intellectual and moral support provided to me by the Department of History at American University, Washington, D.C. When I arrived from England to begin graduate work, I knew little about the career path onto which I had unwittingly stepped. Luckily for me, the Department of History and the College of Arts and Sciences decided I was a good investment and provided me with four years of full and generous funding, as well as with fine teaching and professional training.

The first two faculty members I met in the Department of History, Michael Kazin and Peter Kuznick, became my chief mentors. I am grateful to them both for leading by example as gifted teachers, as historians, as advisers, as cheerleaders, as politically engaged academics, and as generous human beings. I also benefited greatly from the contributions of Vanessa Schwartz, during her time as a faculty member in A.U.'s History Department, and of Roy Rosenzweig. I was fortunate to work with Vanessa as her student and as her research and teaching assistant. In her capacity as an innovative and deeply intelligent cultural historian, Vanessa helped shape many of the questions that drive this book as well as the method by which I answer them. As a member of my dissertation committee, Roy Rosenzweig gave generously of his time, his knowledge of New York history, and his critical judgment, far beyond what I had any right to expect. Michael, Peter, Vanessa, and Roy have all written countless letters of recommendation for me, greatly aiding my successful pursuit of fellowships, grants, and jobs. I thank them all for their support.

Such support helped me receive generous funding from a variety of sources to enable the research and writing of the dissertation and of the book. In addition to the funding I received from American University, I would like to acknowledge the support provided by a Junior Fellowship in Landscape Architecture studies at Harvard University's Dumbarton Oaks center, and by both a Graduate Student Fellowship and a Pre-Doctoral Fellowship at the Smithsonian Institution's National Museum of American History. I would like to thank the senior scholars who guided my research at those institutions: Terence Young at Dumbarton Oaks, and Charles McGovern, Fath Davis Ruffins, and David Haberstich at the Smithsonian. My fellow Fellows at both of those institutions as well as my grad student cohort at A.U. provided much-needed actual fellowship and intellectual support. In particular I received great sustenance from the company of Liz Stewart, Joseph Henning, Louise Mozingo, Peggy Shaffer, Catherine Cocks, Cathy Gudis, Sarah Johnson, Andy Smith, and David Serlin.

The archivists and librarians at Dumbarton Oaks and at the Smithsonian also guided and supported my research in innumerable ways, and I thank them all. A year's funding from A.U. took me to New York to conduct archival research, and, during those eight months, I received invaluable assistance from the librarians at the New York Public Library, especially those in the Map Division, and at the New-York Historical Society and the American Museum of Natural History. I worked as a volunteer researcher at the Museum of the City of New York that same year and was privileged to work with and learn from Barbara Buff, then in the Museum's Division of Paintings and Sculpture. Barbara encouraged my dissertation research, put me in touch with others studying New York's visual culture and history, and appointed herself my honorary Jewish Mother—a figure essential to any British WASP studying New York! During a year's sojourn in Los Angeles while completing the dissertation, I received generous office space and library services support from the Getty Research Institute, making possible the final months of writing.

The Department of History at the University of Toronto has provided me with both a livelihood and the opportunity to develop undergraduate and graduate classes that built on and furthered my research interests. I would like to acknowledge the support shown me by my fellow Americanist Arthur Sheps, by David Hulchanski at the Centre for Urban and Community Studies, and by my students at the university's Scarborough and St. George campuses. My colleagues at Miami University of Ohio in the Department of Communication and the American Studies program have made me most welcome and I am happy to see this book published in my new academic home. Special thanks to Peggy Shaffer and Gary Shulman.

Last, but certainly not least, friends and family in England, the United States, and now Canada provided the bedrock support I could not have done without. Heartfelt thanks to my parents Denis and Anne Blake, my siblings Helen, Robert, and David, and my friends Jane Speare, Bo Priestley, Tessa Wright, Roger Brown, Richard Walker, Liz Shayne, Brooke Bumpers, Gordon Low, Mieke Meurs, Joy Hackel, and Mark Kingwell. My greatest debt, and the one I bear with the deepest thanks and will attempt to repay with the greatest joy, is to my partner and fellow scholar Elspeth Brown. Her love, her ability to make me laugh out loud, and her great intelligence sustain me.

HOW NEW YORK
BECAME AMERICAN,
1890–1924

INTRODUCTION

Now, I do not know New York. I can not interpret it. I do not know what its "message" is. New York is too large to know. Too many things are simultaneously true of it.

FPA [Franklin P. Adams], *Everybody's Magazine*, December 1916

"City of Living Death," "Metropolis of the Western World," "City of Dreadful Height," "World's Prize Borough of Bunk," "Little Old New York": between 1890 and the mid-1920s, urban reformers, newspaper men, city officials, "old" New Yorkers, business boosters, and tourism promoters all pitched their notions of what New York City *was,* what the city "meant," where it fit in American culture and nationhood. Guided by political and commercial interests, each worked to promote a clear image of a city frequently perceived and experienced as unknowable and overwhelming. This book looks at the images and arguments these cultural arbiters, the "spin doctors" of their own time and place, employed to make New York "knowable" to their constituents and consumers, and thus to stabilize the city's image as a verifiable, worthwhile, "American" place. In a period of great tension over immigration and national identity, New York's Americanness became a measure of its national value as well as, potentially, its appeal to tourists. New York's appeal to tourists as a place both to see America and to see the world ultimately won out over characterizations of New York as dangerous, dirty, and downright un-American.

Who cares if a city seems knowable, comprehensible? And why? At least two groups of people care: those invested in attracting new workers, new residents, investors, or tourists to the city and those thinking of visiting the city as tourists, taking up residence, or doing business in the city. A current example of a city with a "knowability" problem is Los Angeles. Ask a typical non-Angeleno her opinion of Los Angeles, and, whether or not she has ever been there, her view of the city is likely to be negative. She might grimace and shake her head at the mere mention of the city. Los Angeles, she might say, is a placeless sort of a place—sprawling, with no discernible center, crisscrossed by multilane freeways, encased in thick layers of smog, and often lacking the basic neighborliness of sidewalks. Furthermore, your informer will tell you (her temperature rising), the city is home to a multiracial population, many of whom are illegal immigrants, and some of whom are surely responsible for the city's reputedly high rate of violent crime and the occasional riot. Most of these opinions, if not based on actual (though usually brief) experiences of Los Angeles, are gleaned from the informational mire of television, movies, fiction, newspaper stories, and the conversational swamp of gossip and myth. All in all, these views are, allowing for technological changes, not too different from the opinions held by many Americans about early twentieth-century New York. Further, I would argue that present-day Los Angeles, like early twentieth-century New York, also veers in the mass media–produced "national imagination" between the categories of a very American place and a very *un*-American place.

What is "American"? What is an "American place"? And why should such an identity, such a label, matter? Of course, notions of what is "American" change over time, contingent as they are on questions of race, ethnicity, ideas of national identity, regional identities and tensions, and the formation of a legally bounded nation state. The naming of a person, place, or thing as "American" is a hegemonic project crucial to the construction, stabilization, and preservation of a national identity. As such, it is a deeply contested project. The interrogation of what is "American" has been the project of American Studies scholarship since the field's inception in the 1930s. The discipline's evolution maps the political and cultural vicissitudes of critical engagement with the meaning of "America" in a century defined by the globalization of American culture and military power and also marked by the domestic fragility of a cohesive national identity.[1] My book investigates the power and cultural importance of representations of Americanness during a period—from the "closing" of the American frontier to the closing of the nation's doors to most immigrants—when the establishment of what (and who) was American took center stage in efforts to develop national markets, set national boundaries, build an industrial workforce, establish American power overseas, and come to terms with a diverse population and electorate. The Americanization of New York was, I argue, central to those efforts.

From the turn of the twentieth century through the 1920s, guidebooks, stereographs, postcards, and tourist maps and brochures gradually made the city visually and practically available to American tourists. When the well-known journalist Franklin P. Adams, in a 1916 article comparing how tourists and residents viewed the city, wrote that New York was "too large to know. . . . Too many things are simultaneously true of it," producers of tourist ephemera were actually in the midst of simplifying the city into a set of convenient itineraries and sites. By the mid-1920s, tourists could certainly experience New York as a coherent place, choosing from a range of itineraries drawn from the plethora of guidebooks and other publications that provided colorful descriptions of the pleasures offered by New York City.

The geometric layout of the city, which should have made New York easier to navigate and to comprehend, in practice added to the city's visual impenetrability. New York was a city founded by traders and designed for commerce, an orientation that has continued to shape the city's culture and built environment. The city commissioners imposed the grid-pattern street plan in 1811, their concerns at the time being the easy parceling and selling of property rather than whatever aesthetic or practical problems were caused by the long, narrow blocks. By the close of the nineteenth century, the relentless grid imposed across almost the entire city had shaped New York's built environment into an increasingly high-walled maze. It was visually oppressive. Unlike Paris, which was radically—some would say brutally—rebuilt and re-planned by Baron Georges Eugene Haussmann in the mid–nineteenth century, New York's street plan allowed for no wide boulevards cutting across the grid and few squares or plazas offering vistas, open sight lines, or spaces from which to gaze upon the city's architecture or population. Manhattan's mostly flat topography only added to the problem. Ironically, it took the development of a specific form of commercial practice—mass tourism—to negate the visual and spatial problems imposed on the city during an earlier commercial era.[2]

It was not just the physical or spatial aspects of New York that made the city seem unknowable in the early twentieth century. As Adams, a.k.a. "FPA," wrote, too many things were simultaneously true of the city. What New York *was* or *meant* lay mostly in the eye of the beholder. However, FPA's particular perspective was that of the resident, in his case a sophisticated "insider" who made his living writing about the city. In the article from which this introduction's epigraph is taken, FPA objected to the way visitors came to New York, saw a few tourist sites, and then returned home assuming they "knew" the city. To the long-term resident insider like FPA, a tourist's estimation of New York would certainly have seemed naive compared to his own nuanced knowledge of the place. However, to those profiting from tourism, keeping New York relatively simple was good business sense.

To those with an interest in selling some aspect of the city, whether for political or commercial gain, it was vital to reduce New York to a single image or interpretation. For much of this period, to the middle-class constituents and consumers courted as much by social reformers as by business boosters, New York's identity lacked clarity, both as experienced at street level and in terms of the city's meaning across the nation. Such lack of clarity worked against the interests of those trying to wring any form of capital from the image of New York. In the chapters that follow, I show not only how and why "so many things" were "simultaneously true" of New York, but also how politicians, reformers, businessmen, and tourism promoters actually contributed to New York's multiple meanings in their respective efforts to assign the city a singular public image. How New York became a coherent, marketable "American" place ultimately resulted from the choices the American public made among these competing versions of New York.

Those versions of New York on offer between 1890 and 1924 drew partly on older perceptions of the city. For example, the popular late–nineteenth century description of New York as a city divided into areas of "darkness and daylight"—the depraved and the demure, the ghastly and the glamorous. Or, from the same era, the popular "bird's eye view" portraits of the city, which provided an imagined view of the city as if seen from the skies above, emphasizing the important buildings, the bridges, and the sheer magnitude of the metropolis. The later nineteenth- and early twentieth-century versions of New York updated those views of the city, making use of the new technologies of graphic representation, such as documentary photography, the halftone process (used to reproduce photographs in books and newspapers), and tightly themed maps. Each version and each image had the potential not only to shape New York's national significance but also to designate New York as a particular *type* of "place": as the exemplar of urban life's numerous ills or of a new urban civilization; as America's representative metropolis or as a city of foreign cultures grafted on to America's shore.

The motivation to resolve New York's identity problems in this period stemmed from the new national role the city assumed, eagerly supported by New York's political and commercial leaders. Between 1890 and 1924, New York became the nation's metropolis, the de facto capital of the United States. The city's natural geography and earlier nineteenth-century industrial and infrastructural developments had established the foundations for New York's early twentieth-century dominance.

Located between the industrialized and heavily populated lower New England states and the commercial and agricultural areas of the Chesapeake and Potomac regions, New York provided a transportation and market hub for much of America's national and international trade. The opening of the Erie Canal between Albany and Buffalo in 1825 strengthened this position by linking the city through to the Great Lakes region and the western interior. New York's location and thriving port made it the center of the nation's commerce, with the leading banks and finance organizations ensconced in the city. As the nation's major conduit for both money and goods, New York soon became the center for commercial information.

By 1900 New York had also achieved cultural dominance as the undisputed center of the publishing industry and home to the nation's leading writers, journalists, and artists. Also headquartered in New York was the burgeoning entertainment business. The city's vaudeville and Broadway theater shows garnered national attention, making New York the natural base for the early film industry, for the radio networks starting in the 1920s, and later for television. All of these geographic and economic factors drew vast populations to New York, both from within the nation and from overseas. As early as 1850, New York was already the major point of entry for European immigration. Between 1880 and 1919, over twenty-three million immigrants arrived from Europe; almost seventy-five percent of them came ashore in New York. Although many thousands moved on to industrial and agricultural employment in the northeastern, midwestern and western states, thousands of others stayed in the city. By the turn of the century, about forty percent of the city's population was foreign-born; by 1930, after the 1924 Johnson-Reed immigration act had brought an end to mass immigration, the city was still home to two million foreign-born residents—not counting the many more of foreign parentage—out of a population approaching seven million.[3]

The nation's official capital, Washington, D.C., did not yet loom large in the national imagination as America's representative city, although Pierre L'Enfant's early nineteenth-century design for Washington had intended to create just such an aura. Capital cities traditionally created greater expectations of this type of symbolic coherence because of their national and international roles. It was important, for example, that Paris be read as "France" and London as "Britain," and rulers of both nations worked hard over the centuries to achieve those ends. In a world still shaped by the power of Europe and the Atlantic world, New York, the entry point for goods and people from Europe, constituted America's public face. At stake, therefore, in the image of New York City was the image of America itself.

Chicago, the obvious comparison city for this time period, did not have an American identity problem. Situated in the heart of the Midwest, providing markets for the rich agricultural areas around it, and the industrial base where many of the nation's raw materials were processed, there was no doubt about Chicago's Americanism. Although individual Chicagoans, such as labor activists, might have been labeled "un-American," city boosters rarely questioned the American identity of "Nature's metropolis." In this period, Chicago, reborn from the ashes of its 1870 fire, was also the "City of Big Shoulders," a reference to the city's burgeoning population of industrial manual laborers. New York, on the other hand, positioned at the edge of the nation, while the metaphorical "center" of so much, in fact existed on the nation's margins. The city on the Hudson had one foot in the Atlantic Ocean, looking east to Europe more often than west to the rest of the nation for its aesthetic and social cues. In an era of growing American nationalism, New York's mixture of American and European culture, style, and population made the city's national identity suspect to an American middle class, residing outside the nation's major urban centers, increasingly committed to an idea of national identity grounded in native-born, Anglo-American values. New York, though an important manufacturing center, seemed to lack the republican, producerist ethic apparently embodied in Chicago. New York was a broker city, a place where powerful men made deals and gambled with the products of places like Chicago.[4]

New York's moral reputation also failed to live up to the dominant middle-class Protestant American ideals of self-control, sobriety, and sexual purity—to the consternation of ministers and social reformers and to the delight of purveyors of racy urban literature and the city's urban amusements. The early decades of the nineteenth century had seen the production of a wealth of descriptive literature about New York, which offered readers a vicarious experience of the seamier sides of city life—the bars, brothels, and crime-ridden areas that presented a mix of pleasure and danger apparently peculiar to city life. With titles like *Lights and Shadows of New York Life, New York By Sunlight and Gaslight, New York by Gas-Light, New York in Slices: By an Experienced Carver,* and various titles purporting to describe the "mysteries" and "miseries" of the city, such guides participated in a rhetoric about cities common on both sides of the Atlantic. Paris and London had similar urban guides, offering glimpses of the "shadows" of Montmartre or the East End.[5]

These guides and city portraits claimed to offer their readers a vicarious experience of the city, of both "its splendors and wretchedness," an accounting so vivid as to make a trip to the city unnecessary.[6] Alternatively, the reader could visit the city, forewarned and thus forearmed about the "vicinity of sin."[7] As James McCabe warned the readers of his 1872 *Lights and Shadows of New York Life,* "The curiosity of all persons concerning the darker side of city life can be fully satisfied by a perusal of the sketches presented in this volume. It is not safe for a stranger to undertake to explore these places for himself. . . . The path of safety which is pointed out in these pages is the only one for either citizen or stranger."[8] Of course, as McCabe and his fellow sensationalist authors well knew, such books catered to the many visitors, usually male, who wanted to seek out the city's shadowy areas during their urban sojourns.

Beginning in the 1890s, the increasingly valuable business of urban pleasure travel constructed a commercial geography of the city beyond the old "darkness and daylight," "sunlight and shadow" dichotomies of nineteenth-century representations of New York. The growing tourist industry in New York during this period demanded both the development of the amenities necessary for tourism and the representation and promotion of the city as "a fine place to visit." The future success and development of the industry also required a more diverse group of visitor-consumers than the white males who voraciously purchased the earlier guides. The businesses of the tourist industry—sightseeing omnibus companies, restaurants, hotels, popular theatres—had to appeal to a mass audience including a broad middle class of men, women, and children from geographically (and to some extent culturally) varied backgrounds. Drawing such a group of visitors to New York required those with a commercial interest in tourism to remake the city's image. The forces of commerce banded together to produce growing quantities of guidebooks, stereographs, souvenirs, postcards, and maps. The hotel industry expanded rapidly, sponsoring the production of large amounts of such tourist ephemera. Companies offering tours of various parts of the city or of its surrounding waterways advertised their services in guidebooks, newspapers, and periodicals.[9]

All these products and services not only drew visitors to the city but also, by the mid-1920s, took them all over the city—from Chinatown to Harlem, and from the downtown skyscrapers to the uptown halls of art and culture. This traversing of the city by visitors eager for entertainment and new sights broke down the old geography of "darkness and daylight," of good and bad areas. By 1932, the Empire State Sightseeing Company offered motor coach tours of the city under the rubric "East Side, West Side, All Around the Town," quoting the song about New York first written in the 1890s and revived in the 1920s. The company's fold-out pamphlet map and brochure depicted an open-armed Father Knickerbocker offering the city to one and all. Lines on the map indicating the tour routes and the photographs on the map's borders suggested that Empire State Sightseeing Company's tours encompassed the whole city: from Fraunces Tavern to Grant's Tomb, from the "East Side Ghetto" to the "Great White Way." As the brochure advised, "To the visitor New York presents two striking spectacles; the panorama that may be seen from the tower of Empire State and the more intimate view of the city, which can be obtained to best advantage only by motor coach lectured tours."

From the turn of the century to the mid-1920s, both social reformers and conservative advocates of a "lost" Anglo-Saxon New York worked hard to present less attractive "spectacles" to New Yorkers and to a national audience: spectacles of poverty, of disease, of dilapidated tenements, of a city and a nation invaded by degenerate and racially unassimilable foreigners. Striking though their images were, from Jacob Riis's photographs of tenement dwellers to maps of "racial colonies," the mavens of the city's consumer culture ultimately won the battle for the hearts and minds of New Yorkers and visitors. Between 1890 and 1924, business leaders helped organize the tourists' view of New York into equally "striking spectacles"—dramatic rooftop panoramas and carefully managed street-level itineraries, both perspectives offering variations of an easily consumable New York, cleverly building on the (negative) attention drawn to the city and its populations by the reformers.

Ultimately, to satisfy the desires of tourists and tourism promoters, New York had to be seen and marketed as *both* American and un-American, treading a fine line between the bold display of difference and the reassuring show of sameness. Tourists came to the city to see the sights, to relax, and to spend money on their pleasures. Coming from all over the United States, thanks to the development of both the nation's rail system and later the roadways, and from overseas, tourists took their impressions of the city home with them. In their verbal accounts, in the postcards they sent home, and in the photographs they took of their trips, tourists acted as a sort of mobile human billboard for New York back in their own communities.

To be marketable, a place—like any other commodity—must have a coherent identity or image. The problem with selling the commodity "place," as British planning historians Stephen Ward and John Gold have argued, is that "it is not readily apparent what the product actually is, nor how the consumption of place actually occurs." Places specifically designed as marketable commodities, such as Disney's amusement parks, more readily lend themselves to selling and marketing. New communities, built from scratch to offer particular amenities and community experiences, are also more easily marketed. Examples include the twentieth century's major "new towns" such as Greenbelt and Columbia in Maryland; Reston in Virginia; and Milton Keynes and Welwyn Garden City in Britain. Disney's new town, Celebration, in Florida, is a more recent example.[10]

Since places are not clearly defined commodities with a clearly defined set of consumers, they must be marketed in specific ways. They need to have a single, strong, and broadly appealing image associated with them, an image expressing what the place "means." In marketing terminology, they require "branding." The history of product branding, as set forth by historian Susan Strasser, closely parallels the chronology I set forth in this book for the recognition of the need to "brand" New York and the ensuing competition between different interests to establish a particular brand image for the city. The United States Trade-Mark Authority (USTMA), formed in 1877 by leading businessmen, lobbied hard for trademark legislation, and eventually succeeded when Congress passed trademark acts in 1881 and 1882. The USTMA, with the support of President McKinley, set up a commission in 1898 to assess the extent of and need for trademarking in the United States. In 1905, as a result of their efforts, Congress passed trademark legislation that protected the holders of brand names and images from infringement by rivals. In the case of New York, as with many other cities, the branding image is often an architectural or engineering icon, such as the skyline, the Flatiron Building, the Empire State Building, the Brooklyn Bridge, or the Statue of Liberty. At different times, these structures have variously connoted modernity, novelty, commercial power, technical know-how, and political freedom. Although all drew public criticism, particularly during the planning and building stages, all quickly became New York icons, as over one hundred years of New York City postcards can attest.

However, since the commodity "place," even in the form of a large city like New York, has an unclear identity as a marketable product, it is also vulnerable to negative images and connotations.

Buildings and bridges are appealing as urban icons because, unlike images of a city's inhabitants, they are less likely to arouse strong negative emotions or be vulnerable to swings in political or moral opinion. For boosters and tourism promoters in New York, the poor and ethnic minority populations constituted the most problematic aspect of the city's evolving public image. In response, to protect their valuable brand, they offered visual and textual versions of New York that either erased or strictly controlled the presence of minority populations.[11]

The history of mass immigration in the early twentieth century provides the other chronology for this book. The members of Congress who wrote the 1924 Johnson-Reed immigration act, and the anti-immigration organizations that lobbied them, took the census of 1890 as the baseline for the quotas they set in the act. The 1890 census represented a more "Anglo-Saxon" America, the moment before the "probationary whites" of the early twentieth century arrived from Southern and Eastern Europe. New York in 1890 saw the publication of Jacob Riis's study of the city's tenement populations, revealing an alarming "other half" largely unknown to the uptown middle and upper classes. By 1924, as Congress passed the new immigration act, guidebook writers were beginning to present the city's increasingly second-generation immigrant neighborhoods as picturesque shopping locations rather than as threatening foreign enclaves, and the city had just celebrated the Silver Jubilee of Greater New York, an occasion created by the politicians and businessmen most interested in re-spinning New York's polyglot population into a selling point for the whole city—ethnic diversity as an important component of, if you will, the brand "New York."[12]

Over the course of the next five chapters, we will explore the connections between public image, politics, business, immigration, national identity, and urban tourism. The first two and the last two chapters show how, as FPA wrote, "too many things are simultaneously true" of New York by examining the concurrent "spins" on New York offered by social reformers and by tourism promoters and businessmen in the 1890s and 1920s. Those chapters pivot around the third chapter's discussion of how New York's first generation of skyscrapers helped incorporate the city into pre-1920 notions of national identity embedded in a distinctly American landscape. The first chapter examines the 1890s as a decade in which social reformers working in New York developed increasingly sophisticated visual representations of their analysis of the city's social problems. I argue that while these representations moved away from the old "darkness and daylight" dichotomies toward a more nuanced, "rational," or "scientific" presentation, by 1900 the message appealed less than the medium. In the second chapter I argue that the reason the reformers' message about New York as a site of social problems appealed less and less to a middle-class audience by 1900 was that the 1890s was also the decade in which boosters and businessmen began to market New York (and other cities) successfully to middle-class tourists. I look at the evolving tourist itineraries of 1890s guidebooks, arguing that they encouraged tourists to get a bigger picture, and a broader experience, of New York, one that drew them away from the seamy "sights and sensations" of New York's tenement neighborhoods. My third chapter argues that efforts to boost New York's image to tourists, as well as generally to the nation, required that the city be understood as an American place and specifically as the American metropolis. I show how boosters managed to "Americanize" New York by associating its distinctively American, bold new skyscraper architecture with the newly Americanized tourist landscapes of the American West.

The fourth and fifth chapters look at the 1920s. In the fourth chapter I show how a conservative postwar anti-immigration discourse about New York and its multiracial population worked to suggest how un-American the city was, while a concurrent counterdiscourse found in the tourist guidebooks of the late 1910s and early 1920s suggested how American tourists might "see the world" in New York's diverse populations and "picturesque" ethnic neighborhoods. The fifth chapter shows how the trends and discourses examined in the previous chapters culminated in an increasingly close relationship between local businessmen and politicians eager to control New York's public image in order to brand and sell the city as both a tourist destination and a modern business center. This new alliance resulted in the promotion of Midtown Manhattan as the city's public face—the city's center for business and pleasure—a process best exemplified in the politico-business committees formed to celebrate the 1923 Silver Jubilee of New York City.

So, holding firmly to this guide to New York's evolution as "a fine place to visit," we will begin our tour, as do so many tourists to New York—by trying to find the best way actually to *see* the city.

1

REFORMING NEW YORK'S IMAGE IN THE 1890s

"It is stimulating . . . to find another stand-point than the pavement for watching the throbbing traffic of the city street," wrote an anonymous author in the popular magazine *Scribner's Monthly* in the spring of 1881. Arguing that viewing the city from street level provided a very limited perspective—"These hollow channels, grooved like Western canons [*sic*], between miles and miles of shops and houses, never let us know more than the immediate neighborhood; there are labyrinths and vistas, but no climax that displays to us the entirety and cohesion of part with part"—the writer concluded that it was preferable to "contemplate the city" from a high rooftop. From such a vantage point the entire city seemed visible; cohesion was attained through the apparent legibility of the city as a whole.[1] As this observer suggested, the problem of seeing New York was also a problem of knowing New York. The visual "climax" sought by the observer was both a visual and an epistemological moment: the subjective instance when the city would make sense.

The difficulty of seeing and knowing the city experienced by the casual street-level observer presented a problem for late-nineteenth century urban reformers as well as for boosters. Both, in order to fulfill their respective political and commercial agendas, required audiences able to perceive clearly the image of the city they offered. Reformers and boosters alike struggled in the 1890s not only to render a particular view of the city but also to make the city legible in a particular way for the middle-class audience whose support—moral, political, or financial—was crucial to the marketing of their respective "versions" of New York. Using photography, maps, statistics, and descriptions of the city's varied streets, neighborhoods, and populations, reformers and boosters employed similar means to ascribe very different meanings to 1890s New York. The reformers drew attention to the problems of quite specific urban areas that they saw as representative of the city's overall identity; for their part, the boosters sketched an overarching, less stark, less focused image of the city. While the two groups thus claimed to offer an interpretation of the whole city to their audiences, both in fact offered differently edited versions of a city increasingly perceived by middle-class observers as unknowable and incomprehensible.

At the close of the nineteenth century, an older, predominantly negative discourse about cities overlapped with an emerging, more celebratory, rhetoric. Urban reformers—the leading edge of America's turn-of-the-century reform age, the Progressive Era—inherited and built on that negative view of the city as the site of poverty and disease, the domain of "darkness," but recast it by means of new social science methods and forms of graphic representation. On the booster side, guidebook publishers and other business owners connected with New York's growing tourist trade helped to construct a new perspective, designed to promote a more positive image. In each case, these opposed discourses attempted to provide a coherent interpretation of the city, rhetorically and visually, by showing the "cohesion of part with part" apparently missing from street-level observations of New York.

The lack of that overall knowledge and vision made the city's meaning and identity unclear. As scholars such as M. Christine Boyer and T. J. Clark have argued, an apparent illegibility and fragmentation characterized the middle-class experience of turn-of-the-century European and American cities.[2] Detailed guidebooks and maps of cities emerged in response to a greater need for spatial explanation: the city map, used by residents as well as visitors, signified a new, more complicated urban age. In addition, the versions of New York represented in these forms reveal the difficulty of describing the city at the century's close. The nineteenth-century visual, spatial, and moral dichotomies of the city proved inadequate by the turn of the twentieth century—the complexities of the city no longer fit into neat separations of good and evil, public and private, native and foreign.

The two very different representations of New York in the 1890s produced by reformers and boosters indicate how the last decade of the nineteenth century witnessed a cultural contest over urban meaning. Historian John Kasson has described this *fin-de-siècle* disruption as a "semiotic breakdown," where external appearances could no longer be predictably anchored to specific meanings. Scholars of urban and cultural history have identified the cause of this "breakdown" as stemming from the shift from an older, more cohesive way of life grounded in family and community links (*gemeinschaft*) to a new, usually urban, existence characterized by anonymity and social disconnection (*gesellschaft*). New York's importance as the nation's largest city and the de facto capital of the burgeoning consumer economy made the city an especially contested site for attempts to resolve issues of urban cultural legibility and meaning.[3]

As New York grew in size, and as distinct areas of manufacturing, business, and residence emerged, many New Yorkers only really knew "their" area of the city—where they lived, where they worked, where they shopped or took their leisure moments, and a few places in between.[4] For most city residents, such everyday itineraries provided only glimpses of sites and lives different to their own class- or ethnicity-bound places of residence and labor. In addition, men and women, certainly from the middle and upper classes, would have known and seen New York in quite different ways. Women from such backgrounds generally stayed close to home, venturing into the city by carriage to visit friends in their homes or to shop at one of the new upscale department stores or to go out to the theatre or a restaurant in the company of their husbands or relatives. Given the growing complexity, size, and differentiation of the city and its various zones of activity, personal experience of the "whole" city was hard to acquire.

In these first two chapters I use the terms *reformers* and *boost-*

ers to identify two broadly defined groups active in shaping New York at the turn of the century. As historians of the city and of social welfare have shown, numerous organizations and individuals committed themselves to a range of reform movements in the mid- and late nineteenth century. From prison and asylum reform to temperance, abolition, and women's rights, the second half of the nineteenth century witnessed broad engagement by middle- and upper-class men and women with the social and moral problems of an industrializing nation.[5] Though perhaps not as known in the history of the city, an emerging class of entrepreneurs and businessmen also played an important role in directing the development of cities such as New York at the close of the nineteenth century.[6] Owners or managers of newspapers, department stores, hotels, manufacturing enterprises, and transportation companies, many of these men saw themselves, like the social reformers, as part of the loosely organized political trend known as Progressivism. However, given their investment in place-based businesses geared toward the rapid turnover of goods and services and their increasing reliance on advertising and public relations efforts, these men focused on improving the city rather than reforming it. That is, they focused on building a more attractive, rather than a more moral, New York: a place in which they could make more money by drawing a larger group of consumers.[7] Boosting New York, certainly in the 1890s, primarily involved drawing the consuming public's attention away from the city's problems and toward its varied pleasures.[8] While chapter 2 will focus on the efforts of these new urban boosters to remake the city's image for tourism and commerce, this chapter focuses on the reformers' version of the city. Social reformers in the 1890s shaped New York's image and meaning by working with the new visual culture and the new ideas of charity of the late nineteenth century, both of which lent themselves to constructing a more "scientific" image of the city.

From his rooftop vantage point, if armed with binoculars or a telescope, the *Scribner's* author we met earlier perched atop a city roof might have trained his gaze on the city's Lower East Side.

Such a view revealed a bulge of land reaching out into the East River, bordered roughly by 14th Street to the north, Division Street to the south, the Bowery and Third Avenue to the west, and the river to the east. The Charity Organization Society, the Association for Improving the Condition of the Poor, and other charitable organizations established themselves on the city's Lower East Side in some of New York's poorest neighborhoods. Making particular use of maps, such urban reform organizations constructed an image of the Lower East Side reminiscent, in its two-dimensionality, of the rooftop view. Together, during the 1880s and 1890s, these organizations also produced a new practice of charity based on techniques of surveillance and quantification developed by the evolving disciplines of the social sciences.

In the early Progressive Era, a new combination of social science research methods, new forms of graphic representation, and urban reform campaigns produced a version of New York as solely the site of urban problems. During the 1890s, a new breed of sociologically inclined reformers amassed evidence from their street-level observations and studies of the city's poorest neighborhoods and translated it into maps, charts, and three-dimensional models. By means of their extensive dissemination of this urban vision—in periodical articles, books, exhibits, and public lectures—the miserable tenement houses and impoverished immigrants of the Lower East Side became a widely recognized representation of New York and of modern city life.

However innovative they may have been, the reformers' graphic representations curtailed the spectator's view, presenting a city mapped and photographed as a site of economic and social decay. This restricted, "scientific," and rather gloomy view of New York would become increasingly unappealing in the new economy of urban pleasure and consumption within which tourism became central in the 1890s. The reformers' view of the city developed alongside the more expansive and celebratory images produced by the boosters and businessmen of the city, which we shall explore in the next chapter. The reformers' version of New York in the 1890s is important, first, because it represents a series of efforts to present a specific, carefully controlled image of the city; second, because even though their message ultimately failed, their methodologies went on to great success and further refinement.

Although differently motivated, the broad dissemination among a middle-class audience of the reformers' images of tenements and immigrants created close links between the narratives of reform and the emerging narratives that saw the city as a site of pleasure and danger.[9] Both narratives participated in a sensationalizing of the city in the latter decades of the nineteenth century and helped to construct the urban geographies of "sunlight and shadow," "darkness and daylight."[10] Such constructions of the city blurred the lines between the exploitation of the poor, especially women, by upper-class sexual adventurers and the moral interventions into those same neighborhoods by men and women from the same class group. Late nineteenth-century American reformers, like the reform-minded urban ethnographers of midcentury England, tried to distance themselves from such sensationalist representations of city life and city populations. To do so, they had to harness and direct the attention of the urban middle classes—those most able to contribute to, and potentially most invested in, the improvement of New York's public image. They also had to find an effective form and style of communication that encouraged a sense of civic responsibility among the middle and upper classes without reproducing the *déclassé* crowd-pleasing techniques of sensationalism.[11]

Getting the Attention of the "Nice People": Reform, Social Science, and the New Visual Culture

Writing about New York City in the *North American Review* in late 1890, reformer and *Evening Post* editor E. L. Godkin admonished his readers, the city's educated classes, for their lack of "municipal conscience." "In no city in Christendom to-day have the poor been left by their more fortunate neighbors and fellow-citizens so completely as in this to the tender mercies of demagogues and thieves and imposters," Godkin fulminated. He viewed his neighbors and peers as guilty of abdicating their class and moral responsibilities toward the poor and thus contributing to what he saw as the general demise of the entire city. They neglected to involve themselves in issues such as housing reform and the provision of proper sanitation, health care, and legal protections because it was easier to dismiss such things as "'politics,' with which clergymen and business men, and 'nice people' generally, cannot be expected to have anything to do." For Godkin, this indifference represented "an immense shame and scandal; but it fully explains the municipal situation at present."[12]

If getting the attention of the city's middle classes was really the key to reforming New York, then what Godkin and other reformers had to address was the relative invisibility of the poor to his middle-class readership. The "nice people" Godkin admonished in 1890 would have had little or no personal experience of the problems he described, nor of the people and neighborhoods associated with these issues. The middle classes did not usually go to working-class areas of the city and had only fleeting contact with people outside their own class or ethnic group, except as domestic servants and employees or through random street encounters. To communicate their view of the city to the "nice people," reformers such as Godkin therefore had to provide their audience with a powerful, concise impression of the poor and their neighborhoods and convince them that the poverty of one part of the city adversely affected the whole—at the very least, in terms of reputation. The decade of the 1890s saw an evolution in the reformers' methods of representation, from the more personal and moral approach we hear in Godkin's tone to a more "scientific," rational representation. In keeping with an increasingly visual culture, reformers in the 1890s learned to employ various types of visual representation to communicate their messages.

The early 1880s and the 1890s saw the rise of the illustrated daily and periodical press, an innovation that presented people, current events, and the city in a more visual and dynamic fashion. In a series of advertisements for major New York newspapers in the *New York Almanac* for 1880, the *Daily Graphic,* in contrast to the advertisements for the other daily papers, aimed to sell itself not on the basis of its political affiliation or independence but by extolling the importance of illustrated journalism: "People love to grasp situations at a glance of the eye. . . . The picture tells a whole story at once. It photographs itself in the memory. . . . Illustrated journalism . . . supplements words, that make dim images on the mind, with pictures, that give form and body and character to the objects described, and transfers a whole scene instantaneously to the imagination. We are fast learning that pictures are something more than objects to lazily enjoy, . . . They are a language."[13] The *Daily Graphic*'s advertisement represented more than just an alternative to its readers; it was a challenge to the other daily newspapers in New York, a challenge not fully taken up until Joseph Pulitzer took over the New York *World* in 1883 and began to illustrate his paper's stories first with detailed woodcut illustrations and cartoons, and later with engravings and halftone reproductions of photographs.

The *Graphic*'s statement also reveals contemporary notions about the superiority of various methods of visual communication over the written word. In particular, this advertising copy suggests the ways in which pictures in general were valued for their ability to convey a great deal of information at once, "instantaneously." *Photograph* is used as a verb in this passage—a picture "photographs itself in the memory"—suggesting both an imprinting effect on the brain and also an immediacy that words lack. Interestingly, this passage makes no claim or suggestion that the images or information conveyed by pictures are any more "real" or "truthful" than those conveyed by words. Its point rests on the idea that images convey information more immediately, and therefore more powerfully, than words.[14]

Different types of images held different currency at the close of the nineteenth century. While readers of daily papers and periodicals in the 1890s were used to interpreting engraved images in fiction or magazine stories and were becoming accustomed to the occasional illustration used in an advertisement, photographs were not widely reproduced in news publications—either periodicals or newspapers—until the mid- and late 1890s, following the perfection of the halftone process by Frederick Ives in the late 1880s.[15]

The widespread use of photographs to reinforce a news item or article about current events in the city—or, indeed, to tell stories on their own—was a recent development. Although photography was part of everyday middle-class life in terms of portrait photographs on the piano or mantelpiece or, certainly in the 1890s, in the form of the stereograph, the use of photography in printed journalism, especially as a means of making an argument, was relatively novel.[16]

However, the use of photographs as documents was not new in the 1890s. In the 1880s, New York's chief of police, Inspector Thomas F. Byrnes, had expanded the Police Department's "Rogue's Gallery" of photographic portraits of arrested criminals first established in 1857. Byrnes's gallery functioned alongside the use of photography by police departments in Europe, techniques that were much discussed in American newspapers and periodicals. The idea of using photography as documentation depended partly on the medium's perceived "reality effect" and truth index at the close of the nineteenth century but also on contemporary discussions that noted the differences between pictorial photography and photographs used "scientifically." By the 1890s, with the rise of both amateur and snapshot photography, writers in photographic and other journals were beginning to discuss the distinctions between different types of photography and their uses.[17]

New York's turn-of-the-century urban reformers made extensive use of both photography and cartography to convey to the public their version of the city. The reformers' perspective on the city evolved in this decade from the confrontational, sometimes sentimental photography of journalist Jacob Riis to the detached abstractions found in their poverty, disease, and housing maps. By the close of the decade, the new social sciences were having a great impact on the study, depiction, and amelioration of poverty in the city. The abstract, rational, and "scientific" methods of the social scientists and the reformers influenced by them were producing detailed maps of the city: a more succinct and distanced representation of the city as the locus of social problems but not, as we shall see, a particularly appealing one.

Depicting the "Other Half": From Photographs to Maps

Journalist and social reformer Jacob Riis's most famous and best selling work, *How the Other Half Lives: Studies among the Tenements of New York,* published in 1890, was based on his lectures and articles about the poor and their conditions in New York City.[18] Riis's images and his narratives, which achieved their greatest effect at the beginning of the decade, were closer to the older nineteenth-century depiction of the city as a place divided into areas of "darkness and daylight," good and evil. Riis's book consisted of twenty-five extensively illustrated chapters describing the rise of tenement buildings, the various neighborhoods in which they dominated, the social and moral problems caused by such housing conditions, and the populations that inhabited them. Although Riis's book purports to be about the tenements and the reasons why decent housing should be provided for the working classes of the city, much of the text and its arrangement differs little from the old urban sketch guides. With fairly lurid chapters on "The Italian in New York," "Jewtown," "Chinatown," "Waifs of the City's Slums," and "The Reign of Rum," Riis's perspective is that of the disdainful middle-class observer, dismayed and slightly exasperated by what he sees—but still eager to provide all the ghastly details to his middle-class readers.[19] While Riis's work is closer in style and tone to the sensationalist "sunlight and shadow" depictions of New York familiar to mid- and late-century readers, he clearly wished his work to be seen in a more scientific light, in keeping with his investigative reporting, his close working relationships with the police and other authorities, and his determination to bring about social and political change. The inclusion of his photographs certainly added to the veracity of a book that was not necessarily regarded as a serious document by all of his readers. *How the Other Half Lives* certainly did not escape criticism from the "serious" press interested in reform issues. A writer in the *London Quarterly Review* opened his review of *How the Other Half Lives* with the comment: "From a superficial reading of this not too scientific book, one might easily get the false impression that New York is one vast slum." While the reviewer acknowledged the power of Riis's book and its interest to housing reformers on the other side of the Atlantic, he qualified his recommendation of the book to "serious" readers by separating Riis's work from contemporary European developments in social scientific analyses of poverty with the comment, "Were Mr. Riis as systematic and statistical as he is entertaining and exceptionally well-informed we could desire no better guide." For this reviewer, the inclusion of Riis's photographs provided the proof necessary to overcome the descriptions of housing conditions, which "would be quite incredible but for the illustrations, most of them reproduced from photographs, by which they are accompanied."[20]

The images in *How the Other Half Lives*, along with the arrangement, style, and tone of his text, place Riis and his work somewhere between the older narrative and visual conventions of the urban sketch and the evolving "scientific" method, language, and graphics of the organized charity movement of the 1890s. Neither Riis nor his publisher drew any distinctions in the list of illustrations at the beginning of the book among original engravings, plans, photographs, and engravings based on Riis's photographs.[21] The titles of the illustrations given in the list are the same as those appearing beneath the images, suggesting that they regarded all of the types of images as equally valid and equally able to indicate the "truth" of Riis's accounts—a somewhat surprising suggestion given that, in 1890, when the book came out, photographs certainly enjoyed a reputation for being closer to the "truth," to "reality," than a hand-drawn sketch or an engraving based on a photograph. This attitude to the images in Riis's book confirms the idea that *How the Other Half Lives* occupies a transitional point between the older, more sensationalist accounts of the city and the emerging "scientific" representations of the city influenced by the new discipline of sociology.[22]

How the Other Half Lives included no maps or panoramic views of the city to show the location of the Lower East Side streets and the other areas described and depicted in Riis's text. The images in *How the Other Half Lives* ranged from the frontispiece engrav-

ing of "Gotham Court," depicting a narrow alley between tenements filled with ragged children and festooned with lines of laundry hung between the window ledges of the buildings to plans of various types of tenement buildings to halftones of Riis's photographs to engraved reproductions of Riis's photographs (fig. 1.1). With its lack of maps, the book gave no indication of where in New York these people and their miserable dwellings might be found. The relation of part to whole was thus entirely absent, contributing to the impression either that these areas were completely separate from the rest of New York or, conversely, that these parts somehow did represent the whole, that the tenement districts "were" New York.

However, in another gesture intended to give his text greater veracity—and to suggest social scientific legitimacy—Riis imagined and wrote about a map depicting the distribution of racial and ethnic groups in the city's tenement districts. More than the photograph, the map serves as the object, the representation, and the medium linking the reformers, the boosters, and the tourists. Maps suggested, then as now, specificity of place and a clear, detailed guide to what one would see in the place depicted. In this instance Riis's imagined map echoed late nineteenth-century city mapping related to social and medical issues at the same time that it foreshadowed the mapping of New York's "racial" minorities by both anti-immigration activists and tourism entrepreneurs in the 1920s. The mapping of social problems and of urban demographic information was becoming familiar in Britain through the work of gentleman sociologist Charles Booth, the beginning of whose multi-volume study of London's poor had been published shortly before Riis's book. Jane Addams's study of poverty in

Fig. 1.1. "Gotham Court" and "Five Cents a Spot," in Jacob Riis, *How the Other Half Lives: Studies among the Tenements of New York* (New York: Charles Scribner's Sons, 1890). These engravings from Riis's original photographs show places he visited in the tenement neighborhoods of New York. Several such reproductions appeared in the book's first edition.

Chicago, using such mapping techniques for the first time in the United States, would not be published for another five years.[23]

Riis employed his imagined map of the city "colored to designate nationalities" to suggest the chaos of a city populated by disparate racial and national groups. Such a map, he argued, "would show more stripes than on the skin of a zebra, and more colors than any rainbow," giving "the whole the appearance of an extraordinary crazy-quilt."[24] The fastest expanding areas of color on this imagined map were the "dull gray of the Jew" and the "Italian red." The red "would be seen forcing its way northward along the line of Mulberry Street," abutting the French quarter and, on the West Side, "overrunning" the black-colored areas, representing the African-American population, forcing that population uptown.[25] The inclusion of this imagined map provided Riis's readers with a vivid image of rampant ethnic otherness spreading unchecked across the city like some noxious seepage or contagion. But the map also served to make his views on the racial geography of the areas *seem* more scientific and, therefore, legitimate.

Social scientific research into poverty and urban problems became significant during the 1890s in a national cultural context that placed great value on realism, authenticity, and facts.[26] The University of Chicago organized the first department of sociology in 1892, giving academic legitimacy to the "scientific" investigation of social issues. In the 1890s periodicals devoted primarily to the sociological study of the city, such as *Municipal Affairs* (founded 1897), first appeared. In an era of increasing anxiety about the stability of the nation as it faced serious political, social, and labor unrest, economic depression, and rising immigration, the factuality of the new social sciences offered a reassuringly rational and coherent approach to managing cultural change.

Sociologists claimed to offer a new, more scientific way to understand society. Based on the presentation and documentation of "facts," the discipline was an attempt to move the observation of society away from the individual, subjective, and nonprofessional writing produced by earlier nineteenth-century observers. However, despite sociology's methodological innovations, the object of the sociologist's gaze differed little from that of previous observers of society and social relations. The focus was still on those populations deemed by their observers to be somehow abnormal. Professor Albion W. Small of the University of Chicago excused this tendency by arguing thus: "To know society it has become necessary to know neglected and despised elements of society. . . . Hence the attention to the defective, dependent, and delinquent classes, which has been so noticeable that many have mistaken this attention for the whole business of sociology." If not sociology's "whole business," the study of such social classes certainly accounted for much of the new discipline's purview. The discipline of sociology developed alongside, and helped shape, new methods of urban reform, especially those focused on urban charity work.[27]

New methods of charity influenced by new sociological theories required a new type of charity worker equipped to operate in the flux of late nineteenth-century urban America. In 1897, Francis Peabody, Professor of Christian Morals at Harvard University's Divinity School, early advocate of sociological studies, and fervent social reformer, gave a speech at a meeting of the United Hebrew Charities, one of the major charitable organizations working in New York's tenement neighborhoods. In his speech Peabody outlined the challenges and distractions facing the "modern charity worker": "a new world—a world of complexity and intensity, of shifting populations and industrial agitations, of enormous increase of wealth and alarming congestion of poverty; a new world, with problems so unprecedented that no wisdom of the past can be sufficient to interpret them."[28] The academic sociologists who constructed the philosophical foundations of the Progressive Era provided the intellectual basis for the new "scientific" charity and its workers, bestowing them with the methods and tools they thought necessary to rationalize the multiple challenges of the modern city.

Adopting the social scientist's new methods of close observation, managerial efficiency, and fact-gathering, the "modern" charity workers of this "new world" were to be "trained experts," Peabody argued, operating in a "new profession . . . which rests on study and research."[29] Their focus on relieving the problems of the poor would be much more effective if they endeavored to "understand and measure" such people. The older methods of poor relief and charity based on moral duty, Christian ethics, and basic class guilt would be gradually pushed aside, according to Peabody's vision, by a new class of reformist technocrat, driven less by a bleeding heart than by a desire for efficiency and quantifiable progress.

Controversy surrounded the new charitable methods proposed by Peabody and others. In the same year that Peabody's speech was published, Jane Addams of Chicago's Hull House spoke against the new type of "systematic charity" in a debate at New York's Nineteenth Century Club.[30] To avoid the image of heartlessness in the eyes of a public still more used to having its heartstrings pulled than to responding to statistics about poverty, it was vitally important that the new breed of charity workers find effective methods to communicate their new ideas.

To that end, and in keeping with the development of the new "ways of seeing" discussed earlier, this first generation of social scientists, and the urban reformers influenced by them, tried to publish their findings in innovative graphic (rather than simply textual) forms. They employed various types of graphs, charts, and maps to represent their research and arguments. Writing in the *Journal of the Franklin Institute* in 1899, Lewis M. Haupt addressed the need to make more easily comprehensible (and thus more palatable) the type of quantified information that the sociologically inclined reformers were busily gathering. While statistics, he claimed, were "invaluable . . . to the progressive man of affairs," their conventional form of presentation as "masses of figures arranged in tabular form" made them "confusing, and often misleading." The solution, Haupt suggested, was to adopt the increasingly popular new methods of "representing statistics by the aid of diagrams, plain, colored or shaded in conventional symbols."[31]

During the 1890s New York's urban reform organizations, especially those focused on tenement housing issues, took on the challenge of visual communication. In particular, their use of maps helped move their communication methods away from the sentimentalism and moralism of late nineteenth-century documentary photography into a more "rational" form of representation. But ultimately, as we shall see, by century's end New York's urban reformers learned that the communication problem they faced was more one of content than of form. The audience for their work was small not so much because the maps or tables of statistics were hard to read but simply because the information about the city they offered was increasingly unappealing in comparison to contemporaneous representations of what the city and its inhabitants offered the middle-class consumer or tourist.

Mapping the Other Half

Progressive-era reformers' focus on environment as the cause of other social problems, their subsequent attention to the location of key urban problems, and their use of newly available statistical information and sociological methods made cartography an ideal medium through which to communicate their arguments. The maps they produced put forward a revealing representation of their version of the city and its meaning at the close of the nineteenth century. An 1899 article by E. R. L. Gould, a leading housing reformer and an economist in the Department of Labor, placed bad housing at the root of all other social problems: "The home is the character unit of society. . . . The relation between humanity and its environment is very close. . . . For all but the exceptionally strong and virile, environment, and especially home environment, determines the trend of life. Populous masses, crowded together one thousand to the acre, as they are in some parts of New York, are absolutely unable to resist the influences by which they are surrounded."[32] The environment of the crowded, poor tenement neighborhoods of New York presented an acute example of the problems reformers such as Gould wished to address. Tenement house reformers soon set about mapping the housing problem, producing what they saw as a scientific representation of the problem and its location.

How solemn sound loved tongues at night

Darby and Joan

An hour of Darkness

Mrs. Washee wanchee you

A warm dinner

Mutual Confidences

The reformers' success depended on their ability to reach the middle-class audience that might, once given clear and detailed information, make the effort to support housing reform. An article in the popular magazine *Harper's Weekly* in January 1895 reproduced and described the city maps prepared by the New York State Tenement House Commission of 1894, whose report, critical of the city's housing for the poor, had just been submitted to the state legislature.[33] Illustrating its findings with photographs, maps, and other diagrams and making extensive use of statistics, the Commission's report was innovative in both style and content. The conditions documented in the report were based on a survey of over eight thousand homes inhabited by 255,033 people.[34] However, despite the Commission's efforts, the Tenement House Act of 1895 incorporated almost none of its recommendations and failed to legislate improvements in the design of tenement houses.

The publication of the Tenement House Commission maps in the issue of January 19, 1895, was therefore unusual not in content but in form—such maps were not the type of image regularly seen in *Harper's Weekly*. *Harper's Weekly* covered the tenement house issue extensively throughout the 1880s and 1890s. The articles ranged from those accompanied by illustrations of the suffering poor intended to elicit sympathy from the reader, such as "Life among the Tenements" from July 1887 (fig. 1.2), to those based on new legislation or campaigns for the improvement in the design and building of tenements, such as "The Tenement House Calamity" from November 1881 or "Model Tenements" from January 1888.[35] The Tenement House Commission maps themselves represented an important milestone in the use of new forms of graphic representation by reformers, and their publication in a

Fig. 1.2. "Life among the Tenements," *Harper's Weekly,* July 23, 1887. This depiction of New York's tenement dwellers coping with the city's July weather presents them as a mix of romantic curiosities and hideous grotesques—much in keeping with *Harper's Weekly's* representations of the poor.

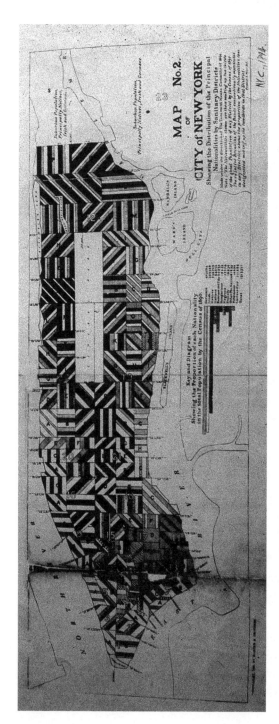

Fig. 1.3. Map No. 2, "Showing the Distribution of the Principal Nationalities by Sanitary Districts," one of a series of maps in Frederick E. Pierce, "The Tenement House Committee Maps," *Harper's Weekly*, January 19, 1895. The social-scientific map contrasted sharply with the cartoon-like images usually seen in the magazine's articles about poverty.

widely read periodical such as *Harper's Weekly* constituted a publicity coup for the Tenement House Commission. The maps provided the type of cartographic representation of the city's racial geography anticipated in Jacob Riis's imagined "crazy quilt" map. The commission's maps, and the report from which they came, suggested the possibility not only of seeing the location of designated problems but also the possibility of exerting some control over what in Riis's imagined map had merely been an image of chaos. However, this set of maps, especially as they appeared in *Harper's Weekly,* was very difficult to interpret coherently and drew on conflicting and problematic sources that undermined their veracity.

The article accompanying the maps, written by their cartographer Frederick Pierce, was illustrated by reproductions of Maps 1, 2, 3, and 6 from the commission's report. Two pages of the magazine were given over to double-page reproductions of Map 1, "Showing Densities of Population in the Several Sanitary Districts June 1, 1894," and Map 2 "Showing the Distribution of the Principal Nationalities by Sanitary Districts" (fig. 1.3). Smaller reproductions of Maps 3 and 6 (showing "Density of the Population by Wards" in 1860 and 1890, respectively) were placed within the text of the short accompanying article by Pierce.

Pierce's first line indicates his faith both in the meaning and power of "facts" gathered by the commission and in the capacity of the maps to represent those facts effectively and powerfully to the reader: "In order to show at a glance certain facts relating to the population of New York City, the committee had prepared the density and nationality maps here reproduced."[36] However, the maps certainly do not convey their meaning "at a glance." To use the maps as their makers apparently intended, the reader must struggle to extract their meaning, peering closely back and forth between the map legends and the maps themselves. The power of the maps (as with most maps)—and of the commission's reports as a whole—lay in the *impression* they gave of having assessed a complex problem, thus giving the appearance of *control* over that problem.

In their stark, rigid representations of the city and some of its inhabitants, made up of crisscrossed lines and shaded stripes, along with the meanings attributed to those graphics, the maps provide another echo of older constructions of the dichotomous city—the domains of "sunlight and shadow," "darkness and daylight." According to the Tenement House Commission maps, there are good and bad areas of the city, problematic and unproblematic spaces. As Pierce writes with reference to the density map, "The darkly shaded portions are districts which to New York of a century ago were suburban settlements; now, it seems almost needless to say, they are about coincident with the tenement house districts."[37] The "dark" areas of the city on these maps represent areas of changing population, equated with physical, moral, and "racial" decline.

Pierce's explanation of the nationality map makes clearer the links among concerns about tenement housing, fears of moral decline in the city, and the new immigration from Eastern and Southern Europe. Based on information from the 1890 census data, the maps plot the location in the city of residents of various "nationalities." The makers of the 1890 census defined nationality according to the mother and constructed a table in the census report showing the result of these findings. Four years later, the mapmakers of the Tenement House Commission of 1894 then used that table as the basis for their nationality map, which Pierce justified by arguing that "at the time of the census over seventy-six per cent of the white population in the city had foreign-born mothers, and over forty per cent were foreign-born themselves. So the latter certainly, and probably a majority of the thirty-six per cent of native-born of foreign mothers, would show the traits of their maternal nationality."[38] However, the Tenement House Commission mapmakers did not include all the nationalities designated in the census report's table. Their interest, it seems, was to map only those "nationalities" with visible "traits" of their origin. As Pierce states, not all "the nationalities given in the [1890 Census] table are plotted. The Scotch, English, Welsh, Scandinavian, and Canadians have not collected in colonies, but are scattered over the city. These, being in small numbers, and perhaps less foreign than the others, were disregarded." The map, then, only represents those "nation-alities" regarded by the mapmakers in 1894 as truly "foreign." It is important to note that the Irish are still regarded as sufficiently "foreign—and by implication visibly racially different from the un-represented Anglo-Saxon and Scandinavian residents—to warrant representation on the nationality map. A woman born in Ireland was in 1894 still regarded as more foreign than one born in Swe-den.[39] By mapping only the more "foreign" populations in the city, these maps contributed directly to arguments about New York's Americanness based in late nineteenth-century notions of racial difference and "whiteness." Such arguments, the "race science" underpinning them, and their effect on New York's public image became more frequently and more overtly deployed after World War I, as we shall see.

The commission's mapmakers further manipulated the origi-nal census statistics in order to emphasize the greater tendency of the newer immigrants—the more "foreign" immigrants—to reside in a particular area of the city. The map shows only those nation-alities "making up two-thirds of the population of any district . . . to bring out in clearer contrast those that do exist to a greater ex-tent." The decision to map and represent the districts in this man-ner occluded the racial and ethnic diversity of many neighbor-hoods. The nationalities were represented by stripes, or bands, which Pierce explained as follows: "The breadth of a band in any district bears the same relation to the sum of the breadth of the dif-ferent bands in that district as the number of the nationality it rep-resents bears to the two thirds of the population in that district." Pierce's confusing explanation of the map's method of representa-tion does little to aid the reader in interpreting the map.

The maps themselves are almost incomprehensible if one tries to understand their method, yet (like most maps) they give the im-pression of great truth and clarity. In this abstracted form, the entire city of New York appears neatly analyzed. The maps show no doubts, no grey areas. Each district appears to have been care-fully measured and scientifically assessed. There is no sense of what the "density" measured and attributed to each area actually meant to the residents of that district; nor is there any room for a discussion of how "nationality," as described by the census and the commission, did or did not relate to the sense of community among different ethnic, religious, or racial groups living in the city's neighborhoods. The paradoxical nature of the maps, and of Pierce's explanation of them, deepens when one compares Pierce's concluding statement to what the maps actually show. Pierce states: "The nationality and density maps should be viewed together. Thus the coincidence of the crowded districts with the German colonies explains the preponderance of that nationality." In fact, the areas of the city mapped as most congested in the density map (based on 1894 figures) do not correspond to the location of residents designated as German by the 1890 census. By the time of publication, in early 1895, the most congested areas—certain neighborhoods of the Lower East Side—corresponded with the tenement districts occupied by Polish and Russian Jews.

The discrepancies among the different sets of figures, between the two main maps themselves, and between the maps and the true state of the areas depicted on the maps in January 1895 ultimately have no bearing on the effect of these maps. The power of the maps as a representation of a particular view of the city, as a perspective on the meaning of New York and the social and cultural changes of the 1890s, resides not in any "truth" index, any correspondence between a cartographic representation and reality, but rather in the *appearance* of factuality, the look of scientific truth.[40]

These maps work in a similar way to Jacob Riis's textual and visual representations of the "other half." Both the maps and Riis's book stand awkwardly between the nineteenth and the twentieth centuries, between old and new methods of constructing arguments about the city, between the old visual metaphors used to define the city and the new visual technologies and means of graphic representation that seemed to offer a more objective way of depicting places and people. As the century drew to a close, the old metaphors of light and dark, of black and white, seemed less appropriate for describing and understanding a city that, with its rapid changes in the appearance of its architecture and the population of its streets, verged on the indescribable, the unrepresentable.

"City of Living Death"

On February 10, 1900, the *New York Times* informed its readers that an exhibition concerning tenement housing would open that evening in the old Sherry's Hotel building on Fifth Avenue: "It is believed that visitors to the exhibition will have placed before them in concrete form a clear and comprehensive statement of existing conditions, so that intelligent action may be taken to remedy them and to prevent their recurrence."[41] The first of its kind in the United States, the exhibit was an extraordinary achievement. Covering three floors, it comprised maps, plans, cardboard models, photographs, charts, and tables of statistics. The exhibit sought to show that tenement housing conditions in New York were worse than in any other city in the United States and that the conditions in the United States overall were worse than in other countries. The tenement house exhibition came on the heels of New York's celebration of the consolidation of the five boroughs in 1898. The extensive citywide festivities had provided an opportunity to boast of New York City's size and status and, in the year of America's victory over Spain, to link the city's self-congratulatory mood to that of the entire nation. The consolidated city placed New York second only to London on the list of large cities. The 1900 exhibition, on the other hand, counteracted such booster bombast by relegating New York City to the bottom of the list of provisions of housing for the urban poor in comparable cities.

Lawrence Veiller, secretary and director of the Charity Organization Society (COS) Tenement House Committee, instigated the exhibit. A professional reformer and social worker, Veiller was more of a politician than many of his tenement house reform cohorts. He also had an eye for publicity and was convinced that the exhibition he envisaged would have a powerful effect on tenement house legislation. Like other members of the organized charity movement in New York at the close of the century, Veiller was frustrated by the unwillingness of the state and city authorities to follow up on recommendations either of the New York State Tenement House Commissions of 1894 or 1899 to revise the building code. The exhibition proved a masterstroke in the attainment of their goal: to garner political attention. After visiting the exhibition, New York Governor Theodore Roosevelt, longtime supporter of housing reform and friend of Jacob Riis, said to COS founder and president Robert DeForest, "Tell me what you want and I will help you get it."[42]

Peter Bacon Hales and Maren Stange have to date provided the major scholarly examinations of the exhibition, particularly as it relates to the history of photography. Stange describes the exhibit as "the most significant and influential event for the development of social documentary photography" in the *fin-de-siècle* era.[43] In her extensive examination of the few extant exhibit materials and other related items, Stange places the photographic materials that appeared in the exhibit within the context of the use of photography as a publicity tool by the increasingly professionalized field of social work. For his part, Hales argues that "though the exhibition lent legitimacy to reform photography, the intention and the result of its display was to move the medium from its primary place as a persuasive tool to a functional, subsidiary role among other modes of social fact gathering." The COS, Hales argues, "used captions which buried the immediacy of the photographs under an incredible body of unassimilable facts. . . . Thus, while the Exhibition transmitted one message about the value of photographs in a reform context, it also promoted a reductionist model of their value and function."[44]

As Stange and Hales note, photography was the least powerful and the least noted representational form at the exhibit. The exhibition's photographs played a subsidiary role to other representational forms—and with good reason. Veiller and his reformist cohorts had learned two important lessons from Riis's use of photographs in 1890 and their first polemical use of maps in 1895: first, that they were running the risk of alienating their audience with photographs that were either too confrontational or too familiar; and second, that a well-designed map with a clear theme could be more effective and more authoritative than the heartrending photographs of ragged children and trash-strewn alleys.

Other than photographs, the exhibit included a set of forty-seven maps, six models of tenement house blocks, charts, tables of statistics, and plans of various types of tenement houses. In addition to the materials concerning New York, the exhibition included photographic and other evidence of housing conditions (and plans for improved dwellings) in other American cities such as Chicago, Philadelphia, and Boston.[45] It also included large amounts of material designed to show that European cities such as London, Edinburgh, and Berlin were ahead of New York and other American cities in the provision of housing for the urban poor and in the construction of suburban working-class housing developments. After its two-week run in New York, the exhibition traveled to Chicago and Boston. In keeping with its international perspective, some of the materials from the exhibit were packed up and sent to the 1900 Paris Universal Exposition.

Press reviews of the exhibition tell two stories. While its opening night drew a large crowd and reviewers present were impressed, the mainstream press ignored the exhibition. Reviews of the exhibition were limited to the reformist publications focusing on charity work. The mainstream press—including the *New York Times,* which had alerted its readers to the exhibition's opening—neglected to review the show. So, despite the exhibition's innovative techniques and apparently powerful argument concerning housing conditions in New York, the city's major papers did not deem the event newsworthy to its varied readerships.

Though the exhibition may have been preaching to the converted, those converts were certainly enthusiastic about what they saw, deeming the exhibit a great success. "The room was packed to its utmost capacity and a large number of people were unable to find entrance," claimed the *Evangelist,* describing the opening night of the exhibition. The *Jewish Messenger* described the exhibit as a "most instructive object lesson for thoughtful citizens." In the popular illustrated magazine *Outlook,* Lillian Betts, who wrote frequently on issues related to urban social problems, described the show as "one of the greatest contributions, if not the greatest, ever made in this or any other country to the proper understanding of the subject of the housing of the poor."[46]

A reading of the reviews and articles about the exhibition also suggests that the maps and models included in the exhibition made a stronger impression than the 1,100 photographs, implying a shift in audience receptivity to photographs employed as tools of reform efforts. Photographs of the type used thus far in New York to contribute visual "truth" to arguments about urban problems had by 1900 perhaps become too familiar. Jacob Riis's images of the poor and their neighborhoods had made a powerful impression ten years before, both standing alone and supported by his lectures, articles, and books. But by 1900, newspapers, periodicals, and print advertisements reproduced photographs of all sorts every day. As Peter Bacon Hales has argued, the use of photography in the annual reports issued by reform agencies and governmental

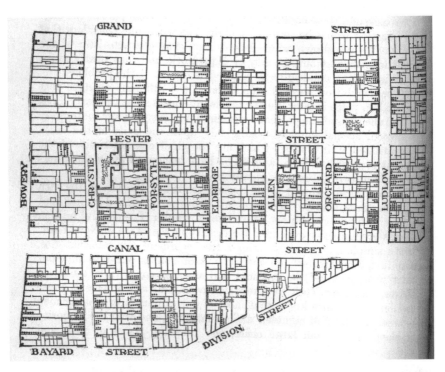

Fig. 1.4. "Poverty map" from the Tenement House Exhibition, 1900. The social-scientific maps attracted a great deal of attention at the exhibition. *The Tenement House Problem,* edited by Robert W. DeForest and Lawrence Veiller, vol. 1, New York: Macmillan and Company, 1903.

committees gradually devalued the photograph's power to shock, persuade, and initiate an effective response from a sympathetic audience. Hales quotes a 1910 review of annual reports in *The Survey* in which the reviewer wrote that "the public soon wearies of pictures of destitute children or desolate tenement interiors."[47] Since, on the other hand, the exhibition's maps functioned without trying to elicit empathy from the viewer, they avoided the potential pitfall of unintentionally eliciting a *negative* emotional response. By 1900, yet more photographs of destitution and desolation might simply have bored the average middle-class viewer. For their part, the maps allowed a certain emotional distance while still conveying a powerful message. They were designed to elicit a focused, rational response to an objective presentation of the "facts" of the matter.[48]

The visual style of the maps suggested the painstaking processes of investigation, fact-gathering, and assessment with respect to the needs of the poor on a case-by-case basis—a methodology on which the organized charity movement prided itself. The parallel sets of forty-seven disease and poverty maps, when displayed one set over the other, as Veiller had intended, covered a large amount of exhibit space, running for 244 feet, with many of the maps measuring forty-two inches in width (fig. 1.4). The maps plotted the reported cases of poverty and contagious diseases on the block level, giving the exact ground plan of each building in each block. Statistics accompanying the maps gave further contextual information such as the number of people living in each building. Covered in black and red dots of varying sizes to signify different levels of the particular problem displayed by each map, visitors saw parts of the city spread out before them, mapped and drawn with details familiar in some ways from other city maps— but tightly themed to show only the presence of diseases or only the presence of certain investigated charity cases.

Veiller intended the maps to work in conjunction with one of the models of a city block displayed nearby. The model was of an existing tenement block on the Lower East Side, bounded (as it was in the years before the Manhattan Bridge) by Chrystie, Forsythe, Canal, and Bayard Streets. The visitor could look at the model of the block and, by referring to the maps, know how many cases of tuberculosis had been recorded from buildings in the block, how many cases of diphtheria, and how many applications had been made to the COS and the United Hebrew Charities for charitable assistance. The other models showed proposals for improved tenements; one depicted a tenement block as it might look if constructed according to the prevailing building code, of which the COS and other housing reform organizations were critical. Betts found the latter model (fig. 1.5) particularly powerful: "To every conscientious man who saw this block there must have come a sense of personal responsibility. The indifference of the mass of citizens to the effort that was made to prevent its passage made the present code possible. This model was labeled 'The Worst Possible Tenement-House Block.' As the two models were contrasted, it was evident to any careless observer that the block of existing tenements, with all its horrors, with all its limitations, was far

Fig. 1.5. "Dumb-bell"–style tenement block from the Tenement House Exhibition, 1900, in support of Veiller's argument that this style was no improvement over the older tenement buildings. Robert W. DeForest and Lawrence Veiller, *The Tenement House Problem,* vol. 1, New York: Macmillan and Company, 1903.

preferable to the block possible under the present law."[49] Betts's comment represented exactly the type of impassioned outrage the exhibit's designers sought to produce in its visitors. Betts implies that were it not for the abdication by middle-class citizens of their responsibilities to their city and its less advantaged citizens, the potentially greater horrors of the block based on the new code might not loom over the Lower East Side.

Once again, with the models as with the maps, the reformers' methods at this exhibition avoided the pitfalls of the earlier representations of the tenement house problem that relied on the viewer's empathy. Most of the models measured three feet wide by five feet long and were eighteen inches in height, and they must have reminded many visitors of doll's houses. Undoubtedly, part of the power of the models was the rather charming effect of miniaturization. Placed on stands in the exhibit room, visitors could walk around each of the miniature city block displays, look at the blocks from every angle, experiencing another version of the thrill of the elevated or "bird's eye" perspective presented by two-dimensional images of the city.[50] Visually appealing in themselves as examples of craftsmanship, the models provided the viewer with a concise, focused distillation of an issue, as the maps did.

Subsequent exhibitions on social and educational themes employed many of the techniques of display and many of the types of material used in the Tenement House Exhibition. In particular, the three-dimensional representation in the form of models became a popular feature of such exhibits. Some shows took this effect further by creating *tableaux vivants,* full-sized reproductions of a working or living space using living models to embody each role silently.[51] Thus the methods of the 1900 exhibition placed it in the vanguard of techniques of graphic display and exhibitionary practice, ones that continued to be developed at world and state fairs and especially in the major history museums of New York.

The COS, fellow reformers or sympathizers who reviewed the exhibit, and certainly Veiller himself intended that visitors to the exhibition would do the necessary work to move from one area of the exhibit to another, comparing the images, tables, photographs, captions, models, and maps one to the other in order to understand the argument made by the organizers and thereby become inspired to act—or at least vote—in favor of further reforms. The exhibition's content intended, therefore, to convey a political and didactic message to its audience, not merely to provide visual or narrative pleasure. Visitors were supposed to experience regret at having failed to vote against the last housing and building laws and to be embarrassed by the negative comparisons made in the exhibit between housing conditions in the United States and those in Europe. As Betts remarked, "The Americans who see this Exhibit at Paris at the Exposition will certainly not view it with pride when the results in other countries are placed beside it."[52] Betts made two rather large assumptions about the Americans sufficiently privileged to attend the Paris Exposition: first, that they would choose to view such an exhibit; and second, that their response would, like hers, be one of shame.

The international comparison was particularly important at the turn of the century. The United States had recently become an imperial power through its war with Spain, and the nation's wealth, as well as the size and commercial importance of its great cities, was increasingly challenging the global economic and cultural dominance of Europe. With New York in particular on the brink of a new national and international role, the exhibition relegated the city to the bottom of a scale measuring care for the poor and attention to the less glamorous aspects of city living. In an article in *Charities Review* after the exhibition had closed in New York, Veiller gave his own account of the show's significance.[53] He critiqued the city's newly celebrated modernity by comparing New York to the one of antiquity's most famous cities: "It has been reserved for New York city, the modern Rome, to duplicate evils of tenement-house structure known in ancient Rome alone among all the cities of the world. In characteristic fashion, she has not only duplicated these evils, but has intensified them to a degree beyond belief."[54] The comparison implied that New York in 1900, like Rome in its heyday, built magnificent, innovative, and beautiful buildings to house its powerful people, its arts, and its amusements, all while neglecting the basic needs of its ordinary residents. Referring to the poverty and disease maps, of which he was especially proud, Veiller warned that they "might well earn for New York city the title of the city of living death. No other words so accurately and graphically describe the real conditions as these."[55]

Going against the emerging booster representations of New York found in guidebooks and other tourist ephemera, a public rhetoric partly occasioned by the formation of Greater New York in 1898, the vision of the city presented at the Tenement House Exhibition insisted on a version of New York in which acute social and physical problems not only dogged the city but also defined it. The exhibition represented the culmination of the efforts of charity organization societies, settlement houses, and other urban reform groups to combine the methodology of social science with photography and other forms of visually representing "facts" in order to present their perspective on and characterization of the city. This gloomy and static representation of the city, even presented in the most "modern" manner at the exhibition, by the beginning of the twentieth century had begun to lose its currency. Depictions of New York as the site of poverty and disease battled unsuccessfully with the impressions and everyday experiences of the city as a "living picture" of human diversity, of architectural and engineering splendors, and of numerous consumer pleasures enjoyed by tourists and the city's middle-class residents. Seen from Fifth Avenue, the theater district, or, best of all, from the roof of one of the new skyscrapers, New York did not appear to be the "city of living death" depicted by Lawrence Veiller at the Tenement House Exhibition. To its promoters, the city on the Hudson increasingly earned the comparison, frequently made in contemporary guidebooks, with the city on the Seine—Paris, City of Light. While the COS's contribution to the Social Economy section at the Paris Exposition of 1900 did well in its category of exhibits, winning the grand prize and an individual gold medal for Veiller for his efforts in organizing the exhibit, it was not a major attraction for visitors to the event.

Visitors to New York in 1900, like those touring the French capital, certainly had many more appealing sights to explore than the Tenement House Exhibition. During the 1890s, while urban reformers amassed statistics, wrote reports, and learned to employ new techniques of visual representation, the promoters of tourism in New York had been engaged in constructing their own set of images and descriptions of the city. Alongside the reformers' version of New York, the boosters' city was drawing middle-class eyes away from the Lower East Side's tenements and toward the city's more elegant commercial and cultural domains. It is to their version of New York in the 1890s that we now turn.

2

TOURISM AND NEW YORK'S IMAGE IN THE 1890s

On New Year's Eve 1891, a reporter for Joseph Pulitzer's newspaper *The World* stood in the glazed rooftop dome of the newspaper's building and described the city view enjoyed by tourists from that vantage point high above the city's streets. "How to See All New York," his headline read the next day, "A Magnificent Picture from the Top of the Pulitzer Building." According to the reporter, the Pulitzer Building was more than just another tall building in Lower Manhattan: it was "The Central and Highest Point of New World Civilization." The view available from its pinnacle was a "Panorama . . . That Every Mind Can Dream Over, But Not Even a Master Hand Can Paint. . . ." The statement's hyperbolic tone fits with the rhetoric of headlines, of course, but also with the early days of the aggressive promotion of mass market commodities and the beginnings of professional advertising. Joseph Pulitzer, his building, and his newspaper played important roles in the promotion of a new image for turn-of-the-century New York City, an image structured by a burgeoning mass consumer culture, of which tourism was increasingly a vital part.

Unlike the precisely detailed, tenement-by-tenement mapping of the social reformers, the emerging literature of urban tourism constructed a sweeping overview of the city, a bird's eye perspective punctuated by specifically defined tourist sites.[1] Tourism's boosters, though using strategies similar to those of the reformers, put forward a very different image of New York in the 1890s. The New York imagined by business and tourist boosters could not have differed more from the New York depicted in the same decade by Jacob Riis and Lawrence Veiller. Hotels, department stores, and guidebook writers sought, like the reformers, to present a coherent, legible view of the city and to focus their audience's attention on particular aspects or areas. Like the reformers, they used maps, detailed narratives, descriptions of the population, and powerful visual images to construct a coherent city image. Like the reformers, these early boosters also amassed facts and statistics about the city to support their version of New York. But, unlike the reformers' city, the boosters' New York consisted of a topography of "sights" located throughout the city, rather than a topography of social problems located in isolated urban pockets. Like those created by the reformers, the boosters' maps also sought to show "the cohesion of part with part," but theirs was a sightseeing cartography, offering maps designed to guide the visitor to the places marked and to draw them into an open, available, consumable city. Ragged children, squalid streets and apartments, crime, disease, and poverty were absent as serious concerns from the tourist ephemera of the 1890s. While guidebooks to the city still mentioned the immigrant neighborhoods and their populations, they downplayed the sites of the "shadows" of New York in favor of the spectacle of new buildings, museums, shopping districts, Central Park, and the image of a generally more elegant American city life. The stops on the tourist itinerary were, literally, the city's selling points.[2]

Merchants, shopkeepers, hoteliers, and members of the municipal government would have heartily endorsed the *World* reporter's extravagant statements. "It seems clear," historian Neil Harris states in his discussion of New York tourism, "that the 1890s was the take-off decade."[3] During this decade, the local business community began to organize itself into groups representing the interests of business owners in a range of service industries. The very active Merchants' Association of New York, founded in 1897, worked with already established organizations such as the Hotel Association of New York City, founded in 1878, and the New York State Hotel Association, founded in 1887, in addition to other associations. As historian Catherine Cocks has shown, once organized, members of these groups more effectively lobbied related businesses such as railroad companies and local and state governments for funds and favorable legislation to help them improve local economic conditions and attract all kinds of visiting consumers to New York City. Learning from the methods employed by other cities, and especially by Chicago during its hosting of the World's Columbian Exposition in 1893, the New York Merchants' Association for example, in conjunction with eastern railroad companies, began offering to their out-of-town members reduced-rate excursion fares to the city. Such fares attracted the businessman or buyer looking for goods in New York's wholesale markets, many of whom brought their wives with them, making the possibility of combining business with pleasure more affordable.[4]

Guidebooks began to address the interests of specifically middle-class families and women, moving beyond the focus on the male visitor passing through the city on business, common earlier in the nineteenth century. Based on the customers they encountered in their own establishments, the city's businessmen recognized the need to appeal to a broad range of tourist-consumers, both men and women, coming to the city in pursuit of middle-class pleasures. As restaurateurs, hotel owners, and department store directors, they were closely involved with the city's consumer culture. New York's development as a center of commercial culture drew middle-class visitors and shoppers into the city, eager to visit Bloomingdale's and Wanamaker's department stores or to gaze upon the millionaires' mansions on Fifth Avenue, as well as visiting established sites such as the Statue of Liberty and the American Museum of Natural History.

The work of tenement house reformers, settlement house workers, health clinics, and temperance crusaders in the city's impoverished immigrant neighborhoods offered two reasons for guidebooks and their tourist clientele to ignore those areas. First, the reformers' success in publicizing urban problems suggested their solutions were well underway, creating the impression that the poor and their neighborhoods needed less attention and sympathy from the middle classes even though most reform legislation was not passed until the early twentieth century. The poorhouses, orphanages, and asylums had been a regular feature of the tourist itinerary in the second half of the nineteenth century. Guidebooks gradually dropped them from their pages as public interest and pride in such welfare institutions faded and as organized charity promoted a less sentimental view of the poor. In addition, the rise of social Darwinism during this period suggested that the poor were "naturally" and irredeemably poor, thus freeing the middle classes from any requirement to "save" them. Second, as guidebook authors pointed out to their readers, the increasing amelioration of urban social problems made poor neighborhoods less attractive as tourist sites offering opportunities for the "slumming" and salacious voyeurism so heralded in the 1870s and 1880s.

Seeing New York from the World

Beginning in the 1890s, visitors to New York could indulge in a new way of seeing the city. Standing on the top of the World Building, their feet planted firmly on one tourist attraction, they could look out over some of the other sites listed in their guidebooks. This perspective worked to present the city as an exciting spectacle, throwing open the curtains to reveal the first scene in the coming show, while at the same time providing the visitors with comfortable distance from the street-level hubbub. Opened in January 1890, the Pulitzer or World Building was designed by the established architect George B. Post, who had also designed, among other important New York edifices, the New York Times Building.[5] The opening of the Pulitzer Building represented the beginning of a new relationship among urban architecture, business, and efforts to promote the city, which matured during the first two decades of the twentieth century. In the 1890s, with businessmen beginning to form effective organizations, a "City Beautiful" movement encouraging a more positive attitude toward the urban environment, and the rapid expansion of white-collar industries in New York bringing greater wealth and new employees to the city, the time was ripe for building the institutions and the professional networks of late-century urban boosterism.[6]

Effective boosting, like effective reform work, required powerful images in the emerging visual culture of the 1890s. The Pulitzer Building created two key types of booster image for 1890s New York: the spectacular view from its rooftop as well as the spectacle of the building itself, created by its size but also by association to the exciting, sensational world of the daily press. Located in "Printing House Square," at Park Row and Frankfort Street, the Pulitzer Building comprised over twenty stories and stood more than 375 feet tall.[7] The Pulitzer was not the city's first skyscraper, nor was it the first tall building offering great urban views to tourists. However, the Pulitzer Building, in both style and function, encapsulated some of the essential features of the cultural and economic changes in New York in the 1890s. First, and perhaps most important, the building signified the power of Joseph Pulitzer and, by implication, of the mass circulation newspapers. By 1890, when the World Building opened to great fanfare, Pulitzer's paper had a daily circulation of 185,672. His rivals—the *Herald,* the *Tribune,* the *Sun,* and the *Times*—boasted circulations of 90,000, 80,000, 50,000, and 40,000 respectively.[8] Such figures indicate a massive reading public, eager for news about themselves and their city, as well as great local power and huge profits for Pulitzer and the other newspaper magnates.[9]

Second, the building helped change the point from which urban visitors obtained their panoramic vistas of New York, moving it from the traditional viewpoint offered by the spire of Trinity Church to the domes, towers, and campaniles built by Mammon. Thus the building represented large shifts in power and culture at the close of the nineteenth century, the confluence of business and tourism being one aspect of that change. Eager for positive publicity in an era suspicious of the growth of corporate power and aware of the attraction their edifices exerted on visitors from outside New York, the owners of new commercial buildings in Manhattan in the 1890s almost always provided public access to their top stories and often included public observation areas in their roofs and towers. The great monied powers in New York at the close of the century were the insurance industry and the country's first mass media, the daily newspapers. These two businesses built the tallest and most impressive buildings of the late 1880s and the 1890s.[10] Their buildings, extensively discussed in the daily and periodical press and starkly visible in the still relatively low-storied city, became the period's great architectural landmarks. So contemporary guidebooks nearly always recommended to tourists a visit to one or more of the tallest commercial buildings.

"One stands there," the reporter continued in his New Year's Eve story from atop the Pulitzer Building, "as it were, within the lower segment of a great circle, and yet it is possible to imagine one at the centre and that with each turn of the head a new sector were formed, with lines marking the visual range as radii and the hills far away as the arc." He described the view from the World Building's dome, segment by segment, as though constructing a panoramic photograph. To support his claims about the view's magnificence, he quoted various out-of-town visitors who had come that New Year's Eve to see the view and to visit the other parts of the building open to the public. The tourists quoted were, of course, uniformly thrilled by the view. Colonel L. J. Hurle of Augusta, Georgia, for example, declared, "The stranger who comes to this city and goes away without visiting the Pulitzer Building misses one of the great sights of the world." Other visitors—from Connecticut, New Jersey, Alabama, Colorado, England, Missouri, and Oregon—also remarked on the tremendous view and how grateful they were to *The World* for allowing them into the dome to see it. Such tourist declarations served as good public relations for the powerful Pulitzer, eager to appear civic-minded in an era suspicious of the conspicuous concentration of wealth and power. For the tourists, the view from Pulitzer's building framed their visit to, and gave perspective on, New York. The view worked to connect commercial institutions with visual pleasure and further anticipated excitement, freeing them from the finger-wagging of the reformers and their demands for civic responsibility.

A pamphlet provided to the building's visitors revealed the edifice's multiple functions and significances in 1890s New York: architectural wonder, tourist attraction, and valuable piece of real estate. The pamphlet acted as a guide to the building, a guide to the city, an advertisement for the newspaper, and an advertisement for the building's available office space.[11] The pamphlet's cover featured a photograph of the Pulitzer Building (fig. 2.1), beneath which were the words "In the path of a million people daily" and a telephone number for the building's agent. Inside the pamphlet the reader could learn facts and statistics about the building, about "points of interest in New York," "Places of Amusement," "Music Halls," and information about the "World's Presses," directing the reader to the many colorful commercial pleasures of New York rather than the black-and-white world of the reformers.[12] To attract advertisers, the pamphlet's last two pages indicated the wide reach of the paper, claiming a circulation of five million per week the previous year. The illustrated advertisement for the Sunday edition showed a white-cuffed man's hand, suggesting an office worker or businessman, spread out over the circulation area of the Sunday paper. His palm covered all of New York City, and his fingers reached out into Vermont, New Hampshire, Massachusetts, Delaware and Pennsylvania.

The pamphlet's back cover appealed to the building's other customer base: real estate agents and businesspeople interested in the availability and suitability of office space in the Pulitzer Building. The advertisement suggested that the implied reader, a "Real Estate Expert," would decide that the Pulitzer Building's location was the best available in "the western hemisphere" because it was in New York and "near the Post Office, Courts and all centres of activity." To the businessman, the appeal was also based on location: "Don't you want [an office] in a popular centre, where your clients and customers can find you without consulting a map or encyclopedia?" The internal features of the building adding to its appeal included the facts that it was open seven days a week, it was "absolutely fire proof," and "its elevators never stop."[13] Like the tourist, the businessman played a key role in the production of New York's new image in the 1890s. Tourists and businessmen had similar concerns about situating themselves in a city suitable for the pursuit of a middle-class lifestyle and an array of suitable urban pleasures. They also shared concerns about understanding

Fig. 2.1. World Building promotional guidebook, c. 1899, front cover. Tourists could read the impressive facts and figures about the building. Reproduced by permission from the Warshaw Collection of Business Americana, Archives Center, National Museum of American History, Behring Center, Smithsonian Institution.

the city's commercial and consumer geography, needing assurance that their sites of business or pleasure enjoyed proximity to the services, populations, and institutions necessary for their success, profit, or enjoyment. The World Building aimed to satisfy both sets of customers, as this pamphlet's various appeals make clear.

The World Building also, of course, represented the editorial and political perspective of Joseph Pulitzer. An immigrant and a Jew, part of New York's first generation of powerful Jewish business leaders, Pulitzer suffered numerous public anti-Semitic attacks, in particular those of Leander Richardson, co-owner and editor of the trade journal, *The Journalist,* which referred to the owner of *The World* as "Jewseph Pulitzer."[14] As an immigrant, as a late nineteenth-century reformist liberal, and certainly as a businessman keen to sell his paper to as many of the city's inhabitants as possible, Pulitzer championed the tenement-dwelling poor and the new immigrants (many of whom, in the 1890s, were Jewish) to an extent unmatched by the other daily papers.[15] However, as his biographers point out, Pulitzer was no radical and consistently opposed any increase in local or state expenditure to solve the problems against which he railed.

Pulitzer's view of the city—what he saw from his window and what the city signified to him—was that of the businessman. As he looked out of his office window on the roofs of his rivals' papers, his field of vision also encompassed City Hall, the banks and insurance companies around Wall Street and Lower Broadway, and the city's growing retail district, which moved during the decade from the "Ladies' Mile" of Broadway and Sixth Avenue between 14th and 23rd Streets further uptown toward 34th Street. From this position he could also see many of his customers, located throughout the array of streets, businesses, and homes within his view. Pulitzer's New York, the businessman's city, was not the striped cartographic landscape of the Tenement House Commission; nor the dark, airless apartment of Jacob Riis's "Italian rag-picker"; nor the measured and tabulated statistical portrait drawn up by the "scientific" charity organizations. New York seen from *The World* and other commercial viewing positions resembled more closely the city depicted, in word and image, in the guidebooks of the late 1880s and the 1890s: a more complex and popular picture of New York, neither "black" nor "white" but, like the halftone images increasingly dominating their pages, combining the various shades of the city. But, as with the halftones, legibility required the right balance of distance and proximity.

Selling the City's New Image

The city presented in New York guidebooks during the late 1880s and the 1890s was a site of commercial consumption edited and described by a corporate, not an individual, author. The New York of George Foster and James McCabe had given way to an image of New York sponsored by a downtown hotel, seen via a souvenir album of views supplied courtesy of a soap company, or published by the local newspaper company and sent with the compliments of the local church.[16] For example, *How to Know New York,* published in 1887 in Boston by the Rand Avery Company, was compiled under the sponsorship of the Grand Union Hotel, though this is not stated explicitly. The guidebook's title page mentions the hotel as the starting point of their itinerary, the second page of the guide is an advertisement for the hotel, the introduction mentions the hotel, and two pages of advice to the reader depict a visitor getting useful information from a hotel clerk at the Grand Union Hotel, at which establishment the reader was recommended to stay while in the city. As business products, largely funded by selling advertising space, the style and content of the guides changed considerably. The city presented to visitors in these publications was a city of hotels, of manufacturing and retail establishments, of commercial institutions featured in the guide itself or pictured in its advertising spaces. The personal tone of an individual author, warning of thrilling urban dangers or extolling the virtues of the city's leading politicians, was replaced by corporate anonymity and the blandness of boosterism.

By the mid-1880s, guidebook publishers were not interested in portraying a city divided into zones of "sunlight and shadow."

For the sake of their advertisers or sponsors, they depicted New York as a safe, entertaining, easily navigable place suitable for the most discerning middle-class visitor. Instead of chapters on the sins and squalor of saloons and tenements, this new generation of guides offered usable itineraries to visitors contemplating a trip to New York and gave guidance as to how best to see the new city "sights."[17] That urban tourism was, by the 1890s, a major aspect of New York's economy, and growing consumer culture encouraged this shift away from the earlier nineteenth-century rhetoric of the dichotomous city. While there are no specific figures to measure how many visitors came to New York in the last two decades of the nineteenth century for the purpose of sightseeing, one can estimate their increasing numbers from the growth in the number, size, and services of hotels in the city, as well as other businesses such as sightseeing companies, whose growth depended on the tourist trade. City directories in 1890 listed 128 hotels in the city, twenty or more of which had been built since 1880. The number and quality of hotels in New York continued to grow through the 1890s and 1910s. By 1895 city directories list 183 hotels; by 1912 more than 200 hotels had the capacity to offer fifty or more rooms.[18]

Some of New York's grandest hotels were built in the 1890s, a few of which endured to accommodate several generations of tourists. The rapidity with which they appeared, their locations, and the facilities they offered all speak to the swift development of the tourist trade in turn-of-the-century New York. These hotels, such as the Hotel Savoy (1891–92) and the Hotel New Netherland (1892–93), were luxury hotels as opposed to apartment hotels. The latter provided permanent residential accommodations but without separate kitchen facilities. All meals were taken in the hotel's communal dining room. Beginning in the late 1880s, apartment hotels grew in number and popularity among well-to-do families wishing for convenient, respectable city addresses without the expense of a full-service household. However, by 1910 their heyday had ended due to the establishment of a range of middle-class apartment houses that allowed for individual housekeeping in the form of kitchens, dining rooms, and sometimes modest servant accommodations within each apartment.[19]

New York's new large hotels, oriented to a "transient" (non-residential) clientele, were built in locations convenient to railroad stations and to tourist amenities. The Waldorf and Astoria hotels joined together in 1897, at the prime location of Fifth Avenue between 33rd and 34th Streets, close to the theater district. The Hotel Savoy and the Hotel New Netherland overlooked Central Park at Fifth Avenue and 59th Street, occupying the southeast and northeast corners of the location, respectively. By the 1890s, the areas around Broadway and Fifth Avenue in the mid-30s, 40s, and 50s, were already quite developed as tourist locations. Herald Square, Longacre (later Times) Square, the middle of Fifth Avenue, and Broadway between 33rd and 59th Streets all offered the amusements and amenities on which tourists relied and which had drawn them to New York in the first place. Soon after the turn of the century, beginning with Macy's in 1902, the major department stores in the shopping district of "Ladies Mile" on Sixth Avenue began to follow other commercial, consumer culture enterprises uptown to Broadway and especially to Fifth Avenue between 34th and 59th Streets.[20]

Following the hotels, the city's theaters and restaurants moved north from the old downtown starting in the 1880s and 1890s. At the turn of the century, land and real estate in the Midtown areas were relatively cheap compared to the overcrowded and expensive downtown areas increasingly given over to business and finance. Beginning with Rudolph Aronson's Casino Theater at Broadway and 39th Street (1882) and the Metropolitan Opera House on Broadway between 39th and 40th Streets (1883), the city's midsection rapidly developed into an entertainment district. The Broadway Theatre at Broadway and 41st Street (1888), the American Theatre at Eighth Avenue and 41st Street (1893), and Oscar Hammerstein's Olympia at Broadway and 44th Street (1895) helped anchor the area and draw other entertainment businesses to Midtown, especially to Longacre Square. According to historian Margaret Knapp, in the 1899–1900 theater season only one of Manhattan's twenty-two theaters was located in Longacre Square; ten years later the majority of the city's thirty-four theaters were both new and located in Times Square, as the area was by then known.[21]

In addition to hotel accommodations and theaters, tourists also came in search of gustatory pleasure and adventure. Starting in the 1890s, restaurants to suit a range of wallets and appetites also began to cluster in the developing hotel and theater district, some leaving their previous locations in Lower Manhattan. Orienting themselves to theatergoers, the restaurants competed to provide dramatic decor and a theatrical celebrity clientele, which in turn drew the spectacle-hungry crowds. Rector's, Delmonico's, Sherry's, Shanley's, Churchill's, Maxim's, and Murray's Roman Gardens all opened between the mid-1890s and 1910 and were situated within walking distance of the hotels, theaters, and public transportation frequented by tourists eager to see sights so unlike those in their hometowns. The coordination of these services and facilities provided the foundation for the further rapid development of Midtown as the tourist's New York and as the new public face of the city by the 1920s.[22]

At the close of the nineteenth century, a wide range of people had reason to visit New York for both short and long stays: shopkeepers and other tradespeople from the New England or midwestern hinterlands coming to purchase wholesale goods in New York's various markets and exchanges, businessmen seeking financial support for new ventures, relatives and friends of the increasing numbers of men and women who moved to New York in search of employment or a new life, and tourists from all over the United States and Europe visiting America's largest metropolis. The growth of service and clerical work in the new economy of department stores, hotels, insurance companies, and banks created work at a range of skill levels for thousands of young men and women. William Leach notes that the number of service workers nationwide increased fivefold between 1870 and 1910. In New York, home to the greatest concentration of such new forms of business, the increase was likely even more precipitous.[23] The nation's booming railroad network, for which New York formed an important hub, brought such workers, as well as consumers and goods, into the city from all regions of the United States.

Guidebooks at the close of the century, serving this wide array of visitors (and new residents) to New York, continued to include as possible sites of interest notorious areas such as Mulberry Bend and the other tenement neighborhoods of the Lower East Side, but not as part of the main itinerary. These impoverished areas, central to the contemporaneous reformers' view of the city and to earlier nineteenth-century guides, became marginal to the new tourist geography of 1890s New York, which was shaped quite deliberately by the business community. The 1890s guidebooks emphasized the city's spectacular aspects: the view of the city from a tall building, the finely dressed Sunday crowds on Fifth Avenue, the national and racial variety of the population, the skyscraper-filled business district, the mansions of Fifth Avenue, and the upscale apartment buildings of Riverside Drive. In these guidebooks we see the beginning of a new version of New York—increasingly referred to in the periodical press as "the new New York"—which would dominate representations of the city in the early years of the twentieth century.

The most impressive guides to the city in this decade in size and quality—and some of the most popular—were those issued by Moses King. Born in England in 1853, King established himself as a publisher of guidebooks and journals based in Cambridge, Massachusetts. King's 1892 *Handbook of New York City* was 1008 pages in length and contained "over 1000 illustrations," almost all of which were halftones.[24] King's *Handbook* was indeed larger, more detailed, better researched and written, and more sumptuously illustrated than any other New York guidebook of its time. In the hyperbolic style familiar from earlier guidebooks, as well as from advertising, King trumpeted his *Handbook*'s size and scope, citing its "index of twenty-four pages with 72 columns, containing over 5,000 items and about 20,000 references." He declared it "the handsomest, the most thorough, the largest, the most costly and the most profusely illustrated book of its class ever issued for any city in the world."[25] With its encyclopedic size and extensive illustrations, King's handbook differed from the majority of late nineteenth-century guidebooks to New York. Most other guidebooks were designed to be carried about the city and were published in a size and format appropriate for that purpose. Unlike King's *Handbook*, they also commonly included maps, usually a fold-out glued to the front or back inside cover. However, King's *Handbook* serves as a representative example of the guidebook trends of the 1890s insofar as King shared with other publishers and authors a fondness for facts and figures about New York, an emphasis on the rooftop view of the city, a desire to promote New York's "cosmopolitan" population, and an appeal to a middle-class audience of both men and women.[26]

King demonstrated an appreciation for quantification similar to that of his social scientist and reformer peers, but, like other guidebook publishers and authors, he employed it as part of a promotional, booster rhetoric. Having enumerated the city's impressive vital statistics, King declared New York "the proud New-World metropolis," the "Empire City of the Western World," and "in all that best distinguishes modern civilization, . . . the rival of the great capitals of the Old World."[27] The notion that New York now rivaled Paris and London as a center of urban splendor and "modern civilization" became a familiar rallying cry among late-century boosters, a nationalist and imperialist claim made with increasing confidence in the early years of the next century.

To emphasize the spectacular quality of the city, to create a strong visual impression on the reader, and to provide a rapid orientation, King constructed his second chapter, "New York of the Present," by alternating pages of text with pages containing photographic views taken from the dome of—where else?—Pulitzer's World Building. The text and photographs, separately and in combination, provided a panoramic, almost cinematic view of the city. By means of this chapter, King achieved in his text what other guidebooks encouraged tourists to accomplish in person upon arriving in the city: to go to the roof of the World Building, or some other tall building, and gaze out at the impressive view of the city, becoming both visually oriented to the city and excited about the coming itinerary.

The text of his "panoramic" chapter moved, topic by topic,

Fig. 2.2. "Looking Southwest from the 'World' Dome," taken from atop the World Building, *King's Handbook of New York* (Boston: Moses King, 1893), was part of the turn-of-the-century representation of New York as an ideal city for middle-class sightseeing—in marked contrast to the depictions of the tenement house reformers, who emphasized the city's social problems.

through statistics and "facts" about the city, its government, its infrastructure, and its population. King continued to emphasize the city's size, scope, and scale. For example, King claimed that New York was "the most cosmopolitan city in the world" by virtue of the number and variety of "nationalities" represented within its borders. "It has more Irish than Dublin, and more Germans than any other German city except Berlin." He added that there were "colonies" within the city, "the French, the German, the Italian, the African, the Chinese, the Hebrew, the Spanish and the Arab colonies."[28] Unlike his guidebook predecessors or reformer contemporaries, King mentioned these foreign colonies not as social problems but as part of the exciting visual spectacle awaiting the tourist. From the number of the members of the judiciary and their annual salaries to immigration figures and facts about the water supply, King provided his readers with a textual, statistical, and "factual" panorama of the city in 1892.

The series of ten rooftop photographs taken from the dome atop Joseph Pulitzer's World Building together provide a visual panorama of the city. Taken in bright sunshine, the photographs clearly show the city stretching upwards and outwards from the confines of its four- or five-storied nineteenth century limits and across the river into Brooklyn, challenging the independence of the sister city. Church spires still reached up above most of the city's buildings, but the new buildings of Newspaper Row next to City Hall Park, one of which was the World Building, had begun to challenge the church's position in the skyline. The Tribune and Times Buildings, in the foreground of the photographs taken looking southwest (fig. 2.2) and west from the World Building's dome, far overshadow the neighboring buildings on nearby Broadway and Chambers Street. In the immediate vicinity of the World Building, the photographs show the streets filled with shops and other businesses, the sidewalks and roads busy with pedestrians, streetcars, carts, carriages, and even one or two very new automobiles. Looking east and south, the photographs depicted an older, more congested, less glamorous city—the locale of warehouses, of manufacturing, and of the East River piers. In these areas one cannot see down to street level, thus lessening the area's visual appeal. Fittingly, these streets, made less visible in this representation, formed the locus of the "shadowy" attractions emphasized in earlier nineteenth-century guidebooks, as well as the focus of reform representations of 1890s New York. The overall impression given by the series of photographs is of a city seemingly without end, its horizon lost in the invisible distance or in the smoky haze that merges with the sky, certainly an impression in keeping with Moses King's grandiloquent descriptions of New York. The city depicted thus contrasted sharply with the squalid, street-by-street, room-by-room images emphasized by Riis and other reformers at this time.

Viewing the city from a rooftop or church tower was not new to the late nineteenth century. Until the mid-1880s, the spire of Trinity Church was the best available viewing point in the city. Situated in Lower Manhattan near Bowling Green and Wall Street, the spire offered good views of the lower section of Manhattan Island and of Upper New York Bay and the Narrows. By the mid-1880s, with tourism to the city increasing yearly, guidebooks could recommend two other sites in Lower Manhattan from which visitors could obtain a "bird's eye view": the Produce Exchange Building, designed by George B. Post and completed in 1884, attaining a height of 224 feet from the sidewalk to the tower, and the Washington Building, built by Edward Kendall in 1885, which after the 1887 addition of a new mansard roof and tower attained a height of 258 feet. Though not exceeding Trinity in overall height, the location of both buildings on the edges of Bowling Green, a few blocks south of Trinity, meant that they offered unsurpassed views of the Battery, the Bay, Castle Garden, and north up Broadway across the expanding city. Such views placed the spectator in the heart of the city's financial district, among the most valuable real estate in the city, surrounded by the commercial institutions that increasingly defined not only the city's identity but also its unique appearance.

Over the next decades, guidebooks, stereographs, and postcards increasingly sold this view of the city, taken from atop one or another large commercial institution, as the defining image of New York. Familiar now as the establishing shot of any film or television show set in New York City, this view from a high point within the city represented the updated version of the old imagined "bird's eye view" of New York. The earlier nineteenth-century bird's eye view depicted New York from a position outside the city, as though seen from high in the air above Governor's Island or Upper New York Bay. The shift in viewing position signified a shift away from an external and remote view of New York, which emphasized the city's relation to the Atlantic world, to one in which the viewer felt part of the city but also in control of, and safely distant from, what he saw. In these newer views, New York City contained all that was visible, all that mattered, suggesting a new pride in the city's rapid growth, its independent power, and its architectural splendor.

The view from the roof oriented the visitor. This perspective (unlike that attainable at street level) provided an excellent starting point to the tourist itinerary because it presented the entire city as a tourist site, readily seen and explored. Pictured or seen thus, the whole city appeared available for consumption by the tourist; all areas of the city seemed equally open, equally interesting territory, not segmented into areas of "darkness and daylight." Simple removal from the "madding crowd" of the street provided the first phase of orientation. As the author of one guidebook suggested, under the heading "A Bird's Eye View of Greater New York," looking out on the city below helped one "to establish the bearings before striking out on detailed explorations. . . . From some such point of vantage the great city and its neighbors lie below like a map."[29] The view did not, of course, actually resemble a two-dimensional paper representation of the city. What made the view "like a map" was the impression of coherence it offered, a spectacular simplification of the city's complexity. The rooftop view allowed the visitor to see the city's street grid, to identify and locate some of its major landmarks, and to obtain a 360-degree view that showed the "cohesion of part with part" missing at street level. Having obtained such a view, the visitor could embark on their itinerary with a greater (though probably fleeting) sense of a sight-seer's geography.

The era of the early tall buildings in New York, the 1890s, when so many of these viewing positions became available to tourists, was also the era when the city reached a size and a complexity re-quiring that visitors carry with them comprehensive city maps. Unlike earlier guides, most guidebooks in this decade included maps. The maps were fairly plain, consisting of the street grid, major transportation lines into and within the city, and a few land-mark tourist sights. In the following decades, tourist maps, pub-lished as separate items, rather than attached to guidebooks, became increasingly colorful and often included photographs or engraved images of significant buildings on the map or as an illus-trated border. By the 1930s, tourist maps were so familiar a part of the tourist's equipment that they could afford to become more humorous than strictly practical, illustrated with cartoon images connoting the characteristics or populations of particular neigh-borhoods. The maps performed not only a practical function but, increasingly, simple encouragement to out-of-towners initially overwhelmed by the size of the city and its population. The maps rendered New York a navigable, legible, and ultimately playful space.[30]

How to See New York: The Itinerary

In keeping with their practical—as opposed to simply vicari-ous—orientation, most 1890s guides provided a one-day or one-week itinerary for seeing the city and its principal sights. Such itin-eraries varied little from one guidebook to the next and changed only to add a new attraction—such as a new architectural feature or place of amusement—or to remove a site that had become *passé*. Publishers apparently assumed that all tourists (business travelers or middle-class families) had the same interests, so a "one size fits all" itinerary sufficed. The guidebook genre had not yet evolved into the themed publications for specific "niche markets" with which we are familiar today. However, the itinerary in most 1890s guides gradually downplayed older tourist sites, such as the reformatories and asylums on the East River islands or the old city prison downtown, popularly known as "The Tombs." The itineraries of the newer guides also marginalized the old "slumming" haunts of the Bowery, Five Points, and the immigrant neighborhoods on the East Side, though they would reappear as major attractions in the 1920s.[31]

The usual recommended route began at the Battery with a visit to the Aquarium at Castle Garden and continued up the West Side on the Sixth Avenue elevated railroad, from which the visitor could get an impression of "the compact building of the city, of its crowded streets, of its richly stocked shops, its handsome churches and theaters, its noise and rush and its industry." From the "el" one could also see Central Park on one's right above 60th Street. Reaching the end of the Sixth Avenue line, the visitor could see the High Bridge over the Harlem River and the larger span of the Washington Bridge. Having seen the West Side of the city, the visitor might then return by the elevated line to walk through Central Park to the American Museum of Natural History near the 79th Street entrance to the park and then east across the park to the Metropolitan Museum of Art. Traveling down Fifth Avenue by stage, perhaps, the sights available included the St. Patrick's Cathedral, the homes of wealthy and famous residents such as the Vanderbilts, and some of the city's largest and most expensive hotels, such as the Plaza at 59th Street. The guide quoted above advised its readers that the city's principal sights could be seen in a day "if the traveler is quick in the use of his eyes and his legs." However, given the list of "principal sights" that followed, the traveler would not have had time to alight from their chosen means of traversing the city for more than a moment.[32]

By the 1890s, the locations on the sightseeing itinerary had changed considerably from the guides of the 1850s or even the 1880s. Writers and publishers placed far less emphasis on the supposedly dangerous or immoral aspects of New York and far more on the city's new buildings, infrastructure, and middle-class pleasures suitable for both men and women. These writers did not entirely drop the older interest in the poorer sections of the city and their nefarious nighttime pleasures, but now they presented such material as part of the "local color" and rich diversity of city sights available to the tourist. One can ascribe this change of emphasis in part to the fact that the older guides had functioned more as opportunities for armchair travel, whereas the writers of guidebooks in the 1890s intended their books as practical guides to the city, to be carried about by various visitors.

As numerous scholars have shown, the turn-of-the-century city became an increasingly mixed-sex space, with more women traveling on their own into cities, and more women occupying the city's everyday retail and business spaces, as both workers and consumers.[33] Publishers of guidebooks, attuned to changes in commercial culture, had to appeal to the female tourist (fig. 2.3). It became increasingly common for guidebooks to include information on hotels catering to women traveling alone or coming to the city as young unmarried workers. By 1903, single female

Fig. 2.3. "Seeing the Sights" postcard (1906) shows an increasingly familiar sight along New York's tourist routes: the sightseeing bus. This bus is carrying a group of well-dressed ladies, part of a new generation of female urban tourists. Reproduced by permission from the Victor A. Blenkle Postcard Collection, Archives Center, National Museum of American History, Behring Center, Smithsonian Institution.

visitors to the city could stay at the Hotel Martha Washington, founded specifically as a women-only hotel. Some other hotels had a floor of the building designated for women visitors only. Guides also offered suggestions of restaurants that would welcome women dining alone at lunch or dinner.[34]

To serve the needs of a greater number and variety of tourists, the guidebooks of the 1890s had to offer something more wholesome than titillating accounts of urban pleasures and dangers. In their efforts to cater to the city's growing number of visitors, these late-century guidebooks occasionally presented the city as if it consisted of nothing but large commercial buildings, churches, and elegant parks, as is the case with much of King's 1892 guide. On the whole, however, they tried to emphasize the city's newest attractions and put a positive spin on older aspects of city life deemed problematic by other contemporary commentators not involved in the business of selling the city—on those areas and populations included in the older guides' domain of "darkness."

The new "spin" on the city offered by these guidebooks is perhaps best seen in their descriptions of, and attitudes to, the city's poor and foreign populations. For example, *Hints for Strangers, Shoppers, and Sight See-ers in the Metropolis,* published in about 1891, gave information about the city common to both late nineteenth-century and early twentieth-century guidebooks—such as statistics and "facts" about the city, a guide to retail areas and establishments, a list of churches, and a table showing the routes of the various elevated railroad stations—but also offered a view of the city's streets and people markedly different from those given by the earlier generation of guidebook writers. One of the first sections of the guide is entitled "The Passing Throng," and it begins by telling the reader, "In no place on this continent can a visitor view such a kaleidoscopic scene as is continually presented by the crowds upon our streets." Offering the city's population as a sight akin to those available at a fair or menagerie, the writer described the picturesque visual pleasures available during a simple walk down the city's streets: "It is no infrequent sight to meet Greeks, Turks, Spaniards, Arabs, Armenians, Finns, etc., in walk-

ing but a few blocks. In fact all these foreigners in their native cos-
tumes are such common sights that the average New Yorker never
gives them a second glance in passing." Such rhetoric made a direct
appeal to visitors unfamiliar with, and possibly intimidated by,
the racial and ethnic diversity of America's large cities. Continuing his rhetoric of the picturesque, the writer described the neighborhoods where these colorful foreigners lived, not as ghettoes of
Europe's and America's bedraggled and criminal but rather as a
sort of residential fairground midway: "whole blocks are occupied almost entirely by adopted citizens of particular countries,
many of whom retain to a great extent their old world habits and
customs, something can always be seen to interest and amuse even
the passing stranger." However, the guide provided neither information about how to reach these areas nor an itinerary for the
"foreign quarters."[35]

The Gate to the Sea, a guide to New York published by the
Eagle Press of Brooklyn in about 1897, also discussed New York's
poor and foreign but discouraged close contact with such peoples
and their neighborhoods. The guidebook began by advising its
readership that New York was an easy city to travel through, due
to its simple grid layout and the ready availability of public transportation. The guidebook showed little sympathy with, or interest in, the poor and immigrant masses of the city, nor in their
neighborhoods. The "bird's eye view" description of the city the
guidebook offered, written (yet again) as though from the roof of
the World Building, included a glimpse of Ellis Island, described
as a place where "thousands of worthless and vicious people, as
well as other thousands of honest, law-abiding and desirable additions to our populace, are landed every month." With a nod to
other tastes in urban tourism, the author suggested: "And, by all
means, see a little of the seamy side of metropolitan life, in order
that the impression of the city shall be true. See the tenement districts of the East and West Side, the crowded, squalid, noisy, ill-
smelling, dirty barracks, where families pay as much in two years
for a room as would give them a home of their own in the health-
ful country. Here vice and crime abound; here the death-rate is

high; here are ignorance, drunkenness, filth, insolence. The effect is depressing and a very short visit suffices." This perspective on the poor and their neighborhoods offered no sympathy, nor did it encourage such a response in the reader. Nor is there any moral outrage over poverty, nor a sense of responsibility toward the poor. At best, the poor and the foreign of the city are part of the vast spectacle of the city, but certainly not an appealing or very important feature. To those determined to look at the "seamy" side of the city, the writer suggested certain streets within the "foreign quarters" that offered easy visual consumption of such sights, such as the "picturesque exhibit in Mott and Doyers streets" of the Chinese community, or Hester Street's Russian Jews, "queer, stunted people, shabby in their dress, dirty in their surroundings, eager in making trades, fiercely jabbering together in the doorways and on the sidewalks."[36]

According to this guide, as with others published at the time, visitors should avoid these neighborhoods not only because they were squalid but because they had lost the notoriety of times past. The effects of urban and social reform on the Lower East Side had created a disappointing result, the writer suggested: "Five Points was at one time the worst place in New York. It is now a place of missions and schools. . . . The Bowery will always remain one of the attractions of New York, though of late years it has become so respectable that it does not offer the facilities for a 'slumming' tour that it once did."[37]

By 1897, when this guide was published, the booster view of the city was already a long way from the perspective of Jacob Riis, whose *How the Other Half Lives* had been published just seven years before. While Riis's text read in many ways like a guide to the city, offering a mix of moral outrage and sensationalism, his work belonged to the earlier generation of "darkness and daylight" guides to New York. In 1897, on the eve of the formation of Greater New York, *The Gate to the Sea* represented the new image of New York as a site of opportunities for middle-class pleasure and business. The guide's very title suggested an elegant resort, and its cover bore a single illustration of a man and woman, both in full riding gear, exercising their horses along a bridle path, perhaps in Central Park. Its pages were filled with photographs of large edifices and carried advertisements for a wide range of local businesses and retail shops. The previous year, the city's largest railroad company had issued a guide to New York promoting the city as a summer resort.[38] With guidebooks such as *The Gate to the Sea,* New York City's image as a middle-class tourist destination rapidly gained ground at the turn of the century.

New York on Display

These new guides presented the city as a show, as a largely visual form of entertainment like the elaborately decorated department store windows that drew the gaze of window shoppers or the midway amusement sections of late nineteenth-century expositions, early precursors to twentieth-century theme parks. The evolving guidebook image represented New York as a series of exhibitionary spaces, like peep shows writ large, in which one was guaranteed certain sights: night life on Broadway, skyscrapers around Wall Street, and conspicuous wealth on Fifth Avenue. This presentation of the "city as theme park" reached its apogee in the tourist literature of the 1920s. Tourist experiences traversing the great fairs and expositions of the late nineteenth century—especially Chicago in 1893—provided a framework for these guided explorations of the city. Guidebooks and maps presented New York as they might present an exposition, explaining how to travel from one area to another, the locations of the different zones of edification or amusement, and how much one could do in a set amount of time. Certainly by the turn of the century, the similarities between city and exposition likely shaped many tourist experiences and expectations of the cities they visited.[39]

This presentation of the city seemingly offered an all-inclusive, multifaceted version of New York. But, like an exposition or a theme park, this version of New York provided a selected view of the city's many aspects. It presented the city's best and most entertaining face. It interpreted (or re-interpreted) almost all areas of the city as potentially entertaining and accessible to the tourist.

However, these guides devoted far more space to, and encouraged visitors to spend more time in, areas of the city becoming standard to the tourist itinerary, such as Fifth Avenue and Broadway. Marginal areas of the city, such as the immigrant neighborhoods, were described but not at length. Tourist access to such neighborhoods quickly came under the control of sightseeing bus companies, with set routes and stopping points in "typical" locations in "Chinatown" or "The Ghetto."[40]

The author of *Hints for Strangers, Shoppers, and Sight See-ers* tells his readers about the various "parades" they could watch in specific areas of the city at various times of the day or week, referencing a much older tradition of urban spectacle—the political parade or festival—re-worked for consumerist ends.[41] On weekday afternoons, for example, one might observe "the daily parades of the fair sex" in the shopping districts along "Broadway, Fourth and Sixth Avenues, between Tenth and Twenty-third streets." On a Sunday morning, Fifth Avenue offered the "Sunday parade" of fashionably dressed churchgoers. In the entertainment districts of Broadway and around the department stores and hotels after dark, one could gaze at the even more splendid nighttime crowd, the "gaily caparisoned army of amusement seekers." The well-dressed crowds, the stores, and the incandescent glow of the streets merged together at night, the author suggested, "the brilliant glare of the electric lights and illuminated show-windows reflecting back from the sparkling jewels and bright eyes of rare and radiant maids and matrons, [making] an entertaining and bewildering living picture." The city and its inhabitants became one massive display, an animated tableau depicting "city life" at its apogee.[42]

Such descriptions of the street crowds acted like a sidewalk "barker," drawing the reader/tourist into the "show." The heterogeneous crowd suggested again the accessibility of the city to all comers, rather than the division of the city into domains of "darkness" and "daylight" or the exclusive territories of the rich or the poor. The contemporary notion of the city as an alienating place was vanquished by the appealing image of an environment in which "all classes are out for inspection and review." However, since visitors generally came to New York, as to any other tourist destination, to see places and people different from themselves, the guidebook writer described the varied street populations as both cosmopolitan and entertaining. On Sundays, for example, one could attend two "shows." The first was offered by the Lower East Side, along the Bowery, "the favorite promenade for the entire heterogeneous cosmopolitan element which constitutes the thickly populated East side."[43] Alternatively, or for contrast, one could watch Fifth Avenue's Sunday parade, offering the "juxtaposition" of "grave judges and reverend divines" alongside "men-about-town, . . . swell members of the demi-monde and pets of the footlights." When described in these terms, the *habitués* of these city "parades" became neither good nor bad, denizens of neither "sunlight" nor "shadow." Together they combined to make the sort of inclusive image of New York promoted by the guidebooks, "each contributing a portion of the light[,] shade and brilliance which makes up a picture that . . . need only to be seen to be appreciated."[44] The nuanced image thus produced suggested a halftone or a photograph, the visual means by which tourists increasingly prepared for, or memorialized, their visits.

Photography was a tool used by visitors themselves, as well as by guidebooks, to depict the city. The wide availability and affordability of the snapshot camera by the mid-1890s meant that tourists increasingly recorded their travel itineraries in images rather than in words. The written travel diary remained a popular form for recording experiences, but snapshots certainly enhanced such memories. Photography was a popular hobby by the close of the nineteenth century, with cameras advertised widely in the daily press and various magazines devoted to the pursuit. One guidebook reminded its readers to record the sights of the city with their cameras, for their own sake and "for your friends and neighbors at home." However, those without cameras could almost always find a postcard bearing an image based on a photograph. First popularized in the 1890s, postcards often served as mementos of favorite sights or as visual records to show the folks at home what they had missed.[45]

In keeping with the trend to record the city visually rather than textually, tourists could purchase booklets depicting New York solely in photographs or lithographs based on photos. These booklets often bore the title "albums" and imitated, in style and shape, the souvenir or keepsake albums common to middle-class homes in the nineteenth century. These albums worked in a similar way to the popular stereograph sets of views. Like the stereograph "tour" of New York, the photographic albums followed the tourist itinerary familiar from most guidebooks and included most of the same sights. However, these souvenir albums had a particular appeal as a virtual tour of the city or as a keepsake of a visit, since they were easier to handle (requiring no special viewing equipment, as stereographs did), and one could more easily share the experience of looking with others. For example, Rand McNally, already at this point dominating the map and guidebook business in the United States, issued a photographic album in 1895, entitled *Greater New York Album: One Hundred Photographic Views of the Greater New York.* The album offered quality halftone photographic reproductions in a large-format, softcover booklet. The images followed an itinerary starting at Battery Park, going north up Broadway and Fifth Avenue to Central Park and then up the West Side to the new homes along Riverside Drive, to Grant's Tomb, up to the Harlem River, and then over to Brooklyn. The album's first image, "A Misty Morning on New York Bay," offered a romantic picture of sailing vessels, with no hint of the city, a rather unlikely first impression of New York. The next four images continued this gentle introduction to the metropolis, offering views of lower New York City taken from the roofs of two of the area's tallest buildings—one image showing "Battery Park and Harbor from Roof of Washington Building" and three taken from the office building at 66 Broadway, offering views south, southwest, and northeast. The views from 66 Broadway gradually brought the viewer's perspective round from views of the Bay up into the city. The last of these three views looked northeast, encompassing the rooftops of Lower Broadway and the surrounding streets. This image hints at the city's size and its congestion, both potentially daunting aspects to the city a visitor might be about to explore.[46]

This album perfectly represented the boosters' greatest aspirations for turn-of-the-century New York: a monumental, dignified city, home to elegant commercial and municipal edifices, with clean, orderly streets. The one image that suggested the presence of poor or working-class New Yorkers and a way of life beyond Broadway and Fifth Avenue, was a picture of Gansevoort Market on the edge of the Lower East Side. However, the image suggested no threat from this "other half." Barely visible in their dark clothing, dotted in among carts piled high with cabbages, crates, and barrels, the vendors and their market instead made a picturesque image of working-class life in the city. This image foreshadows the tactic increasingly adopted by tourism's boosters. Representing New York's poor and foreign, and their neighborhoods, as "picturesque" served as the perfect strategy for dealing with the fact that not all of New York looked like Fifth Avenue, not all New Yorkers straightforwardly embodied the city's new image as an elegant all-American metropolis. Through the early years of the twentieth century, boosters continued to spin representations of the city's poor and immigrant neighborhoods to make them more appealing to middle-class tourist consumers.

The visual construction of New York in the eyes of tourists, city boosters, and business leaders continued to move away from the street-level, confrontational style pioneered by Jacob Riis and the tightly controlled graphics of the tenement reformers. The attempt to present an appealing image of the *city as a whole* to potential investors, consumers, and tourists dictated that images of New York continue to emphasize the city's commercial strength, epitomized by the skyscrapers, and to downplay graphic images of the streets and people that might detract from an overall impression of metropolitan splendor.

New York's national commercial dominance, and the corporate wealth it produced, found greater architectural expression in the first decades of the twentieth century, far outstripping in size, grandeur, and commercial power Pulitzer's World Building. Insurance companies, large corporations, and speculative commercial builders constructed multi-story office buildings in Lower Manhattan that collectively came to form the city's unique skyscraper skyline. As I will show in the next chapter, local and foreign observers of New York, as well as architects and engineers, identified the skyscraper as a uniquely American building style and New York as the center of its development. Pundits described New York's cluster of skyscrapers as an American landscape, akin to the rocky landscapes of the Far West, bolstering boosters' efforts to rid the city of its old reputation as a site of social and moral decay and replacing it with a new image of New York as the nation's representative city, the American metropolis.

3

ARCHITECTURE, AMERICANISM, AND A "NEW" NEW YORK, 1900–1919

In the spring of 1900, as the Charity Organization Society dismantled its Tenement House Exhibition, and as tourists scribbled postcards of New York's sights to the folks back home, the city's public image was about to begin a major refurbishment, one that paralleled New York's remarkable physical transformation over the next twenty years. Between the turn of the twentieth century and the end of World War I, boosters east and west promoted what they argued were the uniquely American characteristics of, respectively, New York City's new buildings and the rocky landscapes of states such as Colorado and Arizona. Establishing each place's status as a definitively American landscape—as judged by their promoters—confirmed a key selling point to their consumers in an era of growing cultural nationalism. The direct visual and metaphorical association made by local pundits, architectural critics, and tourism entrepreneurs between New York's growing cluster of downtown skyscrapers and the dramatic mountainous landscapes of the West proved crucial to New York's "branding" as a prime early twentieth century tourist destination. This Americanization of New York via the representation and interpretation of landscape and commercial architecture moved forward boosters' efforts, starting in the 1890s, to draw middle-class consumers' attention away from the faces, bodies, and buildings of the Lower East Side.

At the start of the twentieth century, writers, illustrators, and photographers noted the emergence of a "new New York."[1] The "old" New York was the city of "darkness and daylight" portrayed in the late nineteenth-century urban guides, a place representative of the most egregious aspects of urban life; the "old" New York also suggested the undemocratic divisions between rich and poor of the "old" world of Europe, rather than the equality, liberty, and opportunity of republican America. By contrast, the "new" city, built roughly between 1900 and the end of World War I, consisted of an increasingly splendid architectural showcase, an international financial center, and the home of the nation's leading industrial and commercial power brokers. An emergent American national culture, distinct from—and confident enough to challenge—European culture, took root in New York's public and private institutions.

The physical transformation of the city, made possible by new wealth, offered the most powerful evidence of a "new" arguably more "American" New York, and served to draw attention away from the city's persistent social problems, potential blemishes on the fair complexion of New York's new face. Numerous construction projects such as the first subway line, additional bridges across the East River, and various new private and public buildings made Manhattan the site of great architectural and engineering innovation, the first phase of the cycle of demolition and reconstruction that would characterize Manhattan in the first half of the twentieth century.[2] "The fair new city lies in the embrace of the old one like the new moon in the old moon's arms," declared literary and cultural critic Randall Blackshaw in *The Century,* in an article sumptuously illustrated by up-and-coming architectural illustrator Jules Guérin.[3] "One might almost fancy that the town had been bombarded by a hostile fleet," he wrote, "such rents and gashes appear everywhere in the solid masonry, ranging from the width of a single building to that of a whole block front," Blackshaw remarked.[4] Rather than focusing on the inconveniences caused by this disruption, authors in popular monthly magazines as well as in the more specialized architectural press focused their attention on what these developments in the built environment, in conjunction with other economic and cultural factors, meant for the city's status and public image. Much of this debate centered on whether or not, and for what reasons, New York City could be regarded as the American metropolis, the nation's de facto capital and representative city. Acquisition of such status would represent a major selling point for the city, another string in the boosters' bow as they worked to brand New York for business and tourism.

Metropolitan status was far easier to confer on the European capitals to which writers on both sides of the Atlantic frequently compared New York. London and Paris, both the long-established capitals of their nations, were centers of political, economic, and cultural power. Paris, especially, formed the national hub in a heavily centralized system of government that had effectively dictated similarly centralized patterns of transportation and commerce. London, overseeing a country whose industrial and commercial development was less centralized around the capital, nevertheless retained a tight political grip both at home and across the enormous British Empire. In comparison with these metropolitan centers, New York—neither politically nor geographically central—ran the risk of appearing almost provincial. However, the city's boosters claimed, New York was rapidly acquiring some of the attributes of a national—and international—metropolis.[5] In a period when these two European capitals defined the modern and the cosmopolitan, the competition with Europe was vital to establishing New York's new status. For New York to compete with the European capitals, its chroniclers would have to work hard to establish its metropolitan attributes, preferably those that distinguished the American metropolis from the dominant European models.

The debate over New York's metropolitan status rested in a larger context structured by tensions stemming from increasing immigration and the resultant debates about "American" identity. Solidifying New York's image as America's representative metropolis meant convincing Americans—non–New Yorkers—that if they visited New York they could "see America."[6] Given the growing image problem presented by a city population frequently represented in guidebooks, newspapers, and magazines as dominated by foreigners, boosters and other pundits in the first two decades of the twentieth century interested in promoting the city's

Americanness turned to New York's built environment to bear that burden of representation. The cartoon accompanying FPA's 1916 article about New York's complexity, about the foolishness of tourists coming to the city and assuming that they had gotten to know it, illustrated more than the new tourist fashion for "seeing America first" (fig. 3.1). With witting or unwitting irony, the cartoon and its caption placed the gung-ho Americanist tourists in the head of the Statue of Liberty: prime symbol of America, located in New York—but built to acknowledge the historical and political connections between the Old World republic (France) and its New World counterpart. Establishing New York's American identity would clearly entail focusing on what seemed most American during the first two decades of the twentieth century—the city's newest signature architectural feature, the skyscraper.

The New Metropolis

The city's identity as a "metropolis" was not self-evident in the early years of the new century. Critics framed the debate around a search for New York's distinctly American attributes. While some located those attributes in the city's commercial character, others argued for its demographic heterogeneity. Leading Progressive-era commentator Herbert Croly, writing in *The Architectural Record,* of which he was co-editor, discussed in detail how New York City might or might not be considered America's metropolis. Croly set a higher standard than did some others for the acquisition of metropolitan status. While he accorded New York the position of the nation's business and commercial metropolis, he argued that to be truly metropolitan the city should also be the social, artistic, and intellectual center of the country. Furthermore, according to Croly, a metropolis should not only reflect national characteristics but also anticipate new ones and remake the old.

Working against New York's metropolitan potential, Croly argued, were not only older national political tendencies that resisted centralization, but also local conditions that contributed to a sense of fragmentation, such as the lack of consistent or coherent urban planning, too great a degree of heterogeneity, and the

SEEING NEW YORK FROM THE HEAD
OF THE STATUE OF LIBERTY.

"So, Mrs. Beebe, you believe in seeing America first?"
"Yes, I DO, and the same with
187 John Henry. None of Yurrup for
him, he says, till he's scratched the
Beebe initials in every nook and
cranny of our noble country."

Fig. 3.1. "Seeing New York from the Head of the Statue of Liberty." This cartoon accompanied an article about New York by FPA (Franklin P. Adams), "It's a Fine Place to Visit, Yes—But I'd Hate to Live There," *Everybody's Magazine,* December 1916. The American tourists choose America over Europe, an option that would never have occurred to members of an earlier touring class.

endemic social divisions—from the "unusual proportion of raw and unapproachable foreigners" to the "set of cliques" that composed New York's higher strata. Croly concluded, however, that "New York is national or nothing" and that the consolidation of the city in 1898, combined with the victory over Spain, had produced "an outburst of national feeling." As an example of New York's connection to "national life," Croly cited President Theodore Roosevelt's New York nativity, claiming that it was "difficult to see how just such a combination of disposition, experience, training and ideas could have come to a head in any other city." New York, Croly concluded, while perhaps not yet a metropolis by all measures, was "the most national of American cities."[7]

In his address before the New-York Historical Society celebrating its ninety-ninth anniversary in 1903, the essayist and popular lecturer Hamilton Wright Mabie challenged some commonly held national beliefs about New York, suggesting that both the city's heterogeneous population and its bold commercialism made it more, not less, American. Mabie referred to the "tradition" of claiming that "whatever New York is, it is not intellectual, religious, moral, homogeneous, beautiful, or American; and New Yorkers have become so accustomed to this state of the provincial mind that they long ago ceased to deny, to explain, or to apologize."[8] Mabie set about to challenge the notion of New York's supposedly "un-American" character by suggesting that what he called the "the spirit of the locality" was its "cosmopolitan" character, a spirit, he argued, that was decidedly American. New York's cosmopolitanism was based on racial diversity and political and religious toleration, Mabie claimed, deploying the term "cosmopolitan" to function alongside other similarly broad terms contributing to a turn-of-the-century racial lexicon. Echoing Croly's argument, Mabie suggested that the city's demographic heterogeneity had, over the years, "given our friends, south and west, the opportunity of saying that New York is the least American of cities because it is the least homogeneous." Mabie argued the opposite.

In challenging the familiar negative assessment of the city's "racial" heterogeneity, Mabie contributed to what became an increasingly familiar debate about early twentieth-century New York. Like some other commentators, Mabie argued that the city's racial diversity constituted its American identity. "It is fair to ask," Mabie contended, "'Which is the most distinctively American, the community in which the citizens are all of one blood, or that in which many races combine to create a new race?' . . . If America stands for a different order of society, a new kind of political and social unity, . . . then New York is the most American of cities." Mabie's promotion of racial diversity can only be regarded as wishful thinking or a plea for tolerance rather than a description of how most early twentieth-century New Yorkers felt about race and immigration. At his time of writing, the number of immigrants entering and residing in Manhattan was increasing rapidly, until by 1910 immigrants made up forty-one percent of the population of New York City, the majority from Southern and Eastern Europe. By the 1920s, opposition to the pluralism and "melting pot" image of New York had increased considerably, with many of Mabie's class actively opposing further immigration. However, Mabie's address certainly laid claim on the city's behalf to key tenets of American political ideology.[9]

In honoring the city, Mabie, like Croly, emphasized New York's commercial character, describing the city as founded by businessmen and first governed by a commercial monopoly, the West India Company. In an era when the older families of the city were making efforts to distinguish themselves from the nouveau riche industrialists, whose money was made and not inherited, Mabie's version of New York's history as well as his promotion of the nobility of commerce aimed to bridge the gap between new and old money in New York's upper echelons.[10] According to Mabie, commerce was democratic and besides, he suggested, some of the European cities so admired by Americans as centers of art and civility, as perhaps "above" commerce, were themselves founded on the riches brought by trade: "Commerce is a peaceful and increasingly honest substitute for the wholesale thieving of feudal times. . . . It is well to remember that Venice, . . . was the first commercial city of a great period; that her palaces were built because the ships that lay at their doors were laden with the treasures of the East."[11] Business and trade, these authors argued, *were* American. New York's profits were not ill-gotten gains such as those acquired by European monarchs and aristocrats; wealth from trade was the product of honest labor, fundamental to the increasing international power of the country. As the undisputed center of the nation's business and trade, New York's metropolitan status, in the eyes of her boosters, was unassailable.

The American Vernacular

National corporations and financial institutions underpinned New York's supremacy as the nation's commercial center. Commerce of all sorts thrived in the city, making use of the presence of large banks, insurance companies, the stock exchange, a huge national and international transportation nexus, local manufacturing facilities, and the nation's largest urban population, which provided a ready supply of both workers and consumers.[12] This commercial strength also created a demand for buildings in which to house the growing executive and white-collar workforce of the city's nonmanufacturing economy. The limited space of Manhattan Island—especially in the lower portion of the city, the commercial and financial center of New York—required architects to build much more on a vertical plane. The resulting "skyscrapers" multiplied and thrived in New York, particularly in the first two decades of the twentieth century, and made perhaps the greatest contribution to debates about the Americanness of New York City.[13]

The city's burgeoning commercial architecture gave rise to a discussion among architects, critics, and opinion-makers of the possibility of a distinctly American architectural style, as well as whether New York might be the center of that development. The terms "skyline" and "skyscraper" were first used in the periodical press in the mid-1890s to describe the new tall office buildings and their effect on the city's horizontal image.[14] Buildings of ten or more stories made a stark contrast in a horizon still mostly made up of five- and six-storied buildings. Previously, the only struc-

Fig. 3.2. "Wall Street Looking toward Broadway," a typical image of the era indicating the extent to which Trinity Church, once the dominant figure in New York's skyline, had become dwarfed by the financial industry's buildings in Lower Manhattan. *New York: The Metropolis of the Western World*, New York: Foster and Reynolds, 1902.

tures to pierce that veil were the steeples and towers of the city's numerous churches. From 1846 until the last decade of the nineteenth century, the steeple of Trinity Church, at 284 feet, was the city's highest point. First eclipsed in 1890 by George B. Post's 309-foot Pulitzer Building on Park Row, the dwarfing of Trinity Church was, in text and image, a much-noted symbol of the city's changing appearance in relation to an apparent shift in its value system from religion to commerce (fig. 3.2). By 1908 one author could remark, in an article entitled "The City of Dreadful Height," that if Trinity Church was noticeable in the skyline at all, it was "conspicuous only as the stub of a broken tooth is conspicuous in a comb."[15]

Despite reservations about the existence of a distinctly American style of architecture, well-known critics such as Barr Ferree did concede that "there has really been developed among us a form of structure which . . . has . . . a character of its own sufficiently definite and distinctive to make it an American type. This is the high office-building."[16] To Ferree, the most important aspect of this new building type was its commercial purpose: "The high building is neither a fashion nor a fad; its popularity rests upon the successful manner in which it fulfils an economic necessity in current affairs." Ferree's praise for the skyscraper's utilitarianism formed the foundation on which other writers, both specialist and popular, based their discussion about the aesthetics of the tall building and its contribution to the positive distinctiveness, the Americanness, of New York. The city was the location of the greatest number of such buildings and thus the place most closely associated with the new verticality of the American city.[17]

Discussions of the new skyscrapers revolved around three major themes: their utility, their Americanness, and their aesthetic appeal. All three themes fit with contemporary American notions of aesthetics in architecture and the decorative arts. Emerging contemporaneously with, but in opposition to, the Beaux Arts style popular at the close of the nineteenth century (the latter exemplified in the 1893 Chicago World's Fair), the American arts and crafts movement gradually gained influence during the prewar

"Flat Iron" Building, New York.

Fig. 3.3. Flatiron Building, a hand-colored 1904 postcard depicting a busy street scene in front of the Fuller Building, nicknamed the "Flatiron." The message ends, "Is not this a very ugly building?" The comment reflects the early twentieth-century debate about the aesthetic value of the city's new tall buildings. Reproduced by permission from the Victor A. Blenkle Postcard Collection, Archives Center, National Museum of American History, Behring Center, Smithsonian Institution.

years, articulating an aesthetic committed to the use of local materials for building, furniture, and housewares and to notions of
beauty grounded in a context of functionalism and utility. By contrast, in this period the European arts and crafts movement was
quickly overshadowed by the early cubism of Picasso and Braque
that had begun to shatter the seemingly unquestionable and "natural" forms of representation. Other painters, sculptors, and photographers were developing the works of a European avant-garde
modernism that did not come to the attention of the general American public until the Paris Exposition of 1925. Until that time,
architects and artists in the United States worked toward an American modernism consciously attempting to construct an aesthetics
different from the European past and present.[18]

Among the opinion-makers of the weekly and monthly periodical press, a consensus developed in the first decade of the century that the "new New York" exemplified in the new commercial office buildings should continue to chart its own architectural
path and break away from the old Europhilia which devalued
American innovations in art and architecture. "What an accent it
gives to the two great highways of the metropolis!" remarked
author and critic John Corbin in a 1903 article in *Scribner's Magazine,* referring to the recently opened Flatiron Building, rapidly
becoming an icon of New York's modernity and originality (fig.
3.3).[19] His answer to those critics who objected to the "American"
qualities of the building was to indicate the Madison Square Garden building, just across the square from the Flatiron, which he
described as "an intelligent variation upon the far-famed campanile of Seville." Corbin was fiercely critical of this type of imi-
tative architecture, and of the vaunted position it held in the eyes
of the public and of architectural critics: "Yet what has a campanile
to do with our past, our present, our future? . . . It is an eternal
monument to the fact that those who made it were not able to work
out the life of their own time and place into new forms of beauty.
Compared with this exquisite exotic from the Old World, no
doubt, the rough young stripling of the New is crude and assertive.
. . . Yet the Spanish tower belongs to an alien people and a van-

ished age. This twentieth century giant, whether ugly or beautiful, stands on the threshold of vigorous new life and of vast architectural possibilities."[20]

Corbin's discussion of New York, like those of many of his contemporary commentators, placed the city within the emergent new geography of space and time whereby Paris and London, the major Old World cities, were no longer regarded as the location of modernity but as the location of the past. "In all the great cities of the world there are interesting and beautiful things, but they are things of a past," wrote Corbin, "of manifold tradition, or things of a present that is scarcely distinguishable from such a past. The life here is the life of a present that looks out to a future, infinite in the variety of its possibilities."[21]

Some journalists and critics valorized Manhattan's new tall buildings because they fit with the city's commercial character and with its physical environment, making them therefore appropriate to their purpose and to their surroundings. Commenting on the new 625-foot Singer Building, the tallest building in the city and in the nation at the time of its completion in 1908, journalist George E. Walsh both dismissed the skyscraper's one European rival in terms of height and claimed a "oneupmanship" for the Singer building based on its canny American practicality: The Singer Building is "a good deal short of the Eiffel Tower, but that was not constructed as an office-building or living place. It was merely a freak for temporary advertising purposes of a great fair. The tower of the new wonder of the New World will be sixty-five feet square, and on each floor there will be ample office-rooms." Walsh and others celebrated New York's tall buildings for their combination of sheer size and utility, of form and function.[22]

Utility was "the governing consideration" of the size and the design of skyscrapers, commentators argued. Engineering problems had hampered the development of tall buildings, but improvements in fireproofing and elevator technology had substantially solved those issues. The solution of such problems had allowed architects to turn to the buildings' exterior and interior decoration. Such buildings provided modern office space, an effec-

tive advertisement for the corporate owner, often a public passage-
way from one street to another, and shops and services so that their
tenants rarely needed to venture outside the building during the
day. Unknown in Europe, the skyscraper was an "American type,"
wrote engineer Herbert Wade, a "building based on pure utility
and special conditions" with "an artistic design and treatment . . .
that to-day justly earns the admiration of European critics."[23]

Architectural critics and commentators almost always linked
the utility of the skyscraper to the idea that such buildings were
both uniquely American and, increasingly, aesthetically appealing.
The pseudonymous "A. C. David" provided perhaps the clearest
example of the relation, in the minds of contemporary architectural critics, of commercial utility, Americanism, and aesthetics.
David's 1910 article in *The Architectural Record* addressed several new commercial buildings on Fourth Avenue between Union
Square and 30th Street. The buildings had been constructed to provide office space, warehousing, and showroom space for some large
manufacturing and importing companies. David praised the design of the buildings to fit a strictly commercial function. He regarded these examples of commercial architecture as not only distinctly American but as a kind of natural evolution from the local
environment.[24] He referred to the buildings as "a normal and natural growth," free from the "perverting and . . . corrupting" effects
of European forms. David closed his article with a Spencerian
interpretation of the success of these buildings, claiming that "they
are absolutely a case of the survival of the fittest—the fittest, that
is, under existing conditions. . . . Any future advance of American
commercial architecture will depend upon a further development
of the ideas and the methods which have made these Fourth Avenue buildings what they are." Assessments such as David's built
on the association of commerce with both national identity and
with New York, thereby implying that these commercial buildings located in Manhattan were both American and natural, an
almost organic expression of New York's metropolitan status.

Land and Nation

While the pundits and boosters commented on New York's status, more adventurous souls explored and described the nation's less traveled areas "out west." Though located at least two thousand miles west of the Hudson, similar concerns preoccupied these journalists and travelers eager to recommend the West as a tourist destination. Like their eastern counterparts, the intrepid interpreters of the West during the pre–World War I period went in search of national symbols but in the more familiar arena of such symbols, the land. During the first two decades of the twentieth century, the architectural boosters of New York increasingly linked the "national" landscape of the Far West to the burgeoning "Americanism" of the city's skyscrapers.

Recent scholarship on the relation between nationalism and landscape imagery places this early twentieth-century American representation of western landscapes within a long European tradition. Geographer Stephen Daniels has described how through the words and images of poets and painters, often conscripted by the state, particular landscapes become part of nationalist iconographies.[25] In early twentieth-century America, both art and commerce designated the landscape of the Far West as the icon of American national identity. In America, as in Europe, particular landscapes have at times better served the purpose of depicting the nation. As Angela Miller has shown, the role played by the mid-century New York school of landscape painters, during a period she refers to as one of "romantic nationalism," was based on the power of the northeastern region to commandeer ideas of nationhood, especially during the Civil War period.[26] Much of what Miller describes as constitutive of this period of nationalism and its popular landscape representations bears a striking resemblance to the factors defining the early twentieth century. There is a parallel between the relation of nineteenth-century landscape imagery and national economic prospects as described by Miller and the similar set of relations at the turn of the twentieth century. Both periods witnessed the nationalist celebration of both the sublime landscape of the wilderness and the burgeoning capitalist market. In the early years of the twentieth century, efforts to incorporate the seemingly unnatural and incomprehensible environments of the Far West and Manhattan into a nationalist iconography brought together these two otherwise dissimilar landscapes. Such efforts were a necessary stage in the development of a twentieth-century American national identity that needed and used the "landscapes" of both skyscrapers and mountains to further American economic and cultural power at home and abroad.

The concerns of the early twentieth-century chroniclers of the Far West were similar to those trying to describe and categorize the "new New York" during the same years. In search of national symbols, they looked to the deserts and mountains for that which distinguished those lands from Europe. In landscape as in urban aesthetics, Europe was still the yardstick against which everything was measured. Like the boosters of New York's emerging skyscraper cityscape, the promoters of the western landscape had to retrain themselves and their audience to perceive these areas as "beautiful" and worthy of the sometimes arduous trip to reach them. By looking for what was distinctly American in the western lands, they freed themselves from a European landscape aesthetic and thus made possible a new way of seeing the land and incorporating it into the nationalist cultural aesthetic demanded by America's changing international status. Their efforts to nationalize the western landscape by reevaluating it and redescribing it with a consciously American vocabulary ultimately provided the metaphorical language with which to certify the Americanness of the unnatural landscape of New York City.

Standing in a settler's ramshackle hut, "face to face with the bare desert," Harriet Monroe, a genteel traveler in Arizona at the turn of the century, cast her mind back to her travels of the previous two summers. Monroe felt "ashamed" of her former European preoccupations as she struggled with her response to the Arizona desert: "It was a most complex emotion, this vision of unachieved glory set against a background of immemorial antiquity. For the desert is old beyond one's dreams of age; it makes

Rome or Nineveh seem a thing of yesterday."[27] She thus described her initially disquieting but important realization that America possessed a history of its own, legible in the lands of the Southwest, still largely unsettled by towns or cities whose newness might detract from the dignified "antiquity" of the desert. Monroe's observation, however, also proposed the role of that region and landscape in an even more glorious future.

Monroe's response to the American Southwest characterizes that of many other travelers and journalists exploring this region in the early years of the twentieth century. Accustomed to equating the aesthetics of landscape with their image of the settled pastoralism of the countryside and towns of Western Europe, early twentieth-century travelers in the American West and Southwest struggled to reconcile a previous generation's ideas about the ugliness and barrenness of those regions with their own perceptions of the apparent beauties of these lands. What had changed to enable the desert and canyon lands, once deemed barren and irredeemably ugly, to be perceived as possessing a beauty comparable to the landscapes of Europe?

A new generation of explorers of the western states and territories, borne in relative comfort to their destinations, made a vital contribution to this early phase of American cultural nationalism by imitating a well-established European method of boosting national identity and national pride: marshalling the nation's landscape as the embodiment of national values, strengths, and characteristics. America's defeat of Spain in the war of 1898 marked the entry of the United States into the elite club of imperialist nations. The U.S. government, with the enthusiastic support of the populace and the presses, had finally claimed for itself the right to dominate the Western Hemisphere.[28] The new sense of national unity provoked by the war came shortly after the very practical uniting of the nation's coasts and interiors by the railroad magnates. The development of railroad connections through the Southwest into southern California and up the Pacific coast completed the links between industry and settlement throughout the West. The railroads provided both the access and many of the amenities necessary not only for industry but also for tourism in these previously little-traveled regions. The period of the greatest expansion and redevelopment of the nation's railroads, from 1890 to 1917, coincided with, and no doubt contributed to, the growing popularity of the West as a tourist destination.[29] The transcontinental railroad companies all advertised excursion trips to the West, and adventurous easterners could buy a complete package including train ticket, hotel accommodation, and sightseeing tours, all provided by the railroad companies. Some of the West's finest hotels in what were to become and remain the most popular tourist destinations in the country—the Grand Canyon, Yellowstone, and Yosemite National Parks—were constructed by railroad companies.[30]

Travel writers and tour promoters increasingly represented the landscapes of the American West and Southwest in the first years of the century as the great American landscape, the ultimate natural representation of American identity. Echoing the contemporaneous claims made for the metropolitan and aesthetic qualities of New York City, fundamental to these assertions about the West was the notion that the landscapes of these regions were entirely different from—but aesthetically equal to or better than—those of Europe. Harriet Monroe, in her account of her impressions of Arizona referred to above, reprimanded herself and other Americans for preferring "months or years of wandering in history-haunted Europe" to explorations of the apparently distinctly American landscapes of the Southwest. The challenge, she and other writers suggested, was not only to perceive the landscape's specifically American beauty but also to wean the touring classes away from their European trips and bring them out west.[31]

The sublime beauties of the undeveloped American West differed from the pastoral attractions of Europe's settled landscapes and from those of the eastern seaboard states. Most middle- and upper-class Americans were more familiar with European standards of natural beauty, either from personal travel experience or from landscape painting. Robert Hill, of the United States Geological Survey, describing the "American Desert" to readers of *World's Work* in 1902, referred to the region as "a strange land of paradox, where each rock and tree and flower and river reverses conventional tenets and laws and conditions for Anglo-Saxon environment, as founded upon ideas preconceived by thousands of years of ancestral experience." He described the "aberrant" features of the desert regions as including many areas "which are apparently a mockery of nature."[32] Hill responded to an apparently "unnatural nature" whose aesthetic appeal he could not deny— nor yet describe.

The beauties of the European pastoral landscape were familiar but, Monroe and others suggested, too comfortable, offering no excitement or challenge. Of Italy Harriet Monroe wrote that "its beauty is self-contained and measurable; one rests in it with profound content," whereas in Arizona "Nature is not conciliatory and charming; she is terrible and magnificent." Such sublime landscapes offered an "unfamiliar and incomprehensible beauty" to Americans raised on European standards of pastoral beauty and their New World counterparts.[33] "One accustomed to the lovely scenery of England, to the soft, caressing beauty of her landscape, is ill prepared to grasp the vastness of the Yosemite, the Yellowstone or the Grand Canyon of Arizona," wrote Robert Hill. "We love what we can understand," Monroe continued, "what history and letters and art have taught us to understand. . . . We prefer to follow other feet,—to see Shakespeare's England and Byron's Switzerland; But no poet has said an adequate word for these unexplored sublimities; . . . to them the mind of man must venture as a pioneer."[34] These chroniclers of the West had discovered a sublime American landscape, whose sublimity paradoxically resided in its seeming unnaturalness. Their responses echoed those of early twentieth-century observers of Manhattan's massed skyscrapers. Both landscapes initially seemed to lack the familiar components of beauty, yet commerce and art ultimately reconciled both with a new, distinctly American aesthetic in the service of national identity.

As Anne Farrar Hyde has argued in her study of the relation between the landscape of the Far West and American national culture at the turn of the century, as American travelers became more familiar with, and enamored of, the appearance of the arid plains, canyon lands, and deserts of the American West, they acquired a language with which to describe it.[35] Hyde argues that early twentieth-century American writers and artists moved away from a descriptive language reliant upon European comparisons and aesthetic standards. Writers stopped describing the mountain ranges, desert rock formations, and climates of the West as American versions of Swiss Alps, or as akin to the turrets and spires of European castles and cathedrals, or as an American Italy.[36] The West, according to Hyde, became "defiantly American," as writers struggled to describe the mountainous and arid lands in a language more appropriate to its newfound national (and potential commercial) value.[37]

However, seeking symbols of national identity in the natural landscape was not an especially "American" impulse. Natural landscapes and geological formations were inextricably tied to constructions of national identity and culture in Europe. England's "white cliffs of Dover," Germany's Bavarian forests, and Switzerland's Alps had all been marshalled by European nations and governments to help define a sense of nationhood and national identity linked to nature. Such images helped to "naturalize" the often political concepts of nation and nationality. Moreover, the language used to describe the American natural landscape in a supposedly more "American" way was, of course, Spanish—the terms *sierra, cañon, mesa,* and *cordillera* had been applied to the region by the previous (European) colonizers of the West and Southwest.[38]

Nonetheless, the seemingly undeniable Americanness of the western landscape—due to its apparent upending of European natural landscape forms—and its soaring popularity with Eastern tourists made the language of this landscape the ideal to which to compare the newfound Americanness of the skyscraper city. If the mesas, sierras, and canyons of the western states represented what distinguished America from Europe, and gave Americans an indigenous landscape and an ancient indigenous past, then what better way to describe and represent the Americanness—the na-

Fig. 3.4. "The skyscrapers helped relieve my loneliness at the absence of mountains." This cartoon was a humorous contribution to the quite serious debate about New York's first skyscrapers, lending credence to the idea that the buildings created a Western-style rocky "landscape," a notion that made the city seem more "American." "Confessions of a Westerner and What He Sees in New York," *The Independent*, September 15, 1917.

tional cultural value—of the skyscraper city of New York but in the language of the natural landscape of the Far West?

Natural, National New York

Upon arriving in New York City in 1912, French author Pierre Loti felt disturbed at how different from Paris the city seemed. Observing the city from his hotel room, he remarked: "When I return from here, Paris will seem just a quiet, old-fashioned little town."[39] To the Frenchman, New York seemed an "infernal abyss, ... almost a nightmare."[40] Loti, accustomed to the ordered uniformity of Haussmann's Paris, expressed consternation at the sight of the city's skyscrapers: "They rise up here and there, as though by chance, alternating with normal . . . buildings; . . . they seem like houses that have caught a strange disease of over-growth and madly shot up to distorted heights."[41] A few years later, however, an anonymous visitor from Laramie, Wyoming, had a very different view of the city. Describing his first impressions of New York, this westerner remarked, "When I came to New York . . . I liked the skyscrapers. . . . They helped relieve my loneliness at the absence of mountains" (fig. 3.4).[42] Both visitors responded to the massed height of Manhattan's skyscrapers and their haphazard arrangement in the lower part of the city—one with horror, the other delighting in the appearance of familiarity.

How could the two visitors have had such different perceptions of New York's built environment? The westerner saw "mountains" where the Parisian saw "modernism." The westerner's claims fit with a new urban discourse that developed during the first decade of the twentieth century that placed the city—in particular New York City—at the heart of a visual and textual rhetoric about the meaning of America, a discourse that sought national symbols for a contested national identity. The visitor from Wyoming offered his readers what by 1917 had become a familiar trope: Manhattan as a version of the Far West's rocky landscape. Naturalizing the skyscrapers—icons of New York's and America's modernity—Americanized New York. The city was thus turned into an acceptable national metropolis for a people hungry for nationalist symbols but not yet ready to see themselves represented by New York's urban skyline.

Loti's statement suggests that New York's status as "the capital of modernism" resituated Paris and New York in both a spatial and a temporal relationship. By describing New York thus, Loti designated the city as the locus of the present, of current trends. In comparison to New York, he says, Paris will now seem "old-fashioned," the location of the *passé*. Geographer James Duncan has described this process as one whereby a "journey in space is a journey in time." Addressing what he calls "sites of representation," Duncan shows how geographical areas are understood to bear temporal properties of past, present, or future. In early twentieth-century America, the representation of Paris as the "past" and New York as the "present" or "future," which repositioned New York (America) in relation to Paris (Europe), was achieved by means of the Americanization of both New York's built environment and western America's natural landscape.[43]

Both skyscrapers and mountains were necessary to the development of an American New York. Civic boosters in the city government and the business community interested in promoting New York's claims to metropolitan status needed first to establish a larger American national identity and set of symbols upon which to base those claims. This work necessitated a cultural separation from Europe through the discovery and celebration of a unique American identity appropriate to an industrialized, urbanizing nation. Early twentieth-century American journalists, photographers, tour promoters, and government officials identified an indigenous, authentic American identity in the natural landscapes of the American West, in the land formations, geology, and climates that most differed from those of Western Europe. This generation of travelers similarly attributed to the native peoples of the West and Southwest a natural, indigenous, and authentically "American" beauty. Like the landscapes they inhabited, white observers had previously regarded Native Americans as ugly and not worth looking at.[44]

The "discovery" and representation of the West as "America"

provided a national imagery, language, and historical foundation on which to base the construction of an acceptably distinct American present. Until the middle of the twentieth century, the ultimate manifestation and location of that American present was New York City. It was therefore vital to Americanize New York by interpreting Manhattan, in word and image, as a natural "American" landscape.[45] Representations of American western landscapes were not entirely new to eastern Americans in the first decades of the twentieth century. Photographs by Timothy O'Sullivan, Carleton Watkins, John Hillers, and William Bell had become familiar from the widely popular published government surveys of the West in the late nineteenth century.[46] These images, as well as the paintings of Albert Bierstadt, Thomas Moran, and Frederick Remington, had depicted the Rocky Mountains, deserts, salt lakes, hot springs, and geysers of the western states and territories. What changed in the twentieth century was, first, the incorporation of these landscapes into a confident cultural nationalism and, second, the ability of a greater number of Americans to visit these areas for themselves as tourists.

At the close of the nineteenth century, the language of the western landscape had been applied pejoratively to the cityscapes of New York and Chicago to describe narrow streets dominated by new tall buildings and to imply the ill effects of the new commercial capitalism on older ways of urban life. Henry Blake Fuller famously described the new middle-class apartment dwellers and office workers of 1890s Chicago as "cliff dwellers" in his novel of that name.[47] He opened his story of the harshness and immorality of urban capitalism by describing Chicago's changing urban landscape as a "tumultuous territory through which . . . the rushing streams of commerce have worn many a deep and rugged chasm."[48] The early years of the twentieth century saw the use of that language shift to construct a celebration of the aesthetic appeal, and the national and international significance, of New York City.

The burgeoning tourist industry provided the most important connection associating images of the West with images of New York. Guidebooks, maps, stereographs, postcards, and bus tours of cities and natural "wonders" constructed a coherent set of images of the nation, ordered in a sequence that allowed the visitor or viewer to see the major designated "sights" of each place within a reasonable amount of time—whether thirty minutes to view a set of stereographs or a week spent visiting a particular place of interest. The appeal to tourists, both domestic and foreign, of cities such as New York or the western states served as a "proof" of the promotion of such sites as representative of the nation.

Guidebooks, postcards, and stereographs proudly associated New York's new urban forms with western landscape features and thus shored up New York's claims as an "American" place. "New York Skyscrapers," the first section of a 1902 New York guide, described the unique impression made by the high buildings as one approached the city from New York Bay. The impact of "these architectural marvels" was further enhanced, the author stated, "as we wander through the downtown streets, and passing from one shadowy cañon into another make our way between the tremendous cliffs."[49] A 1905 pamphlet of New York views distributed as advertising material by the Singer Sewing Machine Company included a photographic view of Broadway, looking south, taken from the St. Paul Building, named the "Grand Canyon."[50] The photograph, by George P. Hall and Company, was reproduced many times in other guidebooks, in stereograph series, and in postcards. Images of downtown Broadway and other streets in Lower Manhattan were routinely captioned as "canyons" in booklets of views issued by guidebook companies or hotels.

The visual trend for photographing the lower part of the city from the roof of a skyscraper or in horizontal format contributed to the perception of New York as an American "landscape" that echoed the West's vertiginous canyons. A reading of the stereograph catalogues issued by two of the largest distributors of such views, Underwood and Underwood and H. C. White and Company, in the early years of the century demonstrates that the vast majority of the stereograph views of New York City were images taken from atop the World Building, the St. Paul Building, the Flatiron, the Singer Building, the Metropolitan Life tower and, a little later, the Woolworth Building. From these vantage points, the city appeared in almost panoramic perspective as an awe-inspiring landscape featuring clusters of skyscrapers set among older, seemingly squat, stores and warehouses. Part of the appeal of these dramatic rooftop views, like those recommended in tourist guidebooks, was the suggestion that one could now see this magnificent cityscape from a perspective previously only imagined. The perspective thus accentuated the suggestion that New York, like the canyon lands and mountains of the West, constituted a sublime landscape. The streets bordering the buildings seen from such a sharp angle might indeed have seemed to resemble the narrow, deep canyons familiar from descriptions and images of Colorado and Arizona.

As William Taylor has argued, the horizontal skyline view of New York marked an iconographic watershed in the development of ways of seeing the city.[51] Surrounded by water and at the entrance to one of the world's great oceans, New York had always lent itself to such horizontal views, often from across one of the rivers or from the Bay. The development of the new tall buildings compounded the preference for this view of the city. Panoramic images taken from photographs were regular features of guidebooks and photographic souvenirs of the city. Taken from a vantage point either in Brooklyn looking across the East River or from across the Hudson, these images presented a jagged horizon of tall buildings, usually identified by name at the base of the image (fig. 3.5). Water below and sky above frame the long narrow strip of land dominated by a series of variously shaped "summits." The skyline image of the downtown skyscrapers removed them from the larger context of the still predominantly low-storied city, creating the impression that this architectural landscape typified the city. The skyscrapers in these early twentieth-century images appeared to form a monumental, unpopulated, silent region similar to the romanticized landscape paintings of the American West by such artists as Albert Bierstadt and Thomas Cole. For tourists to New York City from the West and for easterners familiar with images of the western landscape in their monthly magazines, the

Fig. 3.5. Images such as this double-page skyline helped promote interpretations of Manhattan's built environment as a landscape similar to
that found in the rocky West. *Scenes of Modern New York*, Portland,
ME: L. H. Nelson Company, 1905.

skyline image of New York fit into a developing visual lexicon of
the American landscape in the early twentieth century—a land of
cliff dwellings, mesas, canyons, and sierras.

The jagged irregularity of New York's skyline, a product of
the city's lack of zoning and height restrictions in the pre–World
War I period, contributed to the seeming "naturalness" of the skyscrapers and the possibility of seeing them collectively as a landscape.[52] The location, height, and style of these office buildings was
determined by financial considerations, such as proximity to other
relevant businesses and financial institutions, access to transporta-

Manhattan Life.   Cable.   Columbia.   Standard Oil.   Bowling Green.   Washington.   Produce Exchange.

E HARBOR.

tion, availability and cost of a building plot, and the whims and
wealth of the building's owner. Buildings in Lower Manhattan
were constructed, therefore, without regard to the overall appearance or organization of this section of the city or of Manhattan as
a whole. So this very visible part of the city acquired a haphazard
look, which some observers used to reinforce their representations
of the city both as beautiful and as "natural"—as a landscape.

While some complained that New York would never be as
beautiful as European cities because of its commercial character
and lack of planning, others saw these very features as part of New
York's nascent "natural" beauty. They argued that the skyscraper
had developed and grown in New York to meet local needs; it was,
therefore, "natural," and should not be bound by the "unnaturalness" of strict urban planning. In his 1903 *Scribner's* article, illus-

trated with photographs by Alfred Stieglitz, John Corbin argued that New York's irregular appearance was actually part of its particular beauty. What was needed, he argued, was not a restructuring or redesign of the city, but rather a new way of looking at and representing this urban beauty.[53]

Corbin saw beauty in the city but struggled to find a language and a set of metaphors to express what he saw. Corbin appreciated the novel visual effects of the new architecture on the city's form and appearance—the "surprises of perspective" and the "juxtaposition of masses"—yet employed both European and American landscape metaphors to describe the aesthetic appeal of Lower Manhattan as seen from the Bay. He described the streets as "canyons," the skyscrapers as "cliff-like," and their collective appearance at sunset as resembling the beauty of "a snow-capped Alp." Corbin's metaphoric confusion, similar to that expressed by his contemporaries observing the Far West, suggested that New York's urban landscape was also in the midst of an enthusiastic but as yet incomplete Americanization.[54]

Four years later, with the city's skyline joined by the Times Building in Longacre (soon Times) Square and the Singer Building rising up on Broadway and Liberty Street downtown, the idea grew among the city's boosters that New York's skyscrapers gave the city a "natural" beauty. Others echoed Corbin's suggestion—represented, for example, in Edward Steichen's 1906 photograph of the Flatiron Building—that the city's beauty was best captured through a soft-focus lens, a mist, in some sort of half-light, or in a snow storm. Such effects of light and weather softened the outlines of the buildings and merged the assorted colors of the city into one or two tones, emphasizing the basic shapes and forms rather than the sometimes jarring details of the city and its inhabitants. Such a pictorialist view of the city made it appear more "natural," more part of a landscape.

A 1907 article in *The Craftsman*, the mouthpiece of the American arts and crafts movement, exemplified this discursive trend, celebrating the haphazard appearance of the city's skyline. Addressing a recently published set of etchings of New York skyscrapers by the well-known artist and illustrator Joseph Pennell, the article was entitled, "How New York Has Redeemed Herself from Ugliness—An Artist's Revelation of the Beauty of the Sky-scraper."[55] The author, Mary Fanton Roberts, a frequent contributor to the magazine under the pseudonym "Giles Edgerton," opened her article by describing an approach to New York from across the Bay. Edgerton referred to the "uneven lines" of the city's horizon and to the "canyons" stretching between them. She made the important point that it was only when the individually dissimilar and unrelated buildings were seen in aggregate that they acquired a "picturesque" appearance. The architectural picturesque, she argued, could only come about "in the wake of a real need expressed with intelligence and skill."[56] Like many of her contemporaries, Edgerton connected the utilitarianism of the New York skyscrapers (in terms of their function and their appropriateness to a city with limited land on which to build) to the notion that they were natural to the local environment, and therefore suitably American. From this perspective it seemed a logical step to see the city as an American natural landscape, comparable in form and cultural value to the Far West.[57]

The visual and rhetorical strategies employed by critics, boosters, and American travelers to resituate both the rocky, arid landscapes of the West and the architectural cityscape of New York within an imagined catalogue of national images ultimately relied on the Americanization of commercial culture and its diverse producers. In arguing for New York's metropolitan status, and thus its ability to represent the nation, pundits had to acknowledge what many of them termed its "cosmopolitan" character—that is, the city's racial and cultural diversity. Commerce brought wealth to New York, it built gleaming skyscrapers, and it also brought millions of immigrants in search of the opportunities supposedly available in such an active economic environment. The growth of New York's commercial culture in a business community rapidly diversifying by class and ethnic background provided the connections among architecture, American identity, and metropolitan status in the first two decades of the twentieth century. Seeing America as comprised of diverse national landscapes moved American identity toward a more culturally plural definition.

The image of New York as an all-American landscape, an architectural version of the rocky West, erased from view the day-to-day tensions of the city at street level. In particular, this western, Americanized version of New York made invisible the city's growing immigrant population. While the city's boosters and other image-makers had promoted this architectural reading of the city, approximately fifteen million immigrants, mostly from Southern and Eastern Europe, had arrived in New York. Although not visible in the skyline of the city—or even from the windows of most Manhattan skyscrapers—by the 1920s these newcomers had profoundly reshaped the city's popular culture, politics, and ethnic makeup. Furthermore, the city's immigrant presence put some members of New York's Anglo elite on the defensive, feeding the flames of anti-Semitism and popularizing scientific racism. These anti-immigration elites and their middle-class supporters around the country worked to re-spin older ideas and images of New York as un-American. This time, the charges against New York's Americanism were based less on nineteenth-century anti-urbanism and more on renewed racism and conservatism in the post–World War I period.

Through the 1920s, the city's tourist industry boosters re-deployed this popular (though negative) interest in immigrants by incorporating New York's immigrant neighborhoods into the mainstream tourist itinerary. Guidebooks and travel literature, which in the 1890s had turned tourists away from such areas, in the 1920s promoted visits to New York's Little Italy, Chinatown, the "Ghetto," Little Syria, and other Lower Manhattan neighborhoods. According to the authors and artists producing such materials, these areas and their inhabitants now represented a miniature Europe, or China, or Middle East conveniently located in America. By 1920 the most striking phase of architectural innovation was completed, and a national debate over Americanness and New York's national meaning was just beginning. As people focused more on bodies than on buildings, the city's built environment would increasingly take a back seat to its population.

4

NEW YORK IS NOT AMERICA: IMMIGRANTS AND TOURISTS IN NEW YORK AFTER WORLD WAR I

In contrast to the prevailing sense of New York before World War I, when the city's architecture seemed its greatest new attraction and the burgeoning skyscraper "landscape" its most distinctive feature, by the 1920s observers of New York had lowered their gaze to the streets, as it were, and seemed more interested in assessing New York's status by its population rather than by its buildings. "It is not so much the place . . . as the people," mused renowned British writer and frequent visitor to New York, Ford Madox Ford, in his 1927 book *New York Is Not America,* when considering New York's appeal. He dismissed the urban landscape in favor of the city's diverse urban population.[1]

Ford's book suggested how issues of geography and identity were inextricably linked in the 1920s. To Ford, and to many Americans living west of the Hudson River, heterogeneous, cosmopolitan New York was not America, was not representative of the nation. However, the city's seemingly precarious relation to national culture cut both ways. To social conservatives, New York represented disruptive postwar cultural change and the threat to "old stock" Americans posed by immigrants. On the other hand, for the growing number of Americans spending their vacations as tourists in their own country, much of New York's appeal lay in its exotic, somewhat un-American reputation. For these consumers New York was best marketed as *both* American and un-American.

Despite the Americanizing effects of New York's burgeoning skyscraper landscape, in the postwar period the city still struggled against persistent national doubts about its American identity. During a period of intense anti-immigration campaigning and legislation, New York's reputation as a city of immigrants potentially worked against the efforts of city boosters and tourist industry advocates to sell the city as a suitable middle-class tourist destination. Tourism promoters in New York, using the image of the city's famously diverse population and apparently distinct ethnic neighborhoods, successfully built on old and new fashions for "slumming" in the city's "foreign" quarters. Just as the identity of the city's built environment as American was formed in opposition to representations of distinctly European landscapes, so the identities of various ethnic areas of the city were formed in opposition to the supposed "whiteness" of "native" New York. Boosters and tourism promoters ingeniously used the very aspect of the city that threatened to undermine their business to attract average American tourists.

Locating America, Identifying Americans

National press and political attention to immigration intensified before and after American involvement in World War I. Between 1880 and 1919 over twenty-three million immigrants arrived in the United States, seventeen million of whom entered through New York. The number of immigrants arriving from Eastern and Southern Europe increased exponentially, reaching almost a million as early as 1907. By 1920, almost forty percent of New York City's population was foreign born, with 480,000 Russian Jews forming the largest ethnic group of that population.[2] In 1917 Congress passed a new immigration act that imposed literacy tests on immigrants in an attempt to keep out some of the new immigrants. The war in Europe put an effective stop to the rising trend of immigration due to the practical and political difficulties of population movement during wartime. As the war ended, however, concern rose again in the United States that immigration, static for a few years, would surge once more following the armistice.

At stake in the attacks on New York's Americanness, in the intense campaigns to restrict immigration as well as in the postwar red scare, was a larger crisis of identity and geography: Where was "America" in the postwar world? Was America represented by, and located in, the small town or in the big city? What landscape represented America? Earlier in the century, what had seemed most American, for being the least European, was the rocky landscape of the Far West. However, after World War I, with Europe both fragmented and no longer the dominant political and financial region of the world, what was American had to be defined by means of domestic, not international, comparisons. The anxiety over foreignness was not only about Jews or immigrants; it represented a deeper anxiety about new attitudes, new social mores, deemed "foreign" to a real or imagined America.

Much of the discourse about New York's un-American qualities relied for its credibility on larger national, rather than local, concerns about locating American identity in the postwar period. As numerous scholars have argued, America's postwar prosperity undergirded a renewed conservatism and a refocus on domestic issues.[3] Such self-examination raised questions about who was American and what an American looked like. New York, port of entry for most immigrants and home to the largest urban foreign-born population, became the focus of national attention to matters of identity and race. As the center of the growing advertising and public relations industries, New York was also the national center for image-making. More than any other place at the time, New York City was the location in which the image of America and of Americans was daily created and recreated. From the Gibson girl to the flapper, from the "other half" to the "demi-monde," New York types became national types, the gap between local and national almost imperceptible. It was this imbrication of New York and the nation to which the rest of America increasingly objected. How could New York be the nation's metropolis when a large proportion of its residents looked not "American" but "foreign"? New York's apparent disregard for prohibition, its reputedly risqué cabaret and theater productions, and its tendency to attract "bohemians" and other political and social eccentrics added to the impression that New York could not, and should not, represent America.

An April 1920 editorial exchange between the Philadelphia-

Fig. 4.1. "Leaving the Modern Gomorrah." This Herbert Johnson cartoon supported an editorial critiquing the depravity of New York and warning out-of-town visitors. It appeared originally in the *Saturday Evening Post* and was reprinted with commentary in *Current Opinion* in April 1920. The exchange between the two periodicals reflected the larger debate after World War I about the cultural value of New York City.

based *Saturday Evening Post* and the New York *Globe* suggested the larger parameters for this argument about New York's national metropolitan status. The *Saturday Evening Post*'s editorial, entitled "Gotham and Gomorrah," accused New York of being "unstable and irresponsible," of asserting a negative influence on the city's tourists who went home having adopted "everything cheap and meretricious that the metropolis has to offer, from its Castile-soap pillared hotels to its bogus aristocracy, from the ouija board to parlor bolshevism" (fig. 4.1).[4] In defense of its city, the *Globe* responded that New York was not national in the manner described by the Philadelphia-based periodical; New York did not lead the nation in matters of style and custom. Instead, the city was national by virtue of being "the expression of the great suppressed wish of America." Such a fashionably Freudian explanation of New York's shortcomings must have infuriated the editors of the

Saturday Evening Post, harbingers of a reactionary middle American populism, as no doubt did the *Globe*'s further assertion: "If New York is, on the whole, a vulgar city, it is because the soul of America is tainted with vulgarity."[5] New York was not national in the manner of London or Paris; New York was national as a desirable, consumable product with mass market appeal.

The objections to New York's status as the nation's metropolis flowed not only from Philadelphian sour grapes but also from cities and states outside the Eastern seaboard whose editorial writers and journalists refused to see their cities and local cultures judged by New Yorkers to be parochial and simpleminded, representative of a mass-produced, suburban Babbittry.[6] National culture was now truly national in origin and geography, they argued. New York, populated by the lost and the liminal of the world, should not look down its nose at the stable values and populations of the Midwest. George Ade, a nationally-known journalist, author, and playwright living happily in smalltown Indiana, argued against what he called the "Great Myth" perpetuated throughout the nation that "everything on the wrong side of the Hudson River is Siberia," and that "the sun shines over Fifth Avenue all the time that rain is descending on Omaha." New York, according to Ade, was not only snobbish, its reputation based on myth rather than fact, but also un-American. With thinly veiled anti-Semitism, he described New York's wealth as "more Oriental than Yankee," with "flash, vulgarity, self-advertising . . . more in evidence than rugged New England traits."[7]

New York's large Jewish population made the city a particularly appealing target for out-of-town critics of the city's reputation and image. Anti-Semitism had built steadily throughout the twenty-year period of rapidly increasing immigration from Eastern and Southern Europe. The most commonly expressed fear was that Jewish immigrants from the last twenty years had displaced the more familiar Irish and German immigrants who had arrived in the mid–nineteenth century as well as the old stock "native" Anglo-American population. A lengthy illustrated article in the popular monthly magazine *World's Work* in 1916 described the achievements of the city's inhabitants in recent years, boasting of New York's size, wealth, and cultural progress. The last seven pages of the sixteen-page article dwelled on New York's Jewish population, suggesting a bit crankily that Jews were both too numerous and too successful. They had arrived as "ragged immigrants" twenty years before and were now "many of them . . . millionaires." Jews, the author suggested, were taking over the city: "They are rapidly becoming New York's largest landowners; . . . They are displacing the Irish from the municipal civil service; nearly all the new appointments now made are Jews." The article included various photographs of New York, and three on one page supposedly supported the author's view of the city's Jewish "problem." "The Ghetto" showed a crowded Lower East Side street, with a caption remarking on the great number of Jews living in the city. "Lower Fifth Avenue" ran with the caption "The one-time aristocratic residential section of the city, now almost entirely occupied by Jewish dry-goods firms. Every fourth person in the Borough of Manhattan is a Jew."[8]

Jews had lived in many different areas of the city since the founding of New York in the seventeenth century, but for the purposes of this article it was more convenient to suggest that New York's Jewish community had spread out from one single "Ghetto" area on the East Side and was now taking over many areas of business and employment. In the 1910s and 1920s, New York's Jews did gradually move out of the overcrowded tenement neighborhoods on the East Side to establish communities in other areas of Manhattan, Brooklyn, and the Bronx. Of more concern to the author of this article, however, was the impression that Jews had begun to encroach on areas of Manhattan regarded as the preserve of the city's Anglo gentry. This apparent incursion, whereby immigrant Jews had "demolished the homes of the Knickerbocker aristocracy on Fifth Avenue . . . and replaced them with clothing factories," showed the power struggle behind anti-Semitism and anti-immigration rhetoric in postwar New York.[9] From the mid-1910s, racial and commercial geographies came under increasing scrutiny and reorganization. The 1916 zoning ordinance, new building codes, and the regional plan of the early 1920s, were all attempts to reorder the city and to designate more clearly what—and who—belonged in which spaces. Opponents of further Jewish immigration defined the city's Jewish population, particularly working-class Jews, no matter how long their residence in the city, as foreign interlopers into "American" space and culture.[10]

Mapping Race and Politics

The large patches of red on the "Map of the Borough of Manhattan . . . Showing the Location and Extent of Racial Colonies," issued in 1920 by the A. R. Ohman Company of New York, indicated the neighborhoods inhabited by "Russian, Polish and Other Jews" (fig. 4.2). The map also showed smaller patches of green, yellow, brown, pink, maroon, and black, indicating the presence of other "racial colonies," such as the Irish, the Chinese, and the Italians. The Ohman "Racial Colonies" map was the commercial version of a map first produced by the Lusk Committee the previous summer.[11] State Senator Clayton Lusk headed a committee set up by the New York State Legislature in the summer of 1919 to investigate sedition. Senator Lusk soon went beyond the original rubric for the committee and conducted raids, targeting immigrants as dangerous political radicals, against various institutions in New York City such as the controversial Rand School of Social Science, much like the infamous raids conducted elsewhere in the nation that same year by U.S. Attorney General A. Mitchell Palmer.[12]

The Racial Colonies map, with its carefully demarcated areas of foreign "occupation," suggested the encroachment on all fronts feared by local and national nativists. The uncolored area of Manhattan apparently represented the population that had no race at all: the "white" Anglo population regarded as native to the city. From north and south, from east and west, the colored areas seemed to close in on the spine of whiteness down the center of Manhattan. The map defined ethnic and national groups as racial groups, in keeping with contemporary notions of racial identity. Popular books on racial identity written at the time by anti-immigration-

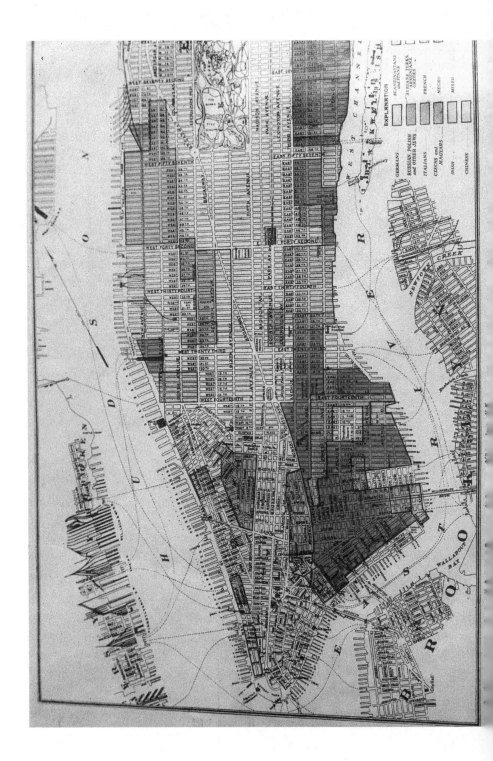

ists and eugenicists, such as Madison Grant's *The Passing of the Great Race* and Lothrop Stoddard's *The Rising Tide of Color,* familiarized a broad American readership with these ideologies. As historian Matthew Jacobson has shown, American society only gradually recognized Jews and other "probationary whites" as fully "white" or "Caucasian" in the years between the Immigration Act of 1924 and the end of World War II. This 1920 map was designed to represent the presence of foreign racial groups, their tendency to live in proximity to one another, and above all to suggest the diminishing space of whiteness. This 1920 map, based on data from 1919, does not suggest the "colored" threat as coming from the city's African-American population. By 1920 Harlem in upper Manhattan was beginning its rapid rise as the nation's black metropolis, due in part to the post–World War I migration of African Americans from the South to northern cities such as New York, Detroit, and Chicago. In 1919 and 1920, with Harlem's sons returning home as war heroes and that generation's push for civil rights not yet a threat to the white establishment, the city's nativists and conservatives could focus their anxieties on the "racial" and political threat posed by European immigrants. The color red on the map, chosen to represent "Russian, Polish and Other Jews," catches the eye most immediately, carrying with it the color's traditional suggestion of danger as well as the more current 1920 association with the political and cultural threat posed by "Reds"— socialists and communists.[13]

Harlem did not require the same type of "re-spinning" needed

Fig. 4.2. Detail of "Map of the Borough of Manhattan and part of the Bronx, showing the location and extent of racial colonies." This 1920 map, published by the Ohman Map Company in New York, presented the city shaded in various colors to suggest the location of certain supposedly identifiable "racial" populations. Use of red shading for the areas for "Russian, Polish and Other Jews" contributed to the demonization of the city's immigrant Jewish population. Reproduced by permission from the collections of the Map Division, The New York Public Library, Astor, Lenox, and Tilden Foundations.

to sell the Lower East Side to tourists. The neighborhood did not become an established white tourist destination until the late 1920s, when Harlem's nightclubs and their black musicians and entertainers appealed to a Prohibition-era white middle class in search of seemingly "exotic" transgressions. In the early and mid-1920s, the preeminent African-American neighborhood of New York— and of the nation—did not have to mount the same arguments about the Americanness of its inhabitants. In fact, leading figures in the Harlem Renaissance in the 1920s drew attention to the fact that Harlem and its black population was American, not "foreign." "The language of Harlem is not alien; it is not Italian or Yiddish; it is English. Harlem talks American, reads American, thinks American," wrote James Weldon Johnson in 1925 as he and others of the "Talented Tenth" pushed Harlem's writers and artists to the attention of the white cultural establishment.[14] Some black Americans may have wished to assert their American identity in the face of fierce competition from European immigrants for jobs and for affordable living space. Johnson's comments do carry an anti-immigrant tone, more than a hint of agreement with the Anglo nativists who had so successfully campaigned to end continued mass immigration from Southern and Eastern Europe. In general, however, New York's blacks and Jews in the 1920s found common cause in supporting each other. The Ku Klux Klan and its less violent political allies ranked both "races" high on their list of undesirables and degenerates in the postwar era.

New York's densely populated immigrant neighborhoods provided an easy target for political scaremongers. The presence in the nation's most important city of such large groups of foreigners, especially Russian Jews tarred by association with the recent Bolshevik revolution, caused widespread alarm. In an inflammatory article in the magazine *Forum* in the spring of 1919, journalist John Bruce Mitchell described the city's Lower East Side as "the breeding place of revolt in the New World." According to Mitchell, few realized the extent or pattern of the geography of Bolshevism in New York: "Have you ever been to Forward Hall on East Broadway, the Manhattan Labour Lyceum at 66 East 4th Street, or the Rand School at 133 East 15th Street?" Mitchell, like Senator Lusk

and other red scare proponents, represented the Jewish neighborhoods of the Lower East Side as the location of increasing danger,
areas fomenting revolt against American political, religious, and
cultural institutions and values.[15]

"Race," Nostalgia, and History

The voices raised in challenge to New York's Americanness
came not only from the pages of national magazines and the Bab-
bitts of the heartland but also from within the city itself. These
voices bore the haughty vowels of the Union and Century Clubs,
of Gramercy Park and Washington Square. The Knickerbocker
and Astor crowds had particular reasons for allying themselves
with the critics of the cowtowns. Since the late nineteenth century,
members of these social elites, many of them "native" New Yorkers and "old stock" Americans, had experienced growing challenges to their economic, social, and cultural dominance in the city
of their birth. By World War I, the population and the power structure of Manhattan seemed increasingly alien to this class of New
Yorkers. As sociologist Frederic Cople Jaher has argued: "Most of
the Old Guard . . . attributed its demise to demagogues who hood-
winked the bovine masses and to robber barons who seized commercial supremacy from a class too noble to adopt their malev-
olence. Beleaguered patricians saw in democracy, immigration,
racial degeneracy, and industrialism the essence of the modern era
and the enemies of the fallen elite."[16] Some members of the old
elites joined forces in business and marriage with the newer industrial and financial elites, but such alliances did not remove the sense
of alienation. Many nouveau riche Anglo railroad entrepreneurs,
bankers, and corporate leaders felt no more comfortable in the
postwar world than did members of the older blueblood or mercantile elites. The old elites responded to this cultural crisis with
efforts to preserve their heritage. Their preservation efforts took
various forms—architectural, spatial, demographic—not the least
of which was a concerted effort to retain the power of their class
and ethnic group by restricting the number of immigrants entering the country.[17]

Old stock New Yorkers, those with the least investment in the city's growing consumer economy, felt the most alienated from the cultural changes taking place in the city they had once called their own. This class group, descendants of the old colonial mercantile elite and of the second wave elite of Mrs. Astor's famous "Four Hundred," had a strong attachment to the city but were devotees of an older version of metropolitan life: a nineteenth-century New York, largely homogeneous in terms of race and religion, with social position clearly demarcated and political power accompanying cultural power. To a generation raised in the 1870s and 1880s, the rapidly changing and increasingly heterogeneous power structure of 1920s New York City, in which political and cultural power was spread across a range of elites and constituencies, was bewildering and threatening.

Old "WASP" New Yorkers, facing increasing anxiety about racial superiority in the face of mass immigration into their city, turned to biology and theories of evolution to bolster their claims to power in the postwar world. In September 1921, New York's American Museum of Natural History (AMNH) hosted the Second International Congress of Eugenics with an accompanying monthlong exhibition. Mary Harriman, wife of railroad magnate and museum trustee Edward H. Harriman and herself founder of the Eugenics Record Office at Cold Spring Harbor, Long Island, contributed twenty-five hundred dollars toward the staging of the exhibit. Other patrons included Herbert Hoover and Honorary President of the Congress Alexander Graham Bell.[18] The 1921 congress and exhibit provided a public forum for old guard New Yorkers and their allies around the country to reassert their political power in the national and international spotlight under the cover of a scientific event at one of the city's most prestigious and cherished institutions.[19] Henry Fairfield Osborn, the driving force behind the 1921 congress and exhibition at AMNH, was a biologist and paleontologist, and became president of the AMNH in 1908, having been a curator at the museum since 1891. Under Osborn's leadership, the AMNH became one of the nation's most important sites for the promotion of eugenics and racial classification and played a major role in the national political debate about immigration.[20]

One of Osborn's chief associates in the popularization of racial and eugenical theories in relation to immigration was his fellow New Yorker and class peer, Madison Grant. Grant, gentleman scholar of natural history, paleontology, and human evolution, knew Osborn both from New York social circles and from their service together on the governing boards of the AMNH and the Bronx Zoo. Like Osborn, Grant came from a well-established and wealthy New York family, with both paternal and maternal roots in the city dating back to colonial times. Madison Grant is best known as the author of the often reprinted and revised treatise on the rise and vaunted decline of the "Nordic" race, *The Passing of the Great Race*, first published in 1916. Osborn wrote two enthusiastic introductions to later editions of the book.[21] In Grant's view, the new immigration of the 1890s and of the early years of the twentieth century represented the lowest racial stocks of Europe, the "sweepings of . . . jails and asylums," which European governments were just as glad to see leave. The "whole tone of American life" had been "lowered and vulgarized" by "this human flotsam."[22]

For both Grant and Osborn, immigration from Southern and Eastern Europe into New York, which they observed around them every day, provided evidence for their racial theories. They believed that immigration by the eugenically inferior "Alpine" and "Mediterranean" races was causing the birthrate of "Nordic" Americans to drop "because the poorer classes of Colonial stock, where they still exist, will not bring children into the world to compete in the labor market with the Slovak, the Italian, the Syrian and the Jew." The passivity of the "man of the old stock" meant that "he is to-day being literally driven off the streets of New York City by the swarms of Polish Jews."[23] To Grant, New York represented the epitome of the dire direction in which the "race" was heading. "Large cities from the days of Rome, Alexandria, and Byzantium have always been gathering points of diverse races, but New York is becoming a *cloaca gentium* [human sewer] which will produce many amazing racial hybrids and some ethnic horrors that will be beyond the powers of future anthropologists to unravel." He argued that the conditions of life in large cities such as

New York threatened the Nordics and Anglo-Saxon old stock Americans: "The 'survival of the fittest' means the survival of the type best adapted to . . . the tenement and factory, . . . From the point of view of race it were better described as the 'survival of the unfit.'"[24]

The New York daily press covered the papers and discussions at the 1921 eugenics congress but showed less interest in the exhibit, which suggests that this anti-immigration elite possessed relatively little power to garner mass publicity.[25] Given the muted criticisms contained in some editorial comments on the congress, it is possible that the editors of the New York dailies deemed the congress's aims wrongheaded or pernicious. It is also possible that, even if individual newspaper owners or editors agreed with some of the aims of the Congress, they simply wished to avoid alienating their readership and advertisers, many of whom were from immigrant backgrounds. More in keeping with the largely pro-immigrant, antiracist politics of the city, *The Sun* and *The World* instead ran front-page stories throughout the month of September 1921 about the resurgence of America's most controversial racist and anti-Semitic organization, the Ku Klux Klan.[26]

During the early 1920s, while immigration debates raged, New York's major dailies had regular coverage of the issues, in particular the problems posed by the three percent quota law passed in early 1921 as a temporary measure to restrict postwar immigration. The quota system meant that boats bearing immigrants from Europe raced to reach New York's quarantine station at the beginning of every month in order to land their human cargo before the quota was filled. Newspapers also reported that the combination of large numbers of immigrants and new laws requiring inspection for physical and mental weaknesses had caused a substantial backlog of immigrants at Ellis Island.[27]

Henry Fairfield Osborn and Madison Grant's mourning for the decline of Nordic civilization fit with the larger sense of loss or embattlement felt by others of their class and generation in New York. The image of old guard New Yorkers Osborn and Grant, ensconced in their museum on the Upper West Side, carefully preserving the remains of sundry dinosaurs while railing against the purported near-extinction of their own species, is telling. Nostalgia for an apparently lost New York, a New York that existed before the new immigration, preoccupied many of the city's upper classes. Largely recalling and extolling the virtues of the 1870s and 1880s, their publications and activities represented another attempt to lay claim to the city and its identity. However, unlike Osborn or Grant, the majority of these writers were not committed to a political program to undo the demographic and cultural changes wrought in the city since the turn of the century. They seemed more resigned to the end of their era and content to describe it nostalgically for their own satisfaction.[28]

Following the Hudson-Fulton celebration in 1909, which commemorated the centennial of Robert Fulton's North River Steamboat and the tricentennial of Henry Hudson's entry into New York Harbor, efforts to preserve New York's Anglo-Dutch past had become more popular. Bastions of the city's old guard such as the City History Club, the New-York Historical Society, and branches of patriotic genealogical organizations such as the Colonial Dames of America sponsored local history and preservation activities. Such activities gained greater momentum in the late 1910s and after World War I with major efforts such as the rebuilding of Theodore Roosevelt's birthplace at 28 East 20th Street following his death in 1919 and the building and opening of the American Wing at the Metropolitan Museum of Art in November 1924.[29] Elaborate events marking an anniversary or other commemoration had become increasingly popular in the early twentieth century. Referencing older traditions of parades and fairs, the historical pageants staged by patriotic organizations in large cities such as New York represented the reassertion of an older order and laid claim to a past frequently not shared by more recent inhabitants.

A New Itinerary and a New Geography

The vast array of images of immigrants in newspapers and popular magazines, while helping to generate support for immigration restriction, also piqued readers' curiosity about such foreign racial types and their cultures. Certainly by the early 1920s, art, fashion, literature, and the tourist industry all catered to a new interest in the "primitive" and in the "picturesque" qualities of peoples and cultures regarded as having retained "old world" ways of life, culture, dress, and language. It was a romantic, consumerist reinterpretation of the racial typing and classifying promoted by anti-immigration advocates.[30]

The 1920s witnessed the maturation of the American consumer economy as a result of higher wages, mass production, the national distribution of material goods, and a highly effective advertising industry. A crucial component of the decade's aura of mass material progress was the automobile. The number of automobiles in the United States grew by a factor of twenty between 1913 and 1931; by the end of the 1920s, over twenty percent of Americans owned cars.[31] This increased mobility, along with increasing leisure time and even paid vacations for some workers, drew more Americans out onto the nation's roadways or railways as tourists. By the early 1920s, guidebooks claimed that New York received about 200,000 visitors per day. While this number probably included a range of regular daily visitors—from suburban shoppers to traveling salesmen—it does indicate both the popularity of New York as a sightseeing destination and the economic value of such visitors to many of the city's businesses.[32]

Representations of New York's immigrant populations and neighborhoods as enhancements to the city's entertainment facilities became increasingly common in the descriptive literature about the city in the mid- and late 1920s. While older guides to the city's attractions had included the immigrant neighborhoods on their itineraries, they did so in terms of "slumming" trips, as slightly risky excursions marginal to the main itinerary, revealing populations largely marginal to the city's life and identity. As new laws gradually reduced the number of new immigrants to a relative trickle, authors and publishers of tourist literature more confidently recommended the city's ethnic neighborhoods to sightseers. By the mid-1920s, as travel writers encouraged their readers to understand, Little Italy, Chinatown, and the "Ghetto" had become part of the mainstream tourist itinerary and were as accessible and as safe to explore as any other area of the city. This growing genre of travel literature, aimed at the burgeoning tourist classes, served to counteract contemporary Anglo-Saxonism and nativism by redescribing New York's immigrant neighborhoods as picturesque and available for consumption.

This commercial spin on erstwhile undesirable populations and neighborhoods took specific issue, in the immediate postwar period, with the images of immigrants produced by eugenicists and nativists calling for immigration restriction. Popular monthly magazines such as *The Saturday Evening Post, Literary Digest, Good Housekeeping,* and *Collier's* ran scores of articles in the 1910s and early 1920s touting eugenicist arguments for immigration restriction.[33] Not only were these articles run in major popular magazines, they were also authored by well-known Americans whose opinions carried great weight: incoming president Calvin Coolidge wrote an article entitled "Whose Country Is This?" for *Good Housekeeping* in 1921; George Creel, who had led the U.S. government's wartime propaganda unit, the Committee on Public Information, wrote an article for *Collier's* magazine the same year entitled "Melting Pot or Dumping Ground?" (fig. 4.3). These articles argued that immigrants from Eastern and Southern Europe were physically and mentally defective, diseased, criminal, and racially unassimilable. Often accompanied by photographs of Ellis Island, or of New York's Lower East Side, these articles posed a threat to the boosters' positive "spin" on the city. To counteract such widespread propaganda about immigrants, guidebook publishers and travel writers promoting the city to middle-class American tourists knew that, despite the obvious contradiction, they needed to market New York as both American and un-American, as offering both the reassurance of familiarity as well as the excitement of difference. Therefore, while promoting the more conventional attractions of the theater district's Great White Way, they also sold Little Italy, Chinatown, and the Ghetto as New York attractions.[34]

Fig. 4.3. "Melting Pot or Dumping Ground?" This image, accompanying George Creel's September 3, 1921 *Collier's* article, is a good example of how anti-immigration advocates used photography to support their arguments about the "degeneracy" of recent immigrants.

One can trace the gradual change in attitude to the city's immigrant neighborhoods by comparing itineraries recommended in guides and travel literature published in the early and mid-1920s. *Rider's New York City,* one of a series of *Rider's* guides to American cities that began publication shortly before World War I, aimed to attract a broad middle-class readership. The editor, author, and compiler Fremont Rider modeled the guides on the well-established Baedeker guidebook series in Europe. Baedekers were part of every American tourist's equipment for seeing Europe in the 1910s and 1920s. As T. S. Eliot suggested in his 1920 poem "Burbank With a Baedeker: Bleistein With a Cigar," the carrying of a Baedeker connoted "American tourist" in pre– and post–World War I Europe. The *Rider's* series imitated the Baedekers, both in the presentation of itineraries tailored to a particular length of stay and in the use of asterisks to denote especially significant sites or highly recommended restaurants and hotels. For middle- and upper-middle-class Americans developing the habit of tourism in their own country, Rider's overt referencing of the Baedeker guides suggested the suitability of the destinations described.[35]

In his 1923 guide to New York, Rider offered both a fourteen-day and a five-day itinerary for visitors with limited amounts of time. His fourteen-day itinerary included a visit to the "foreign quarters" during the afternoon of the sixth day. He listed the Italian quarter, Chinatown, and the "Yiddish and Russian" quarters, giving the street locations of each. But he amended a special note beneath this part of the itinerary: "This excursion involves a rather long walk through narrow, sordid streets, teeming with an overcrowded population, but it is picturesque and quite safe for strangers." Only those visitors most determined to go in search of the urban picturesque were likely to pursue such a backhanded recommendation.

In the five-day itinerary, Rider left out the "Yiddish and Russian" quarters, sending his readers only to the Italian quarter and to Chinatown.[36] The foreign cultures of Italy and China, consumed in the form of immigrant communities in America, were apparently more easily palatable to American tourists. Although both carried somewhat unsavory reputations for violence and gang-oriented skulduggery, guidebook writers could nonetheless more easily promote these two "colorful" cultures as picturesque and quaint. Especially in the period before the 1924 National Origins Act, which effectively closed the door on further Eastern and Southern European immigration, and in the context of the postwar red scare, with anti-Semitic and anti-immigration rhetoric running high, authors and publishers such as Rider more readily excised from their itineraries the predominantly Jewish neighborhoods of New York, which offered the wrong sort of "otherness." Chinatown and Little Italy had more established traditions of satisfying the visiting "slummer" with curio shops, restaurants, music, and festivals, whereas Jewish neighborhoods offered comparatively few opportunities for such consumption.[37]

Rider also mentioned the foreign neighborhoods in his main narrative, organized geographically from south to north. The section describing the sights available "Northeast of City Hall Park" gave brief descriptions of the Italian, Chinese, and Jewish neighborhoods of the Lower East Side, little changed from his 1916 guide to New York. Rider paid little attention to these areas, save to mention the "Italian atmosphere" created in Mulberry Park by the sidewalk markets and the Italian women and children. He reminded his reader that the sightseeing automobiles offered evening trips to Chinatown during which the visitor could enjoy "the picturesqueness of the neighborhood and visit joss houses [Chinese temples] and shops, without fear of annoyance." The "Ghetto" seems least appealing of all in Rider's description, offering a "swarming population" and the oft-mentioned "pullers-in," eager to draw passers by into garment stores. However, the possibility of finding cheap antique brass and copper on Allen Street, in the heart of the "Ghetto," recommended a neighborhood and a population otherwise regarded as having little to offer the tourist.

Beginning in the mid-1920s, guidebook and travel writers more frequently encouraged tourists to explore ethnic neighborhoods on their own, suggesting self-guided walking tours with the aid of a guidebook. Freed from fears of exploring these neighborhoods and the tyranny of the sightseeing bus with its set itinerary and pat megaphone narratives, tourists could create for themselves a more personal experience of the city, a tailored search for ethnic authenticity. After the 1924 Immigration Act, ethnic neighborhoods may have seemed less "foreign" than before the war. By the late 1920s, large numbers of the neighborhoods' inhabitants had grown up in New York or were even born in the city. They formed a more assimilated, more "modern" generation of ethnic New Yorkers. Ethnic neighborhoods in the late 1920s offered a mix of safety, accessibility, and reassuring impressions of assimilation and Americanization while also still offering the thrill of an authentically foreign experience.[38]

In the fall of 1925, *Outlook* magazine published an article by well-known New York Italian-American writer and journalist Edward Corsi entitled "My Neighborhood." The subhead under the title read: "Edward Corsi finds in the polyglot boarding-house of New York the makings of the America of to-morrow. It is an article to make Americans of the old stock pause and think." Corsi's article captured the contradictory argument made by writers encouraging people to visit immigrant neighborhoods that the area was both American *and* foreign: American enough that "Americans of the old stock" should not denigrate its inhabitants but foreign enough that tourists might patronize the neighborhood, making the most of a vanishing "old world" culture.[39]

Corsi quoted an immigrant intellectual friend from the neighborhood who claimed that when the "Great American Novel" eventually appeared, "its background will not be Main Street, but the East Side of New York. Its central figure, furthermore, will not be a Babbitt or a New England farmer or a Kentucky colonel, but an immigrant's son, a child of the melting-pot." His friend insisted that "the East Side, with its peoples from many lands, speaking many tongues, and gradually building a civilization which, in the end, will be ours and not Europe's, is America." Corsi explained his friend's unconventional viewpoint to his implied Anglo, middle-class readership by describing how the limited geography of the city's immigrants affected their concept of "America": "to the Italian mother on Mulberry Street, imprisoned in her four-room flat, or to the overworked Jewish tailor on East Broadway, . . . 'America' is a hodgepodge of toiling millions, tenements, crowded subways, busy sweatshops, and fenced-in playgrounds—in other words the East Side."[40] By implication, his immigrant friend's perspective on America was shaped by his immersion in an immigrant neighborhood.

Both crusaders for immigration restriction and promoters of tourism within New York's "racial" neighborhoods discussed the city's immigrants as physical as well as cultural types. Being able to identify visually a Russian Jew, a Syrian, an Italian, or a Greek was an important aspect of the tourist's encounter with the authentically foreign. Building on the physical, racial typing familiar to middle-class readers from periodical articles and from contemporary notions of race, tourism promoters and torchbearers for the immigrant neighborhoods echoed the images and language of scientific racism.

Tourists came in search of what guidebooks and travel articles referred to as the "real" Jew or the "real" Italian. Hutchins Hapgood, a well-known chronicler of the Jewish Lower East Side, described the "real Jew" as one who "remains steadfastly faithful to the spirit of the old culture, . . . whether he be push-cart peddler, scholar, or worshiper in the synagogue." The location of the "real" Jews, the New York Ghetto, Hapgood argued, "when interpreted by the sympathetic artist," was "deeply picturesque."[41] Edward Corsi encouraged readers to see the foreignness of his immigrant neighborhood, visible not only in "the flags of many colors, [and] the foreign papers on every news-stand, but [also] in the types one meets on the streets—tall blond Nordics, olive-skinned, dark-haired Mediterraneans, long-bearded Semites and Slavs, massive Africans, East Indians, gypsies, Japs, and Chinese." The terms Corsi used, such as "Nordic" and "Mediterranean," borrowed directly from the racial typologies first delineated at the turn of the century by social scientists such as W. Z. Ripley, and further popularized and legitimized by Madison Grant and others. But Corsi warned his readers that the quaint, picturesque Old World as represented in his neighborhood would soon disappear: "America's doors are fast closing, and the tide of a new civilization, . . . which is not Anglo-Saxon or Latin or Slav, but 'American,' is setting in."[42] Corsi suggested that the assimilation deemed so undesirable — even impossible—by immigration restrictionists was indeed occurring. While Corsi seemed to welcome such assimilation in terms of the greater security and respect it brought to immigrants, he also seemed to regret its coming as it would break down the distinct foreign racial types and cultures so appealing to tourists and, apparently, to himself as well.

Unlike the articles and books calling for immigration restriction, tourist literature encouraging ethnic tourism depicted the supposedly available ethnic types, the "real" Jews and Italians and their neighborhoods, using images that avoided visual realism. Instead, guidebooks and travel literature used pencil, charcoal or ink-wash sketches, often by well-known artists, shunning the realism of the photograph. Artists and illustrators, familiar to many readers from their books of sketches or their illustrations in magazines, hired to work on tourist literature included E. H. Suydam, Vernon Howe Bailey, Joseph Pennell, and Loren Stout. The extensive use of pen and ink illustration, at a time when neither cost nor technical complexity inhibited the reproduction of photographic images, came about because, by the postwar period, photographic images of immigrants and their neighborhoods evoked negative connotations in most middle-class Americans. From Jacob Riis's 1890s photographs of New York's tenement neighborhoods and Lewis Hine's images of child labor to eugenicist images of "undesirable aliens," photography had for too long served the aims of the reform movements to allow its successful use by businesses invested in the promotion of the city's immigrant neighborhoods as tourist attractions.[43]

In an early example of this trend, Caroline Singer, an accomplished travel writer, focused her attention in 1921 on an Italian neighborhood in New York's Lower East Side. Singer made specific reference at the start of her article to the contrast between old and new representations of New York's immigrant neighborhoods. The conventional but, she suggested, outdated image of this neighborhood was "framed silhouettes of family groups sitting with hunched shoulders about allotments of piece-work," a reference to the old photographs of the Lower East Side taken by Jacob Riis and other social reformers, still familiar to most of her readers. The new view she and her illustrator, Cyrus LeRoy Baldridge, provided was from the consumer's perspective, taking pleasure in "the pageants of the market-place, the plumed marionettes of Mulberry Bend, and the softly flaring tapers of the holy feast." Baldridge's images of the neighborhood's streets and people emphasized the picturesque details of craggy-visaged old men, cluttered vegetable markets, and dark-eyed, dark-haired young Italian women. The images were captioned either with quotations from Singer's text, adding to the veracity of her account, or with titles such as "A twentieth-century Mona Lisa," "The blind flute-player," and "A Madonna of the balcony," providing another layer of ethnic romance. The use of quality illustrations, with their romantic and picturesque connotations, evoked (as did Rider's guides) the elite pleasures of the European tour, equating New York neighborhoods and their middle-class tourists with well-established but more exclusive travel experiences.[44]

This new tourist literature, whether article, guidebook or collection of travel essays, made direct appeal to a female audience. Writers and publishers knew that American women made up a large proportion of the touring classes and participated in decisions about where to travel and what to do on vacation. Increasingly, starting in the 1920s and growing in numbers in the 1930s, women also wrote guidebooks and travel features, placing more emphasis on assurances of comfort and safety; guidebooks included many more details about shops and shopping, including what one could buy in the small shops and pushcart markets of the Lower East Side. The illustrations accompanying these articles or guidebook chapters featured women and children, not as the victims of poverty but as characters in vibrant neighborhood scenes. The two female authors of *New York in Seven Days,* published in 1925, constructed their tourist narrative through the eyes of a fictional male protagonist guiding a female acquaintance around the city. This knowledgeable male guide reassures his female companion as she hesitates on the borders of Chinatown that he knows "many women" who come to the area "alone or in pairs to shop." The two browse the shops of "Brasstown," a commercial district in the Jewish quarter, and he suggests she return alone on Sunday to see the local Orthodox population of bearded men and bewigged women.[45]

However, the still-thorny issue of urban geography tempered guidebook and travel writers' perceptions of the immigrants as "picturesque." Most regarded such populations as picturesque only when they remained within their ethnically defined neighborhoods. One writer encouraged his readers to experience New York's foreign neighborhoods, to see the "magic and mystery of the Orient" in Chinatown, or the "veritable Naples" of Little Italy. But he also described those same immigrants as a potential threat. Referring to the sight of striking workers marching on Fifth Avenue, he wrote: "There was not an American face in the entire twenty-five thousand. . . . It was an object lesson as to whose are the hands into which we are throwing control of our country."[46]

Mabel Osgood Wright, native New Yorker and popular author, reminisced in her 1926 memoir *My New York* about the version of the city her parents had known and in which she had grown up in the last quarter of the nineteenth century. Taking a taxicab ride around the city, "striving to piece together a patchwork of the city that I knew," she finds only absences and detrimental changes in the places she used to know. Around Fifth Avenue and 23rd Street, instead of the old elegance of the Fifth Avenue Hotel, she sees "the sidewalk procession of the workers from the great loft manufactories." These workers seem racially alien, "of many nationalities, either foreign born or so saturated by alien heredity that no trace of the smelting process was visible"; she sees no evidence of the social qualities she values: they are "gesticulating, aggressive, showing no courtesy to the women of their own breed that swarmed along the gutters, no kindness to the bearded and old that necessity forced among them. To get there first—to get all—was written on every face except those whose dull stolidity seemed to make them progress only by being pushed."[47] At her family's old summer home, fifty miles outside New York, she looks back on her day in the city and concludes that "her" New York no longer exists: "Good night, New York! *My New York, good-bye!*"[48]

If visitors stayed within the geography of immigrant neighborhoods, as promoted by the tourist trade, they could go forth unafraid and relish the opportunity for a form of world travel, moving from one "country" to the next as they strolled around the city. Journalist and author Konrad Bercovici described New York in the mid-1920s as "not a city but a world." Like the anti-immigration campaigners and red scare agitators, guidebook and travel writers mapped the location and borders of New York's immigrant neighborhoods. Bercovici's *Around the World in New York,* for example, took the reader through "Africa," "Greece," "China," and various other "countries."[49] Despite his book's echoes of more conservative versions of the city's foreign geographies, as seen in the "Racial Colonies" map of 1920, Bercovici's imagined map of New York suggested orderly consumer pleasures rather than political or racial threats. Norman Borchardt's illustrations offered pleasing interpretations of Bercovici's text, featuring foreign-looking streets and people whose appearance exuded charm, not menace (fig. 4.4).

This type of literature seeking to boost the city, to promote the

Fig. 4.4. "Picturesque" images such as this of New York's diverse populations in popular travel books and articles were designed to counteract the images and rhetoric of anti-immigrationists and eugenicists. By Norman Borchardt, in Konrad Bercovici, *Around the World in New York* (New York: The Century Company, 1924).

immigrant neighborhoods as attractions, and to locate the urban picturesque had its counterpart in the tourist brochure maps of the late 1920s and the 1930s. Brightly colored and frequently covered in cartoon images or caricatures of the ethnic or urban "types" meant to represent a particular neighborhood, these maps depicted the whole of Manhattan as a site of easy entertainment. Earlier maps designed for tourists were usually fold-out appendices to guidebooks showing only practical information such as the major railroad, elevated, and subway lines and a handful of well-known sites such as the Metropolitan Museum, Trinity Church, and the American Museum of Natural History. Beginning in the late 1920s, map and guidebook publishers, banks, hotels, sightseeing companies, and independent mapmakers issued brochure maps of New York available in bookstores, hotel lobbies, newsstands, railroad offices, and other commercial venues frequented by visitors. Building on the work done by the guidebooks and travel literature of the mid-1920s, by the time these maps were produced new zoning laws had banned garment lofts and their Jewish immigrant workers from Fifth Avenue. The racial "others" now stayed in their own neighborhoods—more convenient for tourists and more acceptable to white, Anglo New Yorkers. These maps presented a city open for exploration by the visitor, designating all parts of the city as equally part of the tourist itinerary.[50]

The open, citywide territories of the tourist maps represented the successful commodification of the city's space by the 1930s. The dominance of New York by a mass consumer economy, underway in the city since the turn of the century, shifted the center of political and economic power away from the old Anglo-Saxon elites toward new immigrant entrepreneurs deeply embedded in the new economy as retailers, bankers, property developers, mass entertainment moguls, and advertisers. As we shall see in the next chapter, the promulgation of the immigrant neighborhoods as tourist attractions on a par with the Metropolitan Museum and Broadway resulted from the successful recasting of New York's image in the mid- and late 1920s by the rising business elites of the city. Working with their class and ethnic peers in the city government, this new breed of boosters reorganized and repackaged New York City, creating a new, less stratified geography.

Throughout the 1920s and into the 1930s, racial categories remained critically important in the United States, but the uses to which they were put shifted. As historians of world's fairs and other "public amusements" have shown, experiencing the "other" as entertainment had a long history by the 1920s, and it continues to be an important aspect of contemporary tourism. Although nativist forces seemed to win the day in 1924, in fact their power to influence the image of New York was already waning. By the mid-1920s, organized commercial forces, led by New York's businessmen's associations, had already amassed far more capital—financial and cultural—than the "old stock" nativists. Conscious of their diverse constituencies, both the city government and the trade associations became adept in the 1920s at marketing both the immigrant neighborhoods and Times Square as native to New York, part of the city's identity as both American and un-American. An important part of that project, running parallel with the re-spinning of the city's "foreign quarters," was the invention of Midtown as New York's brand image, its avowedly American heart.

5

BRAND NEW YORK: MAKING MIDTOWN IN THE 1920s

"It is true that our town is cosmopolitan and that an enormous element in its population is of alien birth," wrote critic James L. Ford in the New York *Tribune* in early 1922, disparaging contemporary fictional portrayals of New York City. "But there is," he continued, "a real New York composed of many different classes and united in a brotherhood that did not altogether go out of existence with the volunteer Fire Department."[1] The cartoon accompanying Ford's article succinctly summed up his objections to the prevailing literary narratives about New York: a writer sits puzzling over what story he can produce involving the stock characters jumbled together as labeled dolls and scenery in a suitcase by his desk. They are all familiar New York "types": the "beautiful settlement worker," the "virtuous district attorney," the "brutal saloon politician," the "honest working girl," and a dreary cutout backdrop labeled "tenements" (fig. 5.1). These characters, and the limited narratives they suggested, described a New York that may or may not have ever existed outside the realm of popular fiction, but they certainly did not adequately represent the complicated characters, "plots," and locations that signified New York in the 1920s.

While Ford's "real New York" of class harmony might have sounded to many just as fictional as the books to which he objected, his rejection of New York narratives based only on the tenement districts and their motley populations fit with growing concerns among members of the city government and the business community over what they saw as the bad press New York re-

Fig. 5.1. The "modern novelist" ponders which stock characters to include in his narrative about the city, supporting the article's argument that contemporary writers were shortchanging the "real" city by reproducing outdated stereotypes of the city and its people. "Workshop of the Modern Novelist." Cartoon from "Misrepresenting New York in Fiction," *Literary Digest* (March 25, 1922).

ceived nationally and sometimes locally. In the early 1920s, businessmen and politicians feared that outdated stereotypes, like the ones depicted in Ford's article, and new New York bogeymen such as gunmen and ghetto Bolsheviks gave outsiders a distorted image of the city, ultimately damaging New York's status and economy. While many in the tourist industry fought this same battle of images by promoting the exploration of other "countries" and cultures on the city's Lower East Side, businessmen and politicians focused their efforts on promoting New York to an audience of both tourists and fellow businessmen through the more mainstream environment of Midtown.

Businessmen and politicians, like the tourism promoters discussed in the previous chapter, aimed in the 1920s to reorient the city's public image through the promotion and management of a particular part of the city. In the post–World War I period and through the 1920s, Midtown gradually developed as the fulfillment of an ideal notion of the modern city: accessible and traversable by public transport utilizing vertical rather than horizontal space, a well-policed area of mixed use (business and pleasure) capable of meeting the varied needs of both the "classes" and the "masses." James L. Ford's "real New York" was by implication not the cosmopolitan city of the Lower East Side, embodied in those of "alien birth." His "real New York" fit better with the particular heterogeneity of Midtown: a deftly controlled and largely privatized "public" space encouraging a range of activities by a multiclass, multi-ethnic urban population, no single group of which overtly dominated the area.

A new boosterism took shape in New York after World War I, more organized and more sophisticated than prewar efforts, the result of a developing, unofficial alliance between the city government and business organizations such as the Merchants' Association of New York and other trade associations. At the national level, Commerce Secretary Herbert Hoover fostered such alliances, specifically courting trade associations in his efforts to bring business and government closer together.[2] As historian Roland Marchand has argued, many businessmen of this generation had gained valuable experience during the war as producers of propaganda and war advertising, utilizing the new medium of radio as well as more familiar printed media: "The rapid proliferation of new media and recollections of the impact of wartime propaganda had made everyone more conscious of public opinion and the power of imagery." New York's businessmen used the communications acumen and advertising expertise for which the city was a national center to develop promotional events and publications that best branded the "real New York" they hoped to sell.[3]

The members of the city government and business organizations involved in this new boosterism generally differed in terms of class and ethnicity from the upper-crust Nordics discussed previously who struggled to maintain a cultural foothold in postwar New York. Many of these new power brokers were the products of mid- and late nineteenth-century mass immigration and Lower East Side "foreign colonies," completely at home with the power plays of ward politics and the mutual back-scratching involved in business. Mayors John Hylan and Jimmy Walker, city and state politician Al Smith, and the ultimate local son of both the business and political networks of New York City, Grover Whalen, came from working-class families. They were deeply embedded in their own "old boy" network, mixing childhood neighborhood loyalties with political and business relations. Taking a certain amount of ethnic and class heterogeneity for granted, these men had grown up, attended school, and came to conduct business in a multiethnic world of ambitious fellow native sons.

This group of city officials, manufacturers, real estate brokers, hoteliers, department store owners, entertainment industry mavens, and insurance company directors were not necessarily more racially tolerant than the nativists to be found in New York's wider political and cultural circles. Rather, as businessmen involved in the industries dominating New York's postwar economy, the new brokers had a greater financial investment in the city's heterogeneous present and future, and in the consumer capitalism that underpinned it. Boosting New York City through Midtown in the 1920s ultimately held great rewards for both politicians and businessmen. But it required shaping the area as the cultural, business, and iconic center of New York City: making it work as real estate, white-collar workspace, pleasure zone, and the city's public face.

Rubberneckers and Reputation

The national periodical press in the 1920s carried numerous articles damning New York as overrun with undesirable aliens, beset by gangsters, and still incorrigibly "wicked."[4] Many of these urban narratives centered on the idea that out-of-towners traveled to New York for a tourist experience, only to be robbed and bamboozled by the sucker-seeking metropolis. Tourism and tourists were, by the 1920s, both the bane and boon of New York. Approximately 200,000 visitors entered the city every day, heading for the shops, restaurants, theaters, movie palaces, and miscellaneous street attractions lacking in their hometowns. Special events, such as conventions or parades, frequently brought in even larger crowds. If each visitor spent only ten dollars per day, the combined revenue for city businesses formed a sizable portion of New York's annual income.

New Yorkers did not commonly hold generous opinions of their many thousands of guests. Locals held tourists responsible for the misrepresentations suffered by their city in national publications. Tourists and out-of-town journalists, New Yorkers complained, came to New York and saw only the gaudiest nightlife of Broadway or the staged "sights" of a "slumming" trip to Chinatown or Harlem. Broadway producer and songwriter George M. Cohan argued, fully aware of the irony, that there was a lot more to New York than Broadway. Those who never veered from the most conventional tourist itineraries and preconceptions distorted the city's image. Such people "take a rubberneck wagon out to the phoney mysteries of the moving-picture Chinatown . . . [and] want the musical show with the least clothes on" so that they can "keep the folks at home awake with tales of the vice and shamelessness they saw."[5]

The very popular *New York Tribune* columnist, FPA, nom de plume of journalist Franklin P. Adams, also took tourists to task, scolding domestic visitors for doing to New York exactly what they accused foreign visitors of doing to America: basing their assessments of the whole place on the small part they actually saw: "You non-New Yorkers resent . . . that Mr. Charles Dickens and Mr. H. G. Wells and Mr. Kipling and Mr. Arnold Bennett base their American comments so largely upon what they see and do in New York. Yet you who tarry a week or two in our delightful city do exactly the same thing. . . . You give a few Broadway blocks a coat of mild vermilion, and tell the folks at home how late you were up every night, and how New Yorkers fling away their money."[6] FPA concluded, perhaps expressing an epistemological relativism ahead of his time, that New York was unknowable: "I can not interpret it. I do not know what its 'message' is. New York is too large to know. Too many things are simultaneously true of it." Although both his scolding of hinterlanders and his neat conclusion no doubt appealed to New Yorkers' sense of superiority, FPA's approach was not likely to challenge misperceptions of New York. To build and maintain a positive and marketable image of the city serving the needs of both tourists and locals required a concerted effort by those experienced in modern techniques of selling, advertising, and media manipulation. It also required the careful maintenance and management of the public and private spaces frequented by tourists, many of them located in Midtown, requiring liaison and agreement between city departments and numerous private businesses and organizations. During the 1910s and 1920s, trade associations representing numerous business interests battled each other and the city government to exert or relax various controls over Midtown's burgeoning entertainment and retail districts that comprised the increasingly distinctive features of New York's public face.

"Selling Points" and Selling Places

Harold Phillips, author of an annually revised guide to New York City, remarked in his 1920 edition that "it is surprising that there are no organized bureaus where we might become better acquainted with Gotham."[7] Other cities or regions, he remarked, had boards of trade and chambers of commerce to disseminate both practical and promotional information about their localities. New York had no such city agency directed to offer information, guidance, or encouragement to business or pleasure visitors to the city. Businessmen's organizations, starting in the 1890s, had taken responsibility for promoting the city, focusing on the provision of services, information, and entertainment to visiting buyers or salesmen. By the early 1920s, the main organization involved in promoting New York was the Merchants' Association of New York (MANY), founded in 1897, which worked increasingly in conjunction with the city government and other organizations. Under the second Hylan administration in the mid-1920s, such cooperation between business and government became more explicit, as seen through events such as the 1923 Greater New York Silver Jubilee celebration. Politicians and businessmen had a shared interest in opposing any nationally held negative views of the city as well as those promulgated locally by their own conservative peers.

At the conclusion of his autobiography, *Mr. New York,* Grover Whalen stated that "the biggest failure of [his] life" was his inability to establish "an official city agency to promote New York." Whalen, born on the Lower East Side in 1886 to a working-class Irish-American family, went on to become general manager of the New York John Wanamaker store, secretary to Mayor Hylan, police commissioner under Mayor Walker, and long-term head of the Mayor's Committee on Receptions. Through his business and political activities, he became the most important link between the business community and successive city governments and worked tirelessly to promote the city. Whalen's greatest achievement was undoubtedly his leadership in organizing and promoting the 1939–40 New York World's Fair.[8]

Although Whalen graduated from New York Law School in 1907, he ultimately pursued a career in retail, rising up through the managerial and executive ranks of the John Wanamaker store at Broadway and Ninth, where he had worked while in school. Whalen's lifelong two-flanked boosting campaign on behalf of New York began in earnest in 1914 when Preston Lynn, the general manager of Wanamaker's, told Whalen that he intended to form a businessmen's committee and wanted Whalen to be secretary, promising him time off from his duties at the store in order to attend to the work. The resulting Businessmen's League, although initially in support of the current mayor, John Purroy Mitchel, elected on an anti-Tammany fusion ticket, ultimately joined forces with the Tammany Hall Democratic Party leadership to back Preston Lynn's candidacy in 1917. However, Lynn's political trajectory was cut short when his employers, John and Rodman Wanamaker, objected to his planned run for mayor, leaving Tammany without a candidate.

Tammany's search for a replacement led them to the Brooklyn courtroom of Judge John F. Hylan, longtime party loyalist and crusader against the "transit interests" and their threats to the treasured five-cent subway fare. Hylan's five-cent fare platform endeared him to the Hearst papers, which were running their own campaign against the "interests." With the full support of the Businessmen's League, Tammany Hall, and William Randolph Hearst, Hylan won a comfortable victory in the fall of 1917. Hylan, never a confident leader, asked Whalen to stay on as his secretary through the inauguration. In this interim period after the election, Hylan soon became reliant on Whalen's superior skills at dealing with the press and at the sort of day-to-day political diplomacy essential to the smooth running of the Mayor's Office. Hylan talked directly with Wanamaker store director Rodman Wanamaker about retaining Whalen in an official capacity as secretary to the mayor, to which Wanamaker agreed, assuring Whalen his career at the store would not be affected. So began Whalen's lifelong shuttling between business and politics, never quite leaving one for the other.[9]

Closer relations between business and government, exemplified in New York in the person and career of Whalen, were fostered at the national level by Commerce Secretary Herbert Hoover's indefatigable director of the Bureau of Foreign and Domestic Commerce (BFDC), Julius Klein. An academically-trained economist and historian, Klein joined the Commerce Department after the war and worked closely with Hoover to solve the distribution problems Hoover believed were at the heart of the postwar economic depression of 1921–22. Historian William Leach has described Klein as very much a man of the postwar consumer economy, "a governmental analogue to the advertising man, the window display manager, the new public relations expert, the securities dealer, and the investment banker, with each of whom he personally identified. He created the connections among the collaborating groups." In his role as director of the BFDC, Klein crisscrossed the nation to address trade associations, promoted American business and advertising in his weekly radio addresses, and supplied the business and managerial elite with reams of information and research intended to help them improve their connections with consumers.[10]

Hoover, Klein, and the businessmen with whom they worked across the nation understood that American towns and cities were also commodities in need of promotion to attract a range of consumers. One of Klein's weekly reports in the BFDC pamphlet series *Domestic Commerce* advised local chambers of commerce and civic leaders how to advertise and promote their communities. Based on a survey conducted by the Commerce Department at the request of the American Community Advertising Association, the report described and tabulated the results of questionnaires sent out to city and state publicity bureaus and to railroad companies involved in community promotion. The report showed some geographical variation in the objectives of community advertising. In the northeast, for example, the top three objectives of community advertising were "prestige and business promotion," "tourists and conventions," and "tourists and business promotion."[11] In New York, the ultimate location of those overlapping objectives and customers was Midtown.

Organized professional campaigns to advertise and promote American towns and cities underpinned the new boosterism of the 1920s. Businessmen, elected city officials, and "admen" pooled their resources to put their places "on the map," drawing investment, business activity, and tourism to their streets and recreation areas. As one 1924 publication put it, "Advertising a city is just like marketing a product." The process involved identifying and selling a place's assets, correcting its liabilities, and developing its "personality" in order to achieve the aims of prestige and goodwill, increasing tourism, and promoting business. The author of this 1924 study advised his readers how to use a broad range of advertising and marketing techniques and media, such as direct mail, radio, movies, expositions, and outdoor advertising. An adman himself, the author argued that only communities that advertised would make progress: "It has become an accepted fact that everything must be 'sold.' Daily you must 'sell' not only yourself but also your services. . . . You must 'sell' your products and your wares."[12] Cities were no different. The American Travel Development Association lobbied the U.S. government in the 1920s to sell the country to itself under the slogan, "Know America." Cities and other communities were "coming to an understanding . . . that their development and their progress is a matter of selling." Beginning in the 1910s and gaining real momentum in the 1920s, the type of business and political coalition encouraged by Hoover, Klein, and the advertising industry came together in New York City to sell a new, improved version of the city.[13]

In 1911, for example, the Merchants' Association of New York formed several new committees in order to carry out more effectively their official purpose: "To foster the trade and welfare of New York." More specifically, the board of directors had concluded that other American cities, such as Chicago, had managed to form larger and better-funded business organizations. It was time for New York's businessmen to meet that challenge. During 1912, MANY conducted an intensive campaign, which doubled the membership within a few weeks.

Two of the new committees formed during this reorganization period, the Convention Committee and the Publicity Committee, went on to play key roles in the promotion of New York over the next two decades.[14] Due to the location in the city of so many corporate headquarters and national leaders of various industries and professions, during the 1920s these two committees came under the influence of men who did much to shape both the image of New York and American big business in general. For example, in 1922, John J. Raskob, vice president of General Motors, joined the Publicity Committee. Eight years later Raskob would provide much of the investment money for what would become New York's best-known publicity icon and a Midtown image anchor, the Empire State Building. In 1928, leading adman Frank Presbrey joined that same committee. Presbrey ran one of the nation's leading advertising firms and wrote *The History and Development of Advertising*, published in 1929; it is still considered a seminal text on American advertising. In 1927, the ubiquitous Grover Whalen became chairman of MANY's Convention Committee, having recently left the Mayor's Office to return fulltime to Wanamaker's as general manager.[15]

In 1914, in his first report to the members of MANY, the

manager of the Publicity Bureau, Robert H. Fuller, stated that the bureau's function was to inform both the general public and the membership about MANY's activities and to "advertise the City and its advantages to the outside world." The Publicity Bureau took over the responsibility of preparing and publishing *Greater New York*, the newspaper-style weekly bulletin issued to the association's members for the past year. The bureau sent the bulletin to other commercial organizations and to libraries. In addition, the bureau arranged to publish articles, photographs, and maps in the daily and Sunday editions of New York City newspapers and in some papers and trade publications outside the city. Every annual report of the Publicity Bureau quantified the fruits of those labors by publishing statistics on the number and length of such stories printed about the work of the Merchants' Association in local and out-of-town newspapers.

That same year, the first report of the Convention Bureau's manager, John R. Young, claimed great success in the bureau's first eight months. He and members of the Convention Committee had managed to book fifty-seven conventions and one trade exposition, all of which were listed in the report. Young estimated that those conventions would bring almost 20,000 delegates to New York City and attract several thousand visitors. He estimated that the delegates alone would spend approximately one million dollars in the city's hotels, restaurants, theaters, stores, and transportation systems. Young also pointed out that those same delegates and convention visitors presented opportunities to MANY members for further business connections, from new sales accounts to real estate deals. Young also made clear his pleasure at the cooperation and assistance of the city administration, which had issued official mayoral invitations to organizations the association was trying to attract to the city and frequently provided official welcomes to conventioneers at the opening of their meetings.[16]

By 1919 MANY's membership numbered almost 6,000, and the mailing list for *Greater New York* had reached 9,000. The Convention Bureau reported that 489 conventions had been held in New York City between April 1918 and April 1919, covering a broad range of organizations large and small: from the American Association of Advertising Agencies to the Women's Benefit Association of the Maccabees. The conventions brought 300,000 delegates who spent over fifteen million dollars in the city—this despite reductions in numbers of attendees and bookings caused by the war. In addition, Convention Bureau Manager John Young reported that the number of other visitors to the city had increased from an average of 200,000 per day to almost half a million. This increase was due, he wrote, both to the increased number of buyers coming to the city in search of scarcer merchandise and to people coming to the city to greet the returning troops entering through the Port of New York.[17] These numbers continued to rise through the 1920s until, by 1929, the city hosted 1,001 conventions, attended by over 800,000 men and women, who spent approximately seventy-five million dollars in the city's hotels, restaurants, and other businesses.[18] During the 1920s, the only area in the city with the capacity to provide facilities for large conventions and other influxes of visitors was Midtown. The area roughly bounded by 34th and 59th Streets to the south and north and Third and Seventh Avenues to the east and west, respectively, was home to the majority of the city's hotels, many of them quite new and thus equipped with facilities such as meeting rooms, telephones, and ballrooms for large gatherings.[19]

Clearly, boosting the city in this manner and attracting visitors of various kinds to New York was of enormous commercial value to the city, specifically to the businessmen of Midtown. The closer relationship between city businessmen and the city government during the 1920s reflected the mutual benefit derived from the promotional work conducted by the trade groups. The mayor and the several thousand businessmen members of the Merchants' Association obviously had interests in common that encouraged cooperation on matters of legislation, municipal policy, and public opinion.[20] These shared interests were best served by the creation of events and occasions that could be used to attract visitors, promote business, and bring good press to the city government. The 1920s saw a number of these civic events and occasions, increasingly handled by the city's trade associations and elected officials—and capably.

"A Remarkable Boosting of New York"

Toward the end of his first term, Mayor John Hylan proposed an exhibit to show the people of New York the achievements of his administration.[21] This initial plan for self-promotion ultimately metamorphosed into an expensive and elaborate Silver Jubilee commemorating the creation of Greater New York in 1898. As historian Brooks McNamara has shown, historical commemoration had often provided opportunities for grand New York occasions. In the 1920s, with both a burgeoning local history movement and a more self-conscious business community eager for the classy "spin" history could provide, historical commemoration became an especially popular basis (or excuse) for municipal and business events.[22] Rather than the New York of poverty-stricken "Bolsheviks" and other foreigners, the Silver Jubilee offered a view of New York as an accomplished, modern, progressive, and harmonious American metropolis.

It seems likely that the idea for the Greater New York Silver Jubilee came after Whalen and Hylan, and perhaps other business associates of theirs, saw the very successful Silver Jubilee celebration staged by the Merchants' Association of New York in November 1922. That event, held in Madison Square Garden, with an attendance of 13,000, was broadcast live over the new medium of commercial radio to about one million potential listeners. Such a skillfully produced and promoted celebration must surely have caught the eye of that consummate stager of events, Grover Whalen.[23] Minutely planned and indicative of Whalen's power both in City Hall and the business community, the city's jubilee the next year was one of the most impressive promotional events ever mounted in New York City.

From its inception, the planned city jubilee met with controversy. Newspapers derided it as a waste of money and, unsurprisingly, as merely a promotion of Hylan and his favorites. City Comptroller Charles Craig, an opponent of Hylan, jeopardized the jubilee by refusing to release city funds to pay for the celebration. However, Mayor Hylan's strong connections to the city's businessmen saved the event. Under the guidance of Grover Whalen and Rodman Wanamaker, already experienced in the mounting of large city events through their joint organizing of welcome ceremonies for the returning U.S. troops after the war, Mayor Hylan got his Silver Jubilee, and the businessmen of New York gained opportunities to promote themselves, their businesses, and their interests in the city.

At an April 6, 1923, meeting of the Advisory Committee to the Mayor's Committee on the 25th Anniversary of Greater New York, there assembled a group of city businessmen representing different trade "teams" assembled by Wanamaker and Whalen to raise money and support for the jubilee following Comptroller Craig's stonewalling. A number of those on the committee were powerful figures in their own fields, experienced in committee work through their roles in the Merchants' Association and other leading trade associations. Included in the roster were Barron Collier, president of the Broadway Subway Advertising Company; William Woodin of American Car and Foundry; Elbert Gary of U.S. Steel; and real estate executive Joseph P. Day.

Mayor Hylan opened the meeting in typically belligerent style by criticizing the newspaper "interests" opposed to the celebration. Arguing that the city government had in the past been a "newspaper government" overly beholden to the city papers, he described his administration as "of, for and by the people," yet also supportive of the business community. Many of the assembled businessmen must have suppressed a smile at the mayor's derisive statements about the newspaper interests. Starting with his election campaign in 1917 and continuing throughout his administration, Hylan's political opponents accurately lambasted him as the puppet of newspaper magnate William Randolph Hearst. Indeed, as the jubilee approached, Hylan relied heavily on the Hearst papers, the *American* and the *Journal,* for positive publicity. Closing his opening statement to the committee, Hylan reported that he had just received a telephone call from Mr. Hearst himself, who had vowed to "go . . . further than probably he would be expected to go, both financially and otherwise, to back up this great celebration." Hylan then left the room, turning the meeting—and with it the planning of the jubilee—over to his two most reliable lieutenants, Rodman Wanamaker and Grover Whalen.[24]

Wanamaker and Whalen were similarly determined that the jubilee would be a success. "Nothing is going to stop this jubilee," Chairman Wanamaker said in his opening remarks. "We are going to have a remarkable boosting of New York City." Whalen, presiding over the majority of the meeting, displayed the organizational and managerial skills that had brought him such success in the Wanamaker store and in political administration. He requested reports from the various trade representatives seated around the table on the pledges of support or funds obtained from their members. Whalen himself read a telegram from Broadway producer Lee Shubert pledging the support of the Producing Managers' Association. Representatives of the waist trade, the Out-of-Town Buyers' Association, the cloak industry, the milliners, the brokers and commission merchants, the Franklin Simon department store, the builders and contractors, Mr. Albert Goldmann of the Bronx Board of Trade, Mr. Ryan of the Queens Board of Trade—all dutifully reported their progress in person. Other trades represented included wholesale notions, wholesale and retail booksellers, the printing industry, musical instruments, and wholesale grocers, in essence the gamut of New York's trade and industry. Larger trade groups such as the Hotel Association of New York City, the New York State Hotel Association, the Society of Restauranteurs and one of the major businessmen's organizations, the Broadway Association, also pledged their members' financial and practical support at the meeting.[25]

At this April meeting, Whalen described in detail the schedule and itinerary of the planned jubilee parade and the exposition at the Grand Central Palace in Midtown. All the city employees, whose numbers Whalen estimated at around 70,000, would participate in the parade, organized into separate departments. The annual Police Parade, which normally took place in early May, was held over so that it could be folded into the jubilee parade, adding to both the pageantry and the vast numbers of city employees represented. Mayors from other cities and governors from other states had been invited, as had President Harding, in whose honor Whalen had planned a presidential banquet. Plans for the content and design of the exposition, also encompassing every department of the city government, were well underway. Whalen also reported to the meeting that "95 to 100%" of the city employees had "volunteered" to work overtime in order to ensure completion of the tasks necessary to the mounting of the jubilee celebration.[26]

Negative publicity about the proposed jubilee put the administration on the defensive. A petulant April 2, 1923, statement from the Mayor's Office responded to criticisms that the event amounted to no more than abject political promotion and was a waste of money. The statement emphasized the civic and educational purposes of the celebration: "All New Yorkers, with the possible exception of self-appointed critics, are very proud of their city. . . . All such New Yorkers are entitled to first-hand information about their city." The statement went on to attack the "harping critics" who had "wilfully misrepresented the present day administration," driven by "their own narrow, selfish ambitions and petty jealousies."[27] Clearly, the upcoming celebration would affect spin control over not only the image of the city but also of the Hylan administration. The Mayor's Office knew that a negative public image of New York City meant a negative image for the administration. After all, someone had to be held responsible for the city's real and supposed shortcomings. The Mayor's Office planned to turn that equation around: someone might as well take credit for twenty-five years of New York City achievements.

On April 27, the Mayor's Office made its first official announcement of the Silver Jubilee and its aims. The statement was broadcast over radio station WJZ by Grover Whalen. He described some of the exhibits visitors could see at the Jubilee Exposition and referred to the official list of the exposition's fifteen purposes: "To boost New York" came first, followed by "To portray New York City in a truthful and accurate manner," "To bring visitors to our city," and "To stimulate business activity." Whalen offered two free exposition tickets to the first five hundred listeners who wrote in. According to the published copy of Whalen's address, he received over 3,000 replies within a few days, from as far afield as Canada, the Midwest, and the Carolinas.[28]

Newspaper comment on the planned jubilee was mixed depending, it would seem from the tone of the comments, largely on the political affiliations of the editor or owner. Opinion varied as to whether or not New York City needed promoting and, if so, which version of the city should be emphasized and which misrepresentations most needed correcting. A collection of press clippings on the jubilee kept by the Mayor's Office recorded the range of press responses but, oddly, not their sources or dates. "It is a detail that the greater city was launched upon its course twenty-five years ago. Let those dance and sing about it who want to," remarked one paper. As 1923 marked Hylan's fifty-ninth and Hylan-supporter and newspaper magnate William Randolph Hearst's sixtieth birthdays, the paper noted, "Why not a huge municipal birthday party— at the city's expense, naturally—to express the upwelling gratitude of the people of New York to those their great benefactors?" Under the heading "No public demand for it," another paper dismissed the planned jubilee as a waste of money that the city did not possess. The idea that the jubilee would help promote New York seemed tenuous to this paper: "In the long run the best advertisement for the city—if the City of New York ever could need an advertisement—is the wise expenditure of the taxpayers' money for the good of the people."

A more sympathetic newspaper heartily endorsed the jubilee, arguing that the celebration would bring thousands of visitors, and thus income, to the city, quoting statistics (sounding very much like those provided annually by the Merchants' Association) about how much the average visitor spent in the city. The jubilee would provide "the opportunity to show them what New York really is. Half the country thinks it knows us as a stamping ground for thugs and demi-mondaines, and a den of 'Wall Street' sharks. They will learn to know us as . . . 'just folks.' They will have a glimpse of the real New York."[29] This "real New York," like that suggested earlier by critic James L. Ford, was imagined as a mainstream, modern city, safe for business and tourism, a New York removed from downtown's shadowy characters still dogging the city's reputation.

The various events comprising the jubilee lasted almost a full month, from late May to late June 1923. Throughout this time, the organizers had set aside particular days to celebrate the various boroughs, the work of specific city departments, as well as the businesses and industries of the city. The celebrations opened on a broiling May 26 with a parade of city employees down Fifth Avenue led by Mayor Hylan, Governor Al Smith, Rodman Wanamaker, Grover Whalen, and other members of the organizing committee, all dressed in top hats and black frock coats. According to press reports, the marchers were greeted enthusiastically by the spectators, with special applause for Grover Whalen, known to all as the main organizer of the event. One paper, *The World,* took great delight in reporting how Governor Smith's popularity overshadowed that of the mayor. The paper related the impromptu serenading of the governor by one of the departmental bands, which halted in front of him at the reviewing stand and broke into "The Star Spangled Banner," followed by "How Dry I Am," the latter a reference to Smith's opposition to prohibition.[30]

Three weeks later, the city's businessmen, who had made the celebration possible with their massive financial and organizational support, had their day with an Industrial Parade on Fifth Avenue, reviewed by Mayor Hylan and a group of visiting mayors. The parade consisted of bands and floats from numerous local businesses. Not surprisingly, the John Wanamaker store fielded a particularly large parade section, led by the men of the John Wanamaker Board of Trade smartly dressed in blazers, bow ties, and straw boaters. They were followed by many other sections, such as the Wanamaker Commercial Institute for Girls and various other boys and girls clubs sponsored by the store.

The major feature of the overall event was the Jubilee Exposition, held in Grand Central Palace, located in Midtown at Park Avenue. The exhibits covered four floors. On each floor elaborate displays demonstrated the work of the city departments. At the Lexington Avenue entrance to the Palace, visitors climbed to the first floor by the building's twenty-five stone steps, which had been covered with silver for the occasion, each step lettered in ascending order with the twenty-five years of Greater New York's existence. At the top of the steps, a large statue of the city's mythical *paterfamilias,* Father Knickerbocker, greeted the visitors. Walking past more statues, potted palms, banks of flowers, and large booths displaying the work of the Mayor's Office and the Board of Estimate, visitors heard the sound of running water as they approached the Electric Jewel Fountain, a centerpiece of the exposition. The official souvenir book of the Silver Jubilee described the fountain as "the most magnificent, artistic and beautiful silvered jewel fountain ever shown" in the United States or abroad. Containing 30,000 cut jewels arranged in a forty-foot-high canopy, the continuously playing fountain was illuminated by a hundred searchlights, eliciting "oh's and cries of delight from every visitor."[31]

The exhibition included all the latest display techniques familiar from other exhibitions, museum galleries, and, of course, department stores. Visual novelties abounded. The Tenement House Department showed large models of tenement houses old and new; the Borough of Manhattan's Bureau of Buildings displayed models of Manhattan's latest skyscrapers and hotels; the Borough of Brooklyn's display featured a scale model of the new boardwalk at Coney Island, complete with miniature amusement park rides, a beach, and ships; life-sized mannequins arranged in elaborate tableaux showed the progress made over the previous twenty-five years by the Department of Correction; various wall- and table-mounted maps of the city used tiny colored electric lights to show city-owned buildings and transportation lines. The Nickel Saving Globe, an eight-foot revolving world globe encircled by a three-coin-wide band of nickels, was meant to show the number of nickels Mayor Hylan had saved the people of New York by preserving the five-cent fare; a twelve-foot-wide Budget Book of 1923, known as the "Giant Open Book" and forming the background shell of the first-floor bandstand, showed the receipts and expenditures of the city's 1923 budget; a large model snowman represented the amount of snow removed from the city's streets by the Department of Street Cleaning the previous winter, during which a record fifty-five inches fell.

All these displays, utilizing color, electric lighting, and craftsmanship of various kinds, showed how much exhibition planners had learned from commercial merchandisers in the previous twenty or so years. Historian William Leach has documented the growth of mutual influence among museum curators, department store managers, and designers. Such crosscurrents resonated beyond these interior spaces to the streets themselves. Businessmen in Midtown's high-class retail areas learned that by redesigning and controlling the appearance and street ambience of their neighborhoods, they could assure their customers that, as museum director, city planner, and former tenement house reformer Robert W. DeForest put it, "to walk with beauty we need not necessarily limit ourselves to trooping through the galleries of our formal collections of art." The heavily trafficked retail and business spaces of the city, increasingly centered in Midtown, were valuable commodities and strategic territories in the efforts to improve and sell New York's public image in the 1920s.[32]

Midtown, Business, and a Usable Past

Just as representations of the Lower East Side had dominated the public image of New York in the 1890s, so representations of Midtown Manhattan came to dominate the public image of the city in the 1920s. However, although Midtown formed much of the public image of the city, and business organizations promoted the area as very much a public space, in fact the relationship between the public and the private in Midtown, and in the area's promotion, was complex. The development of the Midtown area as the city's center of culture and commerce had been underway since the turn of the century. By the early 1920s, the district was firmly established in the national and local mind as the center of the city, the heart of New York for both local residents and visitors.[33]

A number of business organizations, organized in relation to street locations, represented Midtown, each addressing the distinct interests of the businesses in that area. Some examples included the

Broadway Association, the Fifth Avenue Association, the Thirty-Fourth Street-Midtown Association, the Eighth Avenue Association, and the Sixth Avenue Association. While the separate associations occasionally battled each other during this period over issues such as street advertising, ultimately they cooperated with each other and with local politicians to commodify Midtown as the location of the "real New York." This cooperation reflected how Midtown, especially around Times Square, maximized its profitability by erasing boundaries between what in the nineteenth century had been distinct interests and groups. Thus Midtown in the 1920s blurred the boundaries between public and private, business and pleasure, high culture and low culture, the "classes" and the "masses."[34]

To mask some of the tensions inherent in the domination of a supposedly "public" area by private capital, Midtown business organizations touted their "civic" contributions and concerns. Active membership in local trade associations campaigning for street and traffic "improvements" formed part of a business's public relations efforts. By asserting their link to the locality, thereby indicating that they cared about the city and its inhabitants, businesses and corporations legitimized their increasing management and privatization of the city's public space.

Civic-historic occasions like the city's Silver Jubilee provided excellent opportunities for private business to play a very public role, at once promoting the city as a whole and their own spatially specific private interests. As historian Michael Kammen shows, historical pageantry won growing popularity in early twentieth-century America. The concurrent development of local history groups in the United States increased the importance of producing a place-specific pageant rather than a celebration tied to a more abstract or even national historical occasion. Unlike its counterpart in Britain, which tended toward nostalgic recreations of medieval society, "Civic pageantry in American culture," Kammen notes, "came a little closer to fulfilling the quest for a usable past" first called for by critic Van Wyck Brooks in 1918.[35]

However, these civic-historic occasions also functioned as a way of boosting the city—and its current leaders—to the local populace. This might be in an effort to garner votes, or it might serve the less specific but nonetheless crucial purpose of generating a feeling of goodwill and commonality among the citizenry. In a city as diverse and as large as New York in the 1920s, building a common identity among the people of the five boroughs helped mollify factionalism among local politicians and local people with quite different interests and needs. The city's civic and business leaders also realized that any civic pageant apparently boosting New York to New Yorkers would also have a far larger audience, regional and national, eager for news about the metropolis. Events such as the Silver Jubilee, and those discussed below, served both to build community at the local level and to promote the city to outsiders of all sorts. As promotional events they also worked hard to mask local tensions, both historic and contemporary, in an effort to produce an image of the harmonious "real New York" desired by its boosters.

In 1924, on the occasion of its location's hundredth birthday, the Fifth Avenue Association, the most conservative of the Midtown business organizations, staged a series of citywide celebrations. As a souvenir of the centenary (and as a promotional publication), the association published a large-format, colorful, illustrated book, its main text written for them by well-known New York antiquarian and director of the recently founded Museum of the City of New York, Henry Collins Brown. The centennial book was illustrated with old lithographs, maps, photographs, illustrations from nineteenth-century magazines, and several specially drawn, though crude, colored images of Fifth Avenue locations. Brown structured the text as a walk up the avenue, reporting local histories and anecdotes along the way. This section of the publication reiterated the image of Fifth Avenue familiar from guidebooks as the location of wealth and class and as a thoroughfare intimately connected with the history of the city as a whole. Celebrating Fifth Avenue's history, the association urged, was a way of celebrating New York's history.[36]

However, the association was by no means a historical preservation group. Its interests were located firmly in the present. This preference was suggested not only by the opinions presented in the text but also by the contrast between the low-quality images and reproductions provided in the book's historic section and the high-quality images accompanying the sections dealing with the present-day work of the association. The Fifth Avenue Association, like other similar groups and like the City Beautiful clubs and campaigners earlier in the century, aimed to enforce a particular version of civic orderliness on the city's business streets, removing sights, sounds, and persons in conflict with the desired ambience. However, unlike the City Beautiful campaigners or those involved in the founding of Central Park, the aim was not for moral order but rather for the type of order necessary to produce a profitable space of commerce and consumption. The Fifth Avenue Association limited advertising signage, widened sections of the street, prevented the casual commerce of pushcart peddling, encouraged "architectural harmony" along the avenue, and campaigned for the removal of the factories related to the garment industry, also known as the "needle trades," from the avenue.[37] In short, the association acted as a regulator of the avenue's public space in order to protect the business interests of its members. In keeping with this role, in December 1922 the association presented to the City of New York six large bronze traffic control towers located at intersections like Washington Square and 57th Street; they quickly became tourist curiosities. As the association's president and chairman rather chillingly claimed, the organization functioned "in its civic work much like the traffic tower functions in the field of traffic regulation."[38]

The proprietary and regulatory aspects of the association's relation to Fifth Avenue were made explicit in the book's final section, entitled "Fifth Avenue of To-day," by Captain William J. Pedrick, general manager of the Fifth Avenue Association, and Frederick N. Sard, the group's Centennial Director of Research and Publicity. This section opened with an aerial photograph of the portion of Fifth Avenue—from Washington Square to 110th Street—and its neighboring streets "protected through the activities of The Fifth Avenue Association." The aerial photograph suggested both the familiar "bird's eye view" and the perspective obtained by a map. As a bird's eye view, the photograph provided the satisfactions of a grand view, while also endorsing the supposedly benevolent control exerted over the area by the Fifth Avenue Association. As a map-like image, the photograph suggested the association's spatial control while serving to orient and inform a reader less familiar with the size and appearance of the Fifth Avenue area.[39]

In keeping with their proprietary perspective, Pedrick and Sard measured the historical changes along the avenue during the previous century not with reference to social, cultural, or even architectural progress but by the single—and singular—yardstick of real estate. Despite Fifth Avenue's status as an important public space, to the association the area primarily functioned as wealth, as a commodity. The authors claimed that real estate statistics gave an ideal representation of their territory, providing a "bird's eye view which only figures can give, aided by the vivid aerial photograph."[40] Pedrick and Sard offered a view of Fifth Avenue more closely resembling one of the lush brochures issued by property companies selling space in a new office building rather than a commemorative book accompanying a citywide civic-historic occasion.

The avenue's value as real estate had been maintained, the association argued, due to the "civic pride" of its members: "as efficient a check on the wrong kind of commercialism as is historic sentiment." What the authors referred to as "civic pride" might also accurately be described as the political access and financial power of the association's members. Checks on the "wrong kind of commercialism" had indeed resulted from such "civic pride," with just the effect touted by the authors. Examples of such undesirable types of commerce included manufacturing, various forms of which had existed on Fifth Avenue throughout the century celebrated by the association. The garment industry, which maintained numerous sweatshops on Fifth Avenue above 14th Street, became a particular focus of association members' "civic pride." For years, these businesses had spilled out large numbers of garment workers (most of them first- or second-generation Italian or Jewish immigrants) onto the avenue during the noon lunch hour, filling the streets and sidewalks, detracting from the ambience desired by the owners of Fifth Avenue's smarter shops and restaurants. By lobbying the city government for building restrictions and new zoning, the needle trades were eventually banished to the city's West Side, housed in new buildings developed by the Lefcourt Company, one of the city's wealthiest development corporations. The "happy exodus of the garment industries away from Fifth Avenue" allowed more suitable commercial enterprises, from insurance companies to interior decorators, to move into Fifth Avenue, representing commerce "more in harmony with the requirements and prestige of the Fifth Avenue section."[41]

Such control over the ambience of the avenue could only be maintained by constant surveillance and management of the space, something the association's members expected of their organization, according to the authors: "Men to-day believe, as a matter of business logic, that organized vigilance plays a large part in increasing business and realty values."[42] Crucial to the association's power to maintain such extensive private control over public space was its close working relationship with the city government. As the association saw it, the relationship went both ways. The reshaping of Fifth Avenue during the last ten or fifteen years proved, according to the association, that "every community is the builder of its own character and the creator of its own values." Such "character building" could only ensue, the authors argued, echoing the policies of Herbert Hoover and Julius Klein, from alliances between business and government. Without "the organized consensus of its mercantile and industrial interests coupled with the cooperation and support of city authorities," local administrations could do very little to improve public space.[43]

As if to demonstrate the association's power to instigate, maintain, and dominate that kind of cooperation, the association made sure that the avenue's centennial was celebrated both nationally and locally. President Coolidge accepted the Honorary Chairmanship of the Advisory Board; Governor Al Smith and Mayor Hylan sent official messages extolling the virtues of the avenue in their acceptances of honorary chairmanships of the Centennial Committee. The city staged a Centennial Week, November 15 through 22, 1924. Seven committees organized different aspects of the week's celebrations, from merchandise exhibits to street decorations, to essay and poetry contests for the city's schoolchildren, on the theme "Fifth Avenue: Old and New—1824–1924."[44]

Two years later, to celebrate New York's tercentenary, the Broadway Association, demonstrating great contemporary communications acumen, broadcast over the radio station WMCA lengthy booster statements by their leading members, which the association subsequently published in book form.[45] With the title *Broadway, Grand Canyon of American Business,* the publication reiterated the by then familiar assertion of New York's bedrock American identity. Such an assertion was especially important for a New York street associated at the time not so much with business, American or otherwise, but with types of entertainment and behavior still deemed by some middle-class Americans unpalatable and possibly un-American.[46]

Some of the most powerful businessmen in New York and in the nation gave the radio addresses. Among those represented were Adolph Zukor, president of Famous Players-Lasky Corporation, a leader in theater and movie production; A. E. Lefcourt of the Lefcourt Realty company; William L. Colt of the Colt-Stewart automobile company; and S. C. Hemstreet, executive secretary of American Surety. In his introduction to the published volume, Managing Director of the Broadway Association John E. Gratke described the purpose of the enclosed essays in a manner echoing the title's reference to America's sublime landscapes, as providing "a word picture that you too may visualize the vastness and splendor of this titan community." Speaking directly to the public, these commercial leaders appealed to the growing number of Americans with both the money and the time for tourism; at the same time, they promoted the ways in which their own fields of endeavor (automobiles, insurance, finance, electricity, and so on) and big business in general had improved the organization, the look, and the economy of the city.[47]

Unlike the Fifth Avenue Association's centenary book, the

Broadway Association's series of addresses and subsequent publication celebrated a citywide anniversary. As such, the speakers addressed New York as a whole in their broadcasts, though from the perspective of Broadway business. The Broadway Association thus firmly linked their business location, its history, and its development with the city's history. Like the Fifth Avenue centenary, the Broadway Association's involvement with the city's tercentenary blurred the lines between public and private space, between the interests of Broadway businesses and the interests of the city and its citizens.

Radio broadcasting provided the ideal medium through which to construct such a rhetorical space in the 1920s. Advertising quickly colonized the new medium of radio. The first radio advertisement, for a real estate company, was broadcast in 1922 over station WEAF in New York. Soon after, companies began to sponsor whole shows, with the product's name linked to the program's title and advertised throughout the broadcast. In the 1920s, there were no aural boundaries in radio programs between the advertisements and the shows they supported. Ads for a program sponsor's products were usually read over the air by the host or the star of the show, adding celebrity appeal to the product.[48]

Given its large population, New York City and the surrounding area comprised a valuable radio market, as evidenced by the rapid proliferation of powerful and well-financed stations in the area starting in the early 1920s. WEAF began broadcasting in 1922, located atop the eleven-floor Western Electric Building at 463 West Street. In early April 1923, Western Electric's parent company American Telephone and Telegraph took over the station. By 1924 the station has adopted its call slogan "The Voice of Millions." WMCA, the station over which the members of the Broadway Association broadcast their tercentenary messages, used the call slogan "Where The White Way Begins," based on its location at the Hotel McAlpin on Broadway at 34th Street. Station WJZ, owned by Westinghouse and located in Newark, New Jersey, which carried Grover Whalen's message about the Silver Jubilee celebration, began broadcasting in October 1921. Like other New York–area stations, WJZ sought to broadcast music and spoken-word shows likely to appeal to the station's large and diverse audience. WJZ, WHN, and WEAF quickly picked up on the popularity of African-American musicians, bandleaders, and entertainers, bringing 1920s stars such as songwriters Eubie Blake and Noble Sissle, whose "Shuffle Along" was one of Broadway's biggest hits in 1923, to their listeners. Radio historian William Barlow also notes that WJZ aired a weekly African-American drama series, "The Negro Hour," in the late 1920s. By the end of the decade, the nation's first independent African-American broadcasting company, the Harlem Broadcasting Corporation, came on the air from its studios in the heart of the black community at Lenox Avenue and 125th Street.[49]

In their broadcasts, the Broadway Association's members promoted New York City to a wide range of listeners and thus seemed engaged in a civic act. But they also promoted themselves, their businesses, and their shared business location. For members of the Broadway Association, this process must have seemed familiar. Broadway itself, certainly in the Midtown section known as the "Great White Way," perhaps best epitomized the blurring of public and private space in New York at the time. This area of New York's famous thoroughfare drew tourists from all over the United States and the rest of the world to view the unmatched domination of the street by electronic commercial advertising signs.

Reiterating earlier booster and guidebook descriptions of New York's various street and neighborhood cultures, both the Broadway and the Fifth Avenue Associations sold their locations to shoppers, tourists, and fellow investors as spaces resembling expositions in both form and function.[50] More than one speaker in the Broadway Association's broadcasts described New York as a "perpetual exposition," offering something for everyone. Traversing the length of Manhattan Island and beyond, Broadway operated as the central corridor through that exposition. From the vantage point of Broadway, these businessmen suggested, the tourist, the native, or the prospective investor could sample many of the city's entertainments and opportunities. Fifth Avenue shops, according to the Fifth Avenue Association, had "given a new impetus to Democracy in Art" by selling products "judged on their merits alone" and made available to a large consumer base, giving the avenue "the aspect of an international exposition." Like the best of such expositions, the association argued, the "exhibits" were displayed in the most appealing manner in the window displays and showrooms lining the avenue.

The city's grid system of streets, which generally worked against creating a multi-block area of consumption, was mitigated in the Midtown area by changes instigated by the trade associations.[51] Throughout the 1920s, a range of street improvements made the major retail and consumer thoroughfares of Midtown more accessible to the strolling consumer, supporting the trade associations' promotion of the area as an exposition-like space. For example, sidewalks on Fifth Avenue and in the Times Square area were widened, vehicular traffic was brought under closer control by traffic lights or by police direction in addition to the already mentioned improvements of the removal of the garment workers and the tighter restrictions on pushcart vendors.[52] Midtown's function as a space of consumption and as a commodified public space was also managed by more subtle visual cues. Different styles of street advertising (or its complete absence) and window display, for example, suggested which type of consumer a particular street, block, or store would welcome, and what type of behavior was acceptable. The popular theaters, movie palaces, restaurants, cafes, and street vendors of Broadway and Times Square welcomed a broader range of consumers than the exquisitely lit plate-glass windows of Fifth Avenue's *haute couture* and jewelry boutiques or the imposing front steps and porticoed entrance to the Metropolitan Museum of Art. These two areas of Midtown formed different zones, akin to the midway and educational zones of world's fairs or other large expositions, thus supporting the trade associations' comparisons of their business district to expositions.

Linking these two Midtown zones was Forty-Second Street, by the early 1920s certainly one of the most famous streets in America, thanks to its association with the city's theatrical scene. The Forty-Second Street Property Owners and Merchants Association provided the organizational link between the two zones and their respective trade associations, drawing members from both areas. Founded in 1919, this association played an important role in the redevelopment of the Times Square area in the late 1920s and early 1930s. Its officers and directors overlapped with those of the Merchants' Association and with the businessmen involved in the 1923 Silver Jubilee. George Sweeney of the Hotel Commodore was president of the association in the late 1920s. Among his directors were subway advertising maven Barron Collier; Frank Hardart, vice president of Horn and Hardart, the automat café chain; hotelier Frederick Muschenheim; Louis Wiley, business manager of the *New York Times;* and bankers H. C. Holt, T. A. Reynolds, and V. A. Lersner. The overlap between the associations signified the growing dominance of the Midtown area as a center of finance, entertainment, and retail as well as the merging commercial and political interests of the area's business organizations.

In the Forty-Second Street association's 1929 promotional publication, Mayor Jimmy Walker referred to Midtown as "the most important segment of New York." The book, entitled *Mid-Manhattan, The Multimillionarea,* though published by the Forty-Second Street association, promoted "mid-Manhattan" rather than 42nd Street alone.[53] The association thus conflated their locational identity with that of Midtown as a whole. Echoing both the business organizations' version of Midtown-as-exposition, and columnist FPA's comment on New York's unknowability, the book represented Midtown–New York as an entity with multiple, overlapping, and concurrent identities. According to the book's chapter titles, "Mid-Manhattan the Complex" exemplified the city, a place that could also be regarded as the "City of Business Inter-Relationship," "City of Finance," "City of Builders," "City of Hotels," "City of Merchants," "City of Distances," and the "City of Advertising." In keeping with this version of the city, Arthur Williams, president of the New York Edison Company, referred to Midtown as "no longer a geographical actuality."[54] Midtown, he seemed to suggest, was New York.

By 1929, the identities and public images of New York City

and Midtown Manhattan had merged. Through the 1930s, Midtown increasingly assumed the role played by Lower Manhattan earlier in the century—the city's public face, its "brand," for better or worse. With the increase in automobile transportation and domestic tourism, Lower Manhattan became less significant as the entry point into the city. Those arriving by boat into Lower Manhattan encompassed the necessarily well-heeled European tourists or their American peers returning from sightseeing overseas, and the dwindling numbers of immigrants. Especially after the building of the Lincoln Tunnel in 1937, Midtown daily welcomed thousands of the metropolitan area's workers and shoppers in addition to a steady stream of business visitors and tourists from all over the United States.

Midtown also replaced Lower Manhattan as the visual center of the city's skyline. In 1929, at 405 Lexington Avenue, the Chrysler Building, elegant symbol of the new automobile age, became the city's tallest building. It thus finally eclipsed the Woolworth building at Manhattan's southern tip, paean not only to F. W. Woolworth's five and dime store fortune but also to his generation of retail entrepreneurs. The Woolworth Building remained an important New York architectural icon through the 1920s, reproduced in numerous postcard images, but the new skyscrapers of Midtown increasingly drew the crowds to their observation decks and top-floor restaurants. In 1931, soon after the Chrysler Building had wrested the mantle of "the city's tallest" from downtown's Woolworth Building, a group of investors and real estate speculators added the Empire State Building at Fifth Avenue and 34th Street to Midtown's growing cluster of tall office buildings. The newcomer, at 1,250 feet, became the city's (and the world's) tallest building and has remained one of New York's most recognizable icons. Between 1937 and 1940 the group of skyscrapers comprising the Rockefeller Center, the massive office and entertainment center covering the blocks bounded by 49th and 52nd Streets and Fifth and Seventh Avenues, joined the area's roster of landmark buildings. All of these Midtown buildings, seen from most approaches to the city and represented in numerous tourist souvenirs, served as the new brand image of New York and, to a large extent, of America. Since the end of World War I, pundits had discussed New York as the new "world metropolis" in the wake of Europe's comparatively weakened economic power. New York, exemplified in Midtown Manhattan at the close of the 1920s, seemed to Arthur Williams as somehow placeless, "no longer a geographical actuality." To Williams, who identified with the generation who had witnessed "the rise and fall of the hansom-cab," mid-Manhattan also seemed timeless, existing in what he described as a perpetual "day of tomorrows."[55] Williams's statement about time and place echoes and updates the one made in 1912 by French visitor Pierre Loti when he characterized New York as the location of the present, identifying his home town, Paris, as the location of the past. By 1929, the significance of New York (or of Midtown-as-New York) rested even more on its relationship to time rather than on its relationship to place or even on its status as a place. That New York, exemplified in Midtown, was the location of all that was new and modern could by 1929 be taken for granted. All that remained to remark on was the rapidity with which New York constantly reinvented that present—creating the impression, as Williams saw it, that the city existed in a perpetual "day of tomorrows," one step ahead of the rest of the nation and the rest of the world.

CONCLUSION

Had New York by 1924 become American according to the notions of Americanness we have just explored? Well, yes and no. Yes, in that more of New York had come to resemble the commercial city seen by Joseph Pulitzer from his office window, the quintessentially modern city admired by Frenchman Pierre Loti, as well as the better-regulated, better-marketed city shaped by the Merchants' Association of New York and their businessman-politician ally Grover Whalen. No, in that some version of Jacob Riis's "other half" still existed and would continue to exist for the foreseeable future, in parts of one borough or another, representing the foreignness embedded in America's gateway city. And no also in that the mass immigration at the heart of the image wars we have explored in this book had forever changed how New York City looked and sounded; it also changed the food eaten, the Broadway shows attended, the slang exchanged, and the working population thronging the subway cars and sidewalks throughout the city.

But if an American tourist could visit New York in 1924 and, guidebook in hand, explore the stores of Jewish "Brasstown" or the restaurants of Little Italy on the Lower East Side not as part of a risky slumming trip but as the latest additions to a mainstream itinerary, then the alarmingly aberrant New York depicted by the Charity Organization Society or even by post–World War I eugenicists whose lobbying had just passed the National Origins Act no longer held as the dominant national image of New York. At the end of that decade, as the stock market crash and subse-

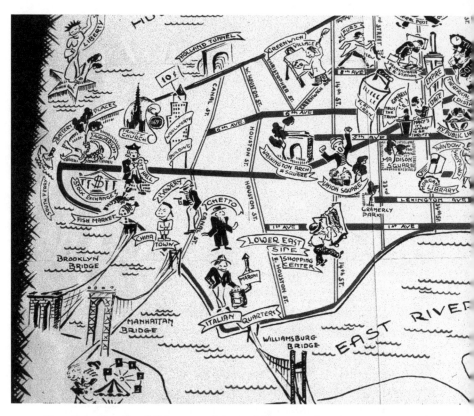

Fig. C.1. Detail of "Cartoon Map of New York City" (New York: H. E. Salloch, 1938). Salloch's tourist map represented the culmination of depictions of New York's neighborhoods as amusing, easily navigable sites where the historic sites and "ethnic types" shown were available for consumption. Reproduced by permission from the collections of the Map Division, The New York Public Library, Astor, Lenox, and Tilden Foundations.

quent Great Depression hit New York and ricocheted throughout America, much that defined modern America found its home in New York: Wall Street, center of the nation's faltering finances and of its economic relations with the rest of the world; Broadway, Times Square, and Radio City, centers of the nation's popular theater; the major commercial radio networks, which entertained and informed Americans coast to coast; and the Empire

State Building, symbol of both New York and America, rising up in the city's center at Fifth Avenue and 34th Street.

New York in the mid-1920s might have become more acceptable to Americans as an American place, but it was not typical of most American cities. In 1924 the city was more populous, had greater physical density, and was home to a larger foreign-born population than any other city in the United States. By 1930 New York had the nation's largest urban Jewish and black populations, evidence of the city's centrality in national and international migration routes. In 1934, when the city elected as mayor of New York City Fiorello LaGuardia, son of Jewish and Italian immigrants, the ascendancy of the Southern and Eastern European immigrant generations of the turn of the century seemed complete.

What helped New York avoid sliding back into its nineteenth-century urban pariah status was that the whole notion of what or who was American had become, from the mid-1920s on, more complicated. Certainly, if one were to measure Americanness by means of the nation's cultural production, the decade or so following the 1924 National Origins Act presented America through works such as Anzia Yezierska's bestselling autobiographical novel *Bread Givers;* the nascent modernism of John Dos Passos's *Manhattan Transfer;* the great range of literary and artistic achievement fostered in Harlem by Alain Locke, Charles S. Johnson, and W E. B. Du Bois; F. Scott Fitzgerald's *Great Gatsby;* Henry Roth's *Call It Sleep;* the architecture of Frank Lloyd Wright; and the music of Billie Holliday, Irving Berlin, George Gershwin, and Louis Armstrong.

In this context of a more complex version of "America," what image defined the brand "New York" by the 1930s? What were the city's "selling points"? Successful alliances between some of the city's businessmen and politicians had commodified New York's diverse population into a version of multiculturalism that allowed them to sell the city as both an American metropolis and as a place like no other in the nation, a delightful diversion. In part, this commodification of diversity represented New York's answer to the post–World War I debates about whether mass immigration should result in assimilation and "100 per cent Americanism" or in the cultural pluralism envisioned by Randolph Bourne, Horace Kallen, and urban sociologist Robert Park. While the ideas of the latter group proved less popular on a national scale, they nonetheless provided a reasonable "spin" for twentieth-century New York.

The tourist maps of New York in the 1930s visually represented the city as the capital of cultural pluralism, emphasizing the sites of both American and "foreign" cultures a tourist might visit during a sojourn in New York. H. E. Salloch's 1938 "Cartoon Map of New York City" provided this impression with a lively, whim-

Fig. C.2. Detail of "Manhattan: First City in America" (New York: S. M. Stanley Co., 1933). Like Salloch's map, this colorful item made history, race, and former social problems (such as the neatly rendered "tenements") accessible and appealing for tourists. Reproduced by permission from the collections of the Map Division, The New York Public Library, Astor, Lenox, and Tilden Foundations.

sical cartography (fig. C.1). Distinctive characters filled his Manhattan, all of them recognizable as the social or racial "types" promised by one's guidebook. For example, the area bounded by First Avenue and the East River and by Houston and 14th Streets he labels the "Lower East Side Shopping Center," signified by a man pushing a rack of clothing through the streets. Below Houston Street, an old man with a long white beard and wearing a full-length black coat and broad-brimmed hat represents "The Ghetto," while the visual referent for the "Italian Quarter" is a man in an ill-fitting jacket and misshapen hat standing next to a street organ. The map also includes a soapbox orator at Union Square and a beret-topped, besmocked painter in Greenwich Village. Similarly, S. M. Stanley Company's pictorial map "Manhattan, First City in America," intended for "the man who learns by looking," situated "The Ghetto" just above Delancey Street on the Lower East Side, signified by a pushcart vendor maneuvering his unwieldy cornucopia of cheap goods (fig. C.2). This map also drew the tourist's attention to the Lower East Side's "Brass Town," by then a popular shopping area for visitors, with an image of a samovar. The map also included historical sites associated with George Washington and Abraham Lincoln, signified with the same visual distinction as the stereotypical images of a chopstick-wielding Chinese fellow near Mott Street and yet another beret-wearing artist in the Village.

The American architectural vision that gave New York its "landscape" of skyscrapers, the engineering technology on which they were based, and their association in the national imagination with New York saw by the end of the 1930s its ultimate showcase: the 1939 New York World's Fair. By the mid-1930s, Grover Whalen and his fellow directors of New York World's Fair, Incorporated, settled on Flushing Meadow in Queens as a suitable site for their planned international exposition "The World of Tomorrow." Locals knew the area as the Corona Dumps, used for twenty years by the Brooklyn Ash Removal Company as a dump for garbage, household ashes, and the dirt and rock dredged up from subway excavations. By 1939, when the New York World's Fair opened, Flushing represented the geographical center of New York City's population, representative of the outer boroughs' share in the identity and image of New York. The siting of the 1939–40 New York World's Fair on the site of the Corona Dumps constituted the biggest makeover project in the city's history, Grover Whalen's finest hour, the culmination of decades of efforts to promote New York City—and also the beginning of the end of the city as embodied solely in Manhattan. But that's another story.

The debate over New York's national significance and its perceived role in the formation and maintenance of a national identity still exhibits a tension based on the marker by which one measures the city's Americanness: its built environment or its population? Throughout the twentieth century and into the twenty-first, the skyscraper architecture of Manhattan has continued to suggest a specifically American identity, despite the proliferation of such buildings across the country and around the globe. As the destruction of the World Trade Center towers on September 11, 2001, suggested, New York's skyscraper landscape does apparently represent "America," American culture, and American economic power to many people who stand in political opposition to the United States. Yet the people in New York affected by the attack on the Twin Towers comprised the polyglot racial, ethnic, and class mosaic that the city now represents, as it did in the early years of the twentieth century.[1] Rich and poor, citizen and noncitizen, busboy and banker, stockbroker and sales clerk—all died in the same manner on September 11, all searched for family and friends in the attack's aftermath, all stood disbelieving in the streets, all pondered the possible causes and responsibilities for that day's events. The attack on New York and the destruction of a major feature of its famous skyline ushered in a new phase for New York's shifting position in the national psyche. In the immediate wake of the attack, the American public and its media placed New York City—both its built environment *and* its people—at the center of representations of national culture, national pride, and national tragedy. New York's rebuilding and rethinking of its cityscape over the next few years will present further opportunities to consider how, when, and why New York—at times—becomes American.

NOTES

INTRODUCTION

Epigraph. FPA [Franklin P. Adams], "It's a Fine Place to Visit, Yes—But I'd Hate To Live There," *Everybody's Magazine* 3 (December 1916): 189.

1. For critical studies of the evolution of American Studies, see Lucy Maddox, ed., *Locating American Studies: The Evolution of a Discipline* (Baltimore: Johns Hopkins University Press, 1999) and Janice Radway, "What's in a Name?" Presidential Address to the American Studies Association, November 20, 1998, reproduced in *American Quarterly* 51, no. 1 (1999): 1–32.

2. Robert Albion Greenlagh, *The Rise of New York Port* (New York: Scribner, 1970); Elizabeth Blackmar, *Manhattan for Rent, 1785–1850* (Ithaca, NY: Cornell University Press, 1989); Peter G. Buckley, "Culture, Class, and Place in Antebellum New York," in *Power, Culture, and Place: Essays on New York City,* ed. John Hull Mollenkopf (New York: Russell Sage Foundation, 1988), 25–52; Frank Monaghan and Marvin Lowenthal, *This Was New York: The Nation's Capital in 1789* (Garden City, NY: Doubleday, 1943); Eric Monkkonen, *America Becomes Urban: The Development of U.S. Cities and Towns, 1780–1980* (Berkeley: University of California Press, 1988); Lloyd Morris, *Incredible New York: High Life and Low Life of the Last Hundred Years* (New York: Random House, 1951); Allan R. Pred, *Urban Growth and City-Systems in the United States, 1840–1860* (Cambridge, MA: Harvard University Press, 1980); Edward K. Spann, *The New Metropolis: New York City, 1840–1857* (New York: Columbia University Press, 1981); and Bayrd Still, *Mirror for Gotham: New York as Seen by Contemporaries from Dutch Days to the Present* (New York: New York University Press, 1956).

3. For the early nineteenth-century economic history of New York, see Robert Albion Greenlagh, *The Rise of New York Port, 1815–1860* (New York: Charles Scribner's Sons, 1939). See also Myron H. Luke, *The Port of New York, 1800–1810* (New York: New York University Press, 1953). On New York's rise as an information and culture center, see Allan R. Pred, *Urban Growth and the Circulation of Information: The United States System of*

Cities, 1790–1840 (Cambridge, MA: MIT Press, 1973). For New York's mid–nineteenth-century development, see Spann, *The New York Metropolis.* For a grand narrative history of New York, see Michael Wallace and Edwin G. Burrows, *Gotham: A History of New York City to 1898* (New York: Oxford University Press, 1999).

4. William Cronon, *Nature's Metropolis: Chicago and the Great West* (New York: W. W. Norton, 1992). See also Daniel Bluestone, *Constructing Chicago* (New Haven: Yale University Press, 1991) and James Gilbert, *Perfect Cities: Chicago's Utopias of 1893* (Chicago: University of Chicago Press, 1991).

5. See James D. McCabe, *Lights and Shadows of New York Life* (Philadelphia: National Publishing Company, 1872) and *New York by Sunlight and Gaslight* (Philadelphia: Douglass Brothers, 1882) and George Foster, *New York by Gas-Light* (New York: W. F. Burgess, 1850) and *New York in Slices: By an Experienced Carver* (New York: W. F. Burgess, 1849). The genre of the urban sketch can be traced back into eighteenth-century England, but it is likely that George Foster and James McCabe were familiar with nineteenth-century sources from London and Paris. Some of the more important of these works include Pierce Egan, *Life in London* (1821) and Charles Dickens, *Sketches by Boz* (1835). Eugène Sue, *Les Mystères de Paris,* serialized in Paris in 1842 and 1843 in the *Journal des Débats,* was rapidly translated into English and made available in book form in America as early as 1843. Numerous volumes bearing titles similar to Sue's soon appeared on both sides of the Atlantic, purporting to offer readers glimpses of the "mysteries" and "miseries" of various cities. For an excellent brief summary of these early and mid–nineteenth-century examples, see Stuart Blumin's introduction in a reprint of George Foster, *New York by Gas-Light and Other Urban Sketches* (Berkeley: University of California Press, 1990). See also Luc Santé, *Low Life: Lures and Snares of Old New York* (New York: Vintage, 1991).

6. James D. McCabe, *Lights and Shadows of New York Life; or, the Sights and Sensations of the Great City* (Philadelphia: National Publishing Company, 1872). Language from title page.

7. Ibid., preface, 16.

8. Ibid., 15–16.

9. For a deeply researched and well-written history of how railroads, hotels, and touring companies contributed to the development of urban tourism in the United States, see Cathrine Cocks, *Doing the Town: The Rise of Urban Tourism in the United States, 1850–1915* (Berkeley: University of California Press, 2001).

10. John Gold and Stephen Ward, eds., *Place Promotion: The Use of Publicity and Marketing to Sell Towns and Regions* (Chichester, United Kingdom: John Wiley and Sons, 1994), 9. See also Stephen Ward, *Selling Places: The Marketing and Promotion of Towns and Cities, 1850–2000* (London: E. and F. N.

Spon/Routledge, 1998) and Gerry Kearns and Chris Philo, eds., *Selling Places: The City as Cultural Capital, Past and Present* (Oxford: Pergamon Press, 1993). On Celebration, Florida, see Andrew Ross, *The Celebration Chronicles: Life, Liberty, and the Pursuit of Property Values in Disney's New Town* (New York: Ballantine, 1999) and Douglas Frantz and Catherine Collins, *Celebration, U.S.A.: Living in Disney's Brave New Town* (New York: Henry Holt, 1999).

11. Susan Strasser, *Satisfaction Guaranteed: The Making of the American Mass Market* (Washington, DC: Smithsonian Institution Press, 1989). See also Richard S. Tedlow, *Keeping the Corporate Image: Public Relations and Business, 1900–1950* (Greenwich, CT: JAI Press, 1979).

12. The term "probationary whites" is used by Matthew Frye Jacobson in his study of the evolving "racial" identities of late nineteenth- and early twentieth-century European immigrants to the United States, *Whiteness of a Different Color: European Immigrants and the Alchemy of Race* (Cambridge, MA: Harvard University Press, 1998).

1   REFORMING NEW YORK'S IMAGE IN THE 1890s

1. "Attics and House-Tops of New York," *Scribner's Monthly* 21 (April 1881): 882.

2. The interdisciplinary scholarly literature related to the topic of urban legibility is extensive. On the development of American cities in the nineteenth and twentieth centuries and the search for visual and social order through planning, see M. Christine Boyer, *Dreaming the Rational City: The Myth of American City Planning* (Cambridge, MA: MIT Press, 1983), especially parts I and II. Studies of European cities have to date provided a more detailed and theoretically informed discussion of the issue of urban legibility. Some of the more important works include T. J. Clark, *The Painting of Modern Life: Paris in the Art of Manet and his Followers* (Princeton: Princeton University Press, 1984); David Harvey, *Consciousness and the Urban Experience* (Baltimore: Johns Hopkins University Press, 1985) and *The Condition of Postmodernity* (Oxford: Basil Blackwell, 1992); Derek Gregory, *Geographical Imaginations* (London: Hutchinson, 1994); and David Frisby, *Fragments of Modernity: Theories of Modernity in the Work of Simmel, Kracauer, and Benjamin* (Cambridge, MA: MIT Press, 1986). John Kasson's essay "Reading the City: The Semiotics of Everyday Life," in his *Rudeness and Civility: Manners in Nineteenth-Century Urban America* (New York: Hill and Wang, 1990) provides a succinct and elegant introduction to some of these ideas in the American context.

3. Kasson, "Reading the City." See also the discussion of German sociologist Ferdinand Tonnies's *gemeinschaft/gesellschaft* formulation in Andrew Lees, *Cities Perceived: Urban Society in European and American Thought,*

1820–1940 (New York: Columbia University Press, 1985) and Robert Wiebe's now-classic account of the American response to the rapid economic, social, and cultural changes of the turn of the twentieth century, *The Search for Order, 1877–1920* (New York: Hill and Wang, 1967).

4. See Charles Lockwood, *Manhattan Moves Uptown: An Illustrated History* (New York: Barnes and Noble Books, 1976). For a discussion of "everyday geographies," see Allan Pred, *Lost Words and Lost Worlds: Modernity and the Language of Everyday Life in Late Nineteenth-Century Stockholm* (New York: Cambridge University Press, 1990).

5. Recent work on the American Progressive Era includes Robyn Muncy, *Creating a Female Dominion in American Reform, 1890–1935* (New York: Oxford University Press, 1991); Peggy Pascoe, *Relations of Rescue: The Search for Female Moral Authority in the American West, 1874–1939* (New York: Oxford University Press, 1990); and Daniel T. Rodgers, *Atlantic Crossings: Social Politics in a Progressive Age* (Cambridge, MA: Belknap Press, 1998).

6. For urban histories that address the role of businessmen and other civic boosters, see Robin F. Bachin, *Building the South Side: Urban Space and Civic Culture in Chicago, 1890–1919* (Chicago: University of Chicago Press, 2004); Max Page, *The Creative Destruction of Manhattan, 1900–1940* (Chicago: University of Chicago Press, 1999); and Catherine Cocks, *Doing the Town: The Rise of Urban Tourism in the United States, 1850–1915* (Berkeley: University of California Press, 2001).

7. For a discussion of the emergence of consumption as an important element in an economy based on mass production, see T. J. Jackson Lears, *Fables of Abundance: A Cultural History of Advertising in America* (New York: Basic Books, 1994); Roland Marchand, *Creating the Corporate Soul: The Rise of Public Relations and Corporate Imagery in American Big Business* (Berkeley: University of California Press, 1998); and William Leach, *Land of Desire: Merchants, Power, and the Rise of a New American Culture* (New York: Vintage Books, 1994).

8. Steven J. Diner, *Americans of the Progressive Era* (New York: Hill and Wang, 1998); Lynn McCree Bryan and Allen F. Davis, eds., *100 Years at Hull House* (Bloomington: Indiana University Press, 1990); Richard Plunz, *A History of Housing in New York City* (New York: Columbia University Press, 1990); Michael B. Katz, *In The Shadow of the Poorhouse: A Social History of Welfare in America* (New York: Basic Books, 1986); Lees, *Cities Perceived;* Paul S. Boyer, *Urban Masses and Moral Order in America, 1820–1920* (Cambridge, MA: Harvard University Press, 1978); David Rothman, *The Discovery of the Asylum: Social Order and Disorder in the New Republic* (Boston: Little, Brown, 1971); and Roy Lubove, *The Progressives and the Slums* (Westport, CT: Greenwood Press, 1962).

9. William R. Taylor, ed., *Inventing Times Square: Commerce and Cul-*

ture at the Crossroads of the World (New York: Russell Sage Foundation, 1991); Kathy Peiss, *Cheap Amusements: Working Women and Leisure in Turn-of-the-Century New York* (Philadelphia: Temple University Press, 1986); and Lewis A. Erenberg, *Steppin' Out: New York Nightlife and the Transformation of American Culture, 1890–1930* (Westport, CT: Greenwood Press, 1981).

10. Judith Walkowitz, *City of Dreadful Delight: Narratives of Sexual Danger in Late-Victorian London* (Chicago: University of Chicago Press, 1992), 15–39.

11. Two of the most important observers of Britain's urban poor during the mid–nineteenth century were Henry Mayhew and Friedrich Engels. The most important works in this regard are Mayhew, *London Labor and the London Poor* (1862; repr. New York: Penguin Books, 1985) and Engels, *The Condition of the Working Class in England* (1845; repr. New York: Penguin Books, 1987). While Mayhew's work was more reformist and Engels's work more in keeping with a developing European political radicalism, both can be regarded as early urban ethnographies, indicating the importance of the city to the emergence of the late nineteenth-century social sciences. See also Deborah Epstein Nord, "The Social Explorer as Anthropologist: Victorian Travelers among the Urban Poor," in *Visions of the Modern City: Essays in History, Art, and Literature,* ed. William Sharpe and Leonard Wallock (Baltimore: Johns Hopkins University Press, 1987).

12. E. L. Godkin, "A Key to Municipal Reform," *North American Review* 151 (October 1890): 422–431.

13. James M. Hudnut, *New-York Almanac for 1880* (New York: Francis Hart and Company, 1880). *The Daily Graphic,* a nationally circulated newspaper, in 1880 became the first newspaper to reproduce a halftone image; it was of a New York "Shantytown." See Alan Trachtenberg, *The Incorporation of America: Culture and Society in the Gilded Age* (New York: Hill and Wang, 1982, 1987), 126.

14. During the 1880s and 1890s, a more discerning sense of the "truth value" of various types of "pictures" would come into play as photography became the illustrative medium of choice across a range of arenas with widely varying agendas. In particular the ability of photography—as opposed to any other pictorial method—to give the impression of reproducing unmediated reality became the medium's currency—and the grounds on which it was challenged.

15. On the invention of the halftone and its significance in the development of mass culture, see David Clayton Phillips, "Art for Industry's Sake: Halftone Technology, Mass Photography, and the Social Transformation of American Print Culture, 1880–1920," Ph.D. diss., Yale University, 1996. See also Neil Harris's essay, "Iconography and Intellectual History: The Halftone Effect," in his *Cultural Excursions: Marketing Appetites and Cultural Tastes in Modern America* (Chicago: University of Chicago Press, 1990).

16. Writing in *The Idler* in 1893, E. A. Jelf discussed the limitations of photography as evidence. Jelf showed his readers how photographic plates could be used to construct images of events that never took place or to show "impossible" situations such as the same man standing and looking at himself or photographed as both the gunman and the victim in a fatal shooting. Jelf stated that the "evidence of photography must then be very warily received [since] it will be seen that photography can prove almost anything." Photography's use as evidence was most valuable, Jelf suggested, when it was employed to record visual evidence the human eye could not perceive, such as subjects in motion: "the position of the four legs of a racehorse at a given moment in time," a reference perhaps to Eadweard Muybridge's contemporaneous experiments in the photography of human and animal motion. See Jelf, "Photography as Evidence," *Idler* 4 (December 1893): 519–525. On the rise of photojournalism, see Michael L. Carlebach, *The Origins of Photojournalism in America, 1839–1880* (Washington, DC: Smithsonian Institution Press, 1992) and his article "American Photojournalism in the Nineteenth Century," in *History of the Mass Media in the United States: An Encyclopedia,* ed. Margaret Blanchard (Chicago: Fitzroy Dearborn Publishers, 1998).

17. See, for example, Edmund R. Spearman, "French Police Photography," *Nature* 42 (October 30, 1890): 642–644. An article in *Outing* magazine discussed the problem of the distortion or misrepresentation of reality apparently peculiar to photography. See Dr. I. Howe Adams, "Photography; or The Munchausen of the Arts," *Outing* 16 (September 1890): 476–480. For the potential for photography to be regarded as "artistic" and something other than merely a mechanical reproduction of reality, see George Davison, "Impressionism in Photography," *Journal of the Society of the Arts* 39 (December 19, 1890): 65–74. For further discussions along these lines, see also "Is the Camera the Friend or Foe of Art?" *Studio* 1 (April 1893): 96–102; H. Van der Weyde, "The Pictorial Modification of Photographic Perspective," *Journal of the Society of Arts* 41 (April 28, 1893): 591–596; and "Photography in Travel," *Around the World* 1 (December 1893): 7–9. There are also rich secondary sources on the complex relationship among photographic representation, the state, and what Allan Sekula has called "instrumental" image-making. See Allan Sekula, *Photography against the Grain: Essays and Photoworks, 1973–1983* (Halifax, Nova Scotia, Canada: Press of the Nova Scotia College of Art and Design, 1984) and Sandra S. Phillips, *Police Pictures: The Photograph as Evidence* (San Francisco: Chronicle Books, 1997).

18. See Jacob A. Riis, *How the Other Half Lives: Studies among the Tenements of New York* (New York: Charles Scribner's Sons, 1891), 3–5. For a detailed discussion of housing reform during this period, see also Plunz, *History of Housing.*

19. See Maren Stange, *Symbols of Ideal Life: Social Documentary Photog-

raphy in America, 1890–1950 (New York: Cambridge University Press, revised edition, 1992).

20. "New York Tenements and Slums," *London Quarterly Review* 78 (April 1892): 48–50.

21. Some doubt persists about the authorship of certain photographs generally attributed to Jacob Riis. For a discussion of what these doubts imply both about Riis and about representations of the poor at the close of the nineteenth century, see Stange, *Symbols of Ideal Life,* esp. 6–10.

22. For Riis's account of the evolution of his use of photography to acquire the evidence he needed to push for changes in housing conditions in New York, see his autobiography, *The Making of an American* (New York: Grosset and Dunlap, 1901), esp. 267–273.

23. See *Hull-House Maps and Papers* (New York, Boston: T. Y. Crowell and Co., 1895), and Charles Booth, *Life and Labour of the People in London,* 17 vols. (London: Williams and Northgate, 1889–1903).

24. Riis, *How the Other Half Lives,* 25.

25. Ibid.

26. For a discussion of late nineteenth- and early twentieth-century realism, see David Shi, *Facing Facts: Realism in American Thought and Culture, 1850–1920* (New York: Oxford University Press, 1995). See also Miles Orvell, *The Real Thing: Imitation and Authenticity in American Culture, 1880–1940* (Chapel Hill: University of North Carolina Press, 1989).

27. Albion W. Small, "Methods of Studying Society," *Chautauquan* 21 (April–September 1895): 52–56. On the history of American social science, see Dorothy Ross, *The Origins of American Social Science* (New York: Cambridge University Press, 1991).

28. Francis G. Peabody, "The Modern Charity Worker," *Charities Review* 6 (March 1897): 18.

29. See Lubove, *The Progressives and the Slums* and Katz, *In The Shadow of the Poorhouse.*

30. Addams's views and those of her fellow debaters were reported in "For Systematic Charity," *New York Times,* December 10, 1897, 5. Peabody described the Belgian labor colonies where "discrimination prevails" by dividing the convicted poor into different classes: "In one place are congregated the infirm but decent, in another the infirm and semi-criminal, in another the able-bodied vagrants, in another the good conduct men." Peabody, "The Modern Charity Worker," 23–24. See Gioia Diliberto's biography of Addams, *A Useful Woman: The Early Life of Jane Addams* (New York: Simon and Schuster, 1999). For a critique of organized charity, written from the point of view of a fictional disenchanted employee, see Konrad Bercovici, *Crimes of Charity* (New York: Alfred A. Knopf, 1917), which has an introduction by John Reed.

31. Lewis M. Haupt, "On the Graphical Presentation of Statistics," *Jour-*

nal of the Franklin Institute 148 (1899): 384–390. For an earlier discussion of how to use statistics and communicate them effectively to a broad public, see Charles F. Pidgin, "How to Make Statistics Popular," *Publications of the American Statistical Association* 2 (September–December, 1890): 107–115. Haupt was critical of the inaccuracy and poor design of some uses of these new techniques. However, his own description of the problem is itself unclear and would have benefited from some visual examples. See also W. Z. Ripley, "Notes on Map Making and Graphic Representation," *Publications of the American Statistical Association* 6 (September 1899): 313–327. Ripley was also the author of *The Races of Europe: A Sociological Study* (New York: Appleton, 1899), one of the founding texts of racial and ethnic classification based on appearance and physical measurements.

32. E. R. L. Gould, "The Housing Problem," *Municipal Affairs* 3 (March 1899): 108–131, quotation 109.

33. Frederick E. Pierce, "The Tenement House Committee Maps," *Harper's Weekly* 39 (January 19, 1895): 60–62.

34. Figures from Plunz, *History of Housing*, 37.

35. Relevant *Harper's Weekly* articles include: "The Mayor and the Tenements," vol. 25, no. 1295 (October 15, 1881): 699; "The Tenement-House Calamity," vol. 25, no. 1300 (November 19, 1881): 775; "Midsummer Night among City Tenements," vol. 27, no. 1384 (June 30, 1883): 410; "Life among the Tenements," vol. 31, no. 1596 (July 23, 1887): 529; "Model Tenements," vol. 32, no. 1621 (January 14, 1888): 31; "Wash Day in the Tenements," vol. 33, no. 1722 (December 21, 1889): 1014; "An Eviction in the Tenement District of the City of New York," vol. 34, no. 1625 (February 1, 1890): 83; "The Tenement House Problem," vol. 39, no. 1986 (January 12, 1895): 423; and "The Language of the Tenement Folk," vol. 41, no. 2092 (January 23, 1897): 90.

36. Pierce, "Tenement House Committee Maps," 62.

37. Ibid.

38. Ibid.

39. In the last decade of the nineteenth century, the Irish were still frequently seen as racially distinct from (and inferior to) other "white" Europeans. The Swedes were classified at this time as "Nordic," seen by turn of the century racial conservatives and some anthropologists as the most highly evolved of the European racial groups. On the history of Irish "racial" identity, see Noel Ignatiev's somewhat polemical study *How the Irish Became White* (New York: Routledge, 1996). For more on studies of "whiteness" and "white" racial identity, see Matthew Frye Jacobson, *Whiteness of a Different Color: European Immigrants and the Alchemy of Race* (Cambridge, MA: Harvard University Press, 1998) and the work that initiated this field of study, David R. Roediger, *The Wages of Whiteness: Race and the Making of the American Working Class* (New York: Verso, revised edition, 1999).

40. For a discussion of the relative truths of maps, see Denis Wood, *The Power of Maps* (London: Guilford Press, 1992). Mark Monmonier is a better-known critic of maps and their meanings, but his discussions tend toward case studies of the uses of maps rather than addressing the larger epistemological and cultural issues raised by cartography. Geographer John Pickles is perhaps the best current example of a scholar combining a background in the use and design of maps as fundamental to his field of study with a critical perspective based on extensive readings in theories of representation and language. See John Pickles, "Texts, Hermeneutics, and Propaganda Maps," in *Writing Worlds: Discourse, Text, and Metaphor in the Representation of Landscape,* ed. Trevor Barnes and James S. Duncan (New York: Routledge, 1992). See also J. B. Harley, "Deconstructing the Map," ibid., and Mark Monmonier, *How to Lie with Maps* (Chicago: University of Chicago Press, 1991); Geoff King, *Mapping Reality: An Exploration of Cultural Cartographies* (New York: St. Martin's, 1996); and Jeremy Black, *Maps and Politics* (Chicago: University of Chicago Press, 1997).

41. "Tenement House Show," *New York Times,* February 10, 1900, 7.

42. Lawrence Veiller, *Reminiscences,* Columbia Oral History Project, 20. As quoted in Lubove, *The Progressives and the Slums.* Roosevelt subsequently appointed DeForest chair of the 1900 New York State Tenement Housing Commission, which drafted the important and effective 1901 housing law. DeForest later became president of the Russell Sage Foundation, the National Housing Association, and other housing and welfare organizations.

43. Stange, *Symbols of Ideal Life,* 28.

44. Peter Bacon Hales, *Silver Cities: The Photography of American Urbanization, 1839–1915* (Philadelphia: Temple University Press, 1984), 250–252.

45. The archives of the Tenement House Exhibition are contained within the Community Service Society (CSS) Papers, Rare Book and Manuscript Library, Columbia University. Veiller, in his capacity as secretary of the Tenement House Committee of the COS and organizer of the exhibit, sent form letters to charitable organizations and builders of model homes across the United States to request photographs of housing conditions good and bad in their cities and photographs and plans of model homes. See Letters from Lawrence Veiller, October 14 and 25, 1899, in CSS Papers, Box 166, Folder "The Exhibit—1899–1900."

46. *Jewish Messenger* and *Evangelist* reviews can be found in a collection of press clippings regarding the exhibit in the CSS Papers, Box 166, Folder "The Exhibit—1899–1900." Lillian W. Betts, "The Tenement-House Exhibit," *Outlook* 64 (March 1900): 589–592, quotation 589.

47. Margaret Byington, "Fifty Annual Reports," *Survey* 23 (March 26, 1910): 970–977 quoted in Hales, *Silver Cities,* 253–254.

48. This shift in method and medium can also be seen as part of the "mas-

culinizing" of urban social reform work. Women's reform groups or female-dominated organizations were seen by their male peers as employing irrational emotional methods.

49. Betts, "Tenement House Exhibit," 590.

50. For a discussion of miniaturization, see Susan Stewart, *On Longing: Narratives of the Miniature, the Gigantic, the Souvenir, the Collection* (Baltimore: Johns Hopkins University Press, 1984). Dimensions of the models given in Lawrence Veiller, letter to Patrick Geddes, CSS Papers.

51. See the images accompanying the advice and examples in Evart G. Routzahn and Mary Swain Routzahn, *The ABC of Exhibit Planning* (New York: Russell Sage Foundation, 1918). Evart Routzahn was associate director of the Department of Surveys and Exhibits at the Russell Sage Foundation.

52. Betts, "Tenement House Exhibit," 592.

53. Lawrence Veiller, "The Tenement-House Exhibition of 1899," *Charities Review* 10 (March 1900): 19–27.

54. Ibid., 19.

55. Ibid., 21–22.

2   TOURISM AND NEW YORK'S IMAGE IN THE 1890s

1. Neil Harris, "Urban Tourism and the Commercial City," in *Inventing Times Square: Commerce and Culture at the Crossroads of the World,* ed. William R. Taylor (Baltimore: Johns Hopkins University Press, 1996), 75. See also Dean MacCannell, *The Tourist: A New Theory of the Leisure Class.* (New York: Schocken, 1976), and John Sears, *Sacred Places: American Tourist Attractions in the Nineteenth Century* (New York: Oxford University Press, 1989). The scholarship on tourism is sparse, though growing steadily. On nineteenth- and early twentieth-century American tourism, see Marguerite Shaffer, *See America First: Tourism and National Identity, 1905–1930* (Washington, DC: Smithsonian Institution Press, 2001) and Catherine Cocks, *Doing the Town: The Rise of Urban Tourism in the United States, 1850–1915* (Berkeley: University of California Press, 2001). The limited amount of historical scholarship on tourism is largely focused on the American West, though Cocks's multicity project has begun to address that imbalance. For a study of tourism in the West, see Hal Rothman, *Devil's Bargains: Tourism in the Twentieth-Century American West* (Lawrence: University of Kansas Press, 1998). For recent work by social scientists on urban tourism, see Dennis R. Judd and Susan S. Fainstein, eds., *The Tourist City* (New Haven: Yale University Press, 1999).

2. On turn-of-the-century New York and the development of leisure, see Nan Enstad, *Ladies of Labor, Girls of Adventure: Working Women, Popular Culture, and Labor Politics at the Turn of the Twentieth Century* (New York: Columbia University Press, 1999); Kathy Peiss, *Cheap Amusements: Working Women and Leisure in Turn-of-the-Century New York* (Philadelphia: Temple

University Press, 1986); John Kasson, *Amusing the Million: Coney Island at the Turn of the Century* (New York: Hill and Wang, 1978); David Nasaw, *Going Out: The Rise and Fall of Public Amusements* (New York: Basic Books, 1993); and Elizabeth Blackmar and Roy Rosenzweig, *The Park and the People: A History of Central Park* (Ithaca, NY, and London: Cornell University Press, 1992). For comparable work on Chicago, though less focused on working-class women, see Lauren Rabinovitz, *For the Love of Pleasure: Women, Movies and Culture in Turn-of-the-Century Chicago* (New Brunswick, NJ: Rutgers University Press, 1998).

3. Harris, "Urban Tourism." The national organization, the American Hotel Association, was founded in 1910, and became the umbrella organization overseeing the city, state, and regional hotel associations. See David Watkin, *Grand Hotel: The Golden Age of Palace Hotels, An Architectural and Social History* (London: J. M. Dent, 1984).

4. See Merchants' Association of New York, *Annual Report* (New York: MANY, 1906). For more on this topic, see Timothy B. Spears, *100 Years on the Road: The Traveling Salesman in American Culture* (New Haven: Yale University Press, 1995) and Cocks, *Doing the Town.*

5. "The New York 'World,'" *Harper's Weekly* 134 (January 18, 1890): 43–44.

6. On the City Beautiful movement and other aspects of late–nineteenth-century urban planning, see David Schuyler, *The New Urban Landscape: The Redefinition of City Form in Nineteenth-Century America* (Baltimore: Johns Hopkins University Press, 1986); James Gilbert, *Perfect Cities: Chicago's Utopias of 1893* (Chicago: University of Chicago Press, 1991); and M. Christine Boyer, *Dreaming the Rational City: The Myth of American City Planning* (Cambridge, MA: MIT Press, 1983).

7. As Carl W. Condit and Sara Bradford Landau point out, there is some debate about exactly how many stories the Pulitzer Building had: "The story count varies from one report to another; eighteen is a number often cited in contemporary accounts. The *World,* however, stretched the count to twenty-six, which included two below-grade levels, fourteen full stories in the tower, three above-ground mezzanine stories, six stories in the dome, and the lantern observatory level. Whatever the number, the *World* was the tallest building yet constructed in the city and easily overtopped the spire of Trinity." See Landau and Condit, *Rise of the New York Skyscraper, 1865–1913* (New Haven: Yale University Press, 1996), 199.

8. Figures from N. W. Ayer and Son, *Directory, Newspapers and Periodicals* (Philadelphia: IMS Press, 1982).

9. For histories of the New York press, see George Juergens, *Joseph Pulitzer and the New York World* (Princeton: Princeton University Press, 1966) and Frank M. O'Brien, *The Story of the Sun* (New York: D. Appleton

and Company, 1928). For arguments by historians about how the mass press contributes to the construction of a version of the city and to a mass audience for current events, see Peter Fritzsche, *Reading Berlin 1900* (Cambridge, MA: Harvard University Press, 1996); Vanessa Schwartz, *Spectacular Realities: Early Mass Culture in Fin-de-Siècle Paris* (Berkeley: University of California Press, 1998); and David Henkin, *City Reading: Written Words and Public Spaces in Antebellum New York* (New York: Columbia University Press, 1998). Pulitzer's great rival, William Randolph Hearst, did not arrive in the city until 1895, when he moved from San Francisco to New York and bought the *New York Journal.* The competition between the *Journal* and the *World* came to define a new type of sensationalistic journalism, dubbed "yellow journalism" at the time—a label based on one of the first sources of the two papers' rivalry—the popular comic strip character known as the "Yellow Kid."

10. For example, the Equitable Life Assurance Company building of 1870 had five stories, reaching a height of 142 feet from the curb to the roof at its highest point. Equitable added another two stories to the building in the 1880s. Equitable's great rivals, the Mutual Life Insurance Company and the New York Life Insurance Company, competed fiercely to have the grandest and tallest company building in the city. The competition began in the 1870s and continued on into the twentieth century. Through the 1890s, developments in building technologies as well as increasing corporate wealth continued the race on and on, with insurance companies and newspapers in the lead into the next century. Three of the tallest and most discussed buildings in Manhattan at the close of the century were the Home Life Insurance Company building of 1894, which reached a height of 256 feet in a massive (for the time) sixteen stories; the record-setting Manhattan Life Insurance Building of 1895, which reached a height of 348 feet; and the American Surety Company Building of 1896, which stood at approximately 312 feet. For details of these and other late nineteenth-century skyscrapers, see Landau and Condit, *Rise of the New York Skyscraper.*

11. *Information for Visitors* (New York: New York *World,* c. 1899). From National Museum of American History (NMAH) Archives Center's Warshaw Collection of Business Americana, New York City Boxes, Box 23.

12. On the development of urban commercial amusements, see Peiss, *Cheap Amusements;* Nasaw, *Going Out;* Kasson, *Amusing the Million;* and Rabinovitz, *For the Love of Pleasure.*

13. For an excellent example of the selling of a particular building and its location over time, see the series of advertisements for the Fifth Avenue Building produced by the N. W. Ayer advertising agency. These can be found in the NMAH Archives Center's N. W. Ayer Collection.

14. Juergens, *Joseph Pulitzer,* 245. For a discussion of Pulitzer's views on immigrants and the poor during the early years of his editorship of the paper, see esp. chs. 8 and 9.

15. See Juergens's discussion of Pulitzer's politics in the chapters cited in the previous note. Also, see Pulitzer's published statement in the first issue of the paper following his purchase of the *World*, May 11, 1883, 4.

16. Other examples are *New-York Compliments of Joseph Biechele Soap Company, Canton, Ohio* (c. 1884); *The Gate to the Sea* (Brooklyn, NY: Eagle Press, c. 1897). The *Eagle*, the daily newspaper of Brooklyn, also ranked among the important and widely read papers of the New York area. The title page of this guide is stamped "Compliments of the Third Universalist Church, North Henry Street and Nassau Avenue. Look for the Pink Sheets." The pink sheets in question were stapled in the center of the guide and contained information about the church and its services as well as advertisements for Brooklyn businesses and manufacturers.

17. The transition from the "sunlight and shadows" image of New York to the booster's more positive image of the 1890s did not happen overnight. Earlier guidebooks from the 1840s and 1850s had provided basic factual information about the city, such as transportation to and within New York. In the 1870s, particularly around the national centennial celebration in 1876, visitors could buy guides to New York that offered a mixture of the familiar practical information combined with a more detailed narrative about New York's history and guidance about the various parts of the city recommended as tourist sights. See, for example, *Great Metropolis, 1846* (no publisher); *Nelsons' Guide to the City of New York and Its Neighbourhood* (London: T. Nelson and Sons, 1858); *New York Illustrated* (New York: D. Appleton and Co., 1869); Robert Macoy, *History of and How to See New York and Its Environs* (New York: Robert Macoy, 1876); *The Guest's Handy Book and Guide to Points of Interest in New York City* (New York: Hotel Publishing and Advertising Company, 1886).

18. See Landau and Condit, *Rise of the New York Skyscraper,* 338. For further information and more illustrations of some of these late nineteenth-century hotels, see Robert A. M. Stern, Gregory Gilmartin, and John Montague Massengale, *New York 1900: Metropolitan Architecture and Urbanism, 1890–1915* (New York: Rizzoli International, 1983). For an excellent fictional account of the growth of the hotel business in turn-of-the-century New York, see Stephen Millhauser, *Martin Dressler* (New York: Vintage, 1997).

19. Landau and Condit, *Rise of the New York Skyscraper,* 338. See also R. W. Sexton, *American Apartment Houses, Hotels, and Apartment Hotels of Today* (New York: Architectural Book Publishing Company, Inc., 1929).

20. On the history of the American hotel and its relation to tourism and leisure, see David Watkin, *Grand Hotel;* Catherine Donzel, Alexis Gregory, and Marc Walter, *Grand American Hotels* (New York: Vendome Press, 1989); Jeffrey Limerick, Nancy Ferguson, and Richard Oliver, *America's Grand Resort Hotels* (New York: Pantheon, 1979); Jefferson Williamson, *The American*

Hotel (New York: Knopf, 1930); Irvin S. Cobb, *"Who's Who" plus "Here's How!"* (New York: Hotel Waldorf-Astoria Corporation, 1934); and Lucius Beebe, *The Ritz Idea: The Story of a Great Hotel* (New York: privately printed, 1936).

21. Margaret Knapp, "Introductory Essay: Entertainment and Commerce," in *Inventing Times Square,* ed. Taylor, 120–132. See also Lewis A. Erenberg, *Steppin' Out: New York Nightlife and the Transformation of American Culture, 1890–1930* (Westport, CT: Greenwood Press, 1981); Jack N. Poggi, *Theater in America: The Impact of Economic Forces, 1870–1967* (Ithaca, NY: Cornell University Press, 1968); Stephen Jenkins, *The Greatest Street in the World: The Story of Broadway, Old and New, from Bowling Green to Albany* (New York: Putnam, 1911); and Alfred L. Bernheim, *The Business of the Theatre: An Economic History of the American Theatre, 1750–1932* (New York: Actors Equity Association, 1932; repr. New York: Benjamin Blom, 1964).

22. George Rector, *The Girl From Rector's* (Garden City, NY: Doubleday, Page and Co., 1927); Lewis, Scribner and Company, *Where and How to Dine in New York* (New York: Lewis, Scribner and Co., 1903); Ahrens Publishing Company, *A Pictorial Survey of the Hotel and Restaurant Markets* (New York and Chicago: Ahrens Publishing Company, Inc., 1930); Scudder Middleton, *Dining, Wining, and Dancing in New York* (New York: Dodge Publishing Company, 1938); Selmer Fougner, *Dining Out in New York and What to Order* (New York: H. C. Kinsey and Company, 1938); and John F. Mariani, *America Eats Out: An Illustrated History of Restaurants, Taverns, Coffee Shops, Speakeasies, and Other Establishments that Have Fed Us for 350 Years* (New York: Morrow, 1991).

23. See William Leach's discussion of the growth of service-oriented employment, *Land of Desire: Merchants, Power, and the Rise of a New American Culture* (New York: Vintage Books, 1994), ch. 5. See also Angel Kwolek-Folland, *Engendering Business: Men and Women in the Corporate Office, 1870–1930* (Baltimore: Johns Hopkins University Press, 1994) and Susan Porter Benson, *Counter Cultures: Saleswomen, Managers, and Customers in American Department Stores, 1890–1940* (Urbana: University of Illinois Press, 1990).

24. Moses King, *King's Handbook of New York City* (Boston: Moses King, second edition, 1893). For a brief commentary on King's guides to New York and their popularity over the years, see A. E. Santaniello's introduction to *King's Views of New York, 1896–1915, and Brooklyn, 1905* (New York: Benjamin Blom, 1974). See also King's *New York: The Metropolis of the American Continent* (Boston: Moses King, 1893) and *King's Photographic Views of New York* (Boston: Moses King, 1895).

25. King, *King's Handbook,* preface, 3.

26. See other guides to New York published in the 1890s, such as *Godey's Illustrated Souvenir Guide to Chicago, World's Fair and New York* (Chicago: E. Lockwood and Co., 1893); *"How To Get There" in New York* (New York: Hall Publishing Company, 1897); and *The Sun's Guide to New York* (New York: R. Wayne Wilson and Company, 1892).

27. King, *King's Handbook*, 46–47.

28. Ibid., 50.

29. New York Information Agency, *Hints for Strangers, Shoppers and Sight See-ers in the Metropolis*, uncorrected proof (New York: New York Information Agency, c. 1891.), 9; *The Gate to The Sea*, 7.

30. See chapters 4 and 5 for discussions of this later commercial cartography.

31. Moses King, *New York: The Metropolis of the American Continent* (Boston: Moses King, 1893); Brooklyn Daily Eagle, *The Sun's Guide to New York; A Visitor's Guide to the City of New York* (Brooklyn, NY: Brooklyn Daily Eagle, 1899); Herbert Foster Gunnison, *A Visitor's Guide to the Greater New York* (Brooklyn, NY: Eagle Press, 1896); *The Guide of Guides* (New York: Davis and Hopp Bros., 1896); Gustav Kobbé, *New York and Its Environs* (New York: Harper and Brothers, 1891); and Ernest Ingersoll, *A Week in New York* (New York: Rand, McNally and Co., 1892).

32. *The Gate to the Sea*, 8–12.

33. See Elaine Abelson, *When Ladies Go A-Thieving: Middle-Class Shoplifters in the Victorian Department Store* (New York: Oxford University Press, 1992) and Peiss, *Cheap Amusements*. See also Rabinovitz, *For the Love of Pleasure;* Kwolek-Folland, *Engendering Business* Benson, *Counter Cultures;* and Leach, *Land of Desire*.

34. On the founding of the Hotel Martha Washington, see the circular issued by the hotel, *Hotel Martha Washington* (New York: Woman's Hotel Company/Hotel Martha Washington, 1903).

35. New York Information Agency, *Hints for Strangers*, 6. See also *Godey's Illustrated Souvenir Guide* and *The Sun's Guide to New York*. To compare the language of this and other guidebooks' descriptions of the streets and neighborhoods with the descriptions and layouts of tableaux of foreign peoples and nations at late nineteenth-century fairs, see Timothy Mitchell, *Colonizing Egypt* (New York: Cambridge University Press, 1988) and Robert Rydell, *All the World's a Fair: Visions of Empire at American International Expositions, 1876–1916* (Chicago: University of Chicago Press, 1984) and *World of Fairs: The Century-of-Progress Expositions* (Chicago: University of Chicago Press, 1993).

36. *The Gate to the Sea*, 6–13.

37. Ibid., 36. See similar comments in, for example, *Godey's Illustrated Souvenir Guide* and *The Sun's Guide to New York*.

38. New York Central and Hudson River Railroad Company, *New York as a Summer Resort* (New York: New York Central, 1896). See also Ingersoll, *A Week in New York* and Moses Sweetser, *How to Know New York* (New York: J. J. Little and Co., 1895).

39. Michael Sorkin used the image of a theme park to organize a collection of essays on current American city developments. See Michael Sorkin, ed., *Variations on a Theme Park: The New American City and the End of Public Space* (New York: Hill and Wang, 1992). See also Robert Rydell, *World of Fairs* and Tony Bennett, *The Birth of the Museum: History, Theory, Politics* (New York: Routledge, 1995).

40. Pamphlets issued by some of these early bus companies can be found in the Warshaw Collection of Business Americana, New York Boxes, Archives Center, NMAH.

41. See Susan G. Davis, *Parades and Power: Street Theatre in Nineteenth-Century Philadelphia* (Philadelphia: Temple University Press, 1986); David Waldstreicher, *In the Midst of Perpetual Fetes: The Making of American Nationalism, 1776–1820* (Chapel Hill: University of North Carolina Press, 1997); and Simon P. Newman, *Parades and the Politics of the Streets: Festive Culture in the Early American Republic* (Philadelphia: University of Pennsylvania Press, 1998).

42. *Hints for Strangers,* 6. Similar accounts of the city's populations as sights in themselves, as "parades," can be found in *The Sun's Guide to New York.* See also Leach, *Land of Desire,* chs. 2 and 5, esp. 143–145, for his discussion of the style and psychology of department store displays, especially the role of Joseph Urban as the progenitor of many of the most splendid techniques. For more on the streets and shops of the late-century city as show and spectacle, see Schwartz, *Spectacular Realities* and Rosalind H. Williams, *Dream Worlds: Mass Consumption in Late Nineteenth-Century France* (Berkeley: University of California Press, 1991).

43. Ibid., 7–8.

44. Ibid., 7.

45. See Brian Coe and Paul Gates, *The Snapshot Photograph: The Rise of Popular Photography, 1888–1939* (London: Ash and Grant, 1977) and Susan Stewart, *On Longing: Narratives of the Miniature, the Gigantic, the Souvenir, the Collection* (Baltimore: Johns Hopkins University Press, 1984). See also Victor A. Blenkle Postcard Collection, Archives Center, NMAH; Postcard Collection, Division of Collections, National Building Museum, Washington, D.C.; Postcard Collection, Museum of the City of New York.

46. For other examples of early visual souvenirs of New York, see Smith, Bleakley and Company, *Pictorial New York and Brooklyn* (New York: Smith, Bleakley and Co., 1892); A. Wittemann, *Select New York* (New York: A. Wittemann, 1889, 1890, 1898), *New-York* (New York: A. Wittemann, n.d.) and

East River Bridge (New York: Wittemann Brothers, c. 1884); Rand, McNally and Company, *[New York] From Recent Photographs* (New York: Rand, McNally and Company, 1895); Moses King, *King's Photographic Views of New York* (Boston: Moses King, 1895); and Rudolph M. De Leeuw, *Both Sides of Broadway* (New York: The De Leeuw Riehl Publishing Company, 1910).

3   ARCHITECTURE, AMERICANISM, AND A "NEW" NEW YORK, 1900–1919

1. The clearest representation of this phrase and its meaning can be found in John C. Van Dyke, *The New New York* (New York: Macmillan, 1909).

2. Max Page has referred to this process, linking New York's architectural history to Baron Haussmann's rebuilding of Paris, as one of "creative destruction." See Page, *The Creative Destruction of Manhattan, 1900–1940* (Chicago: University of Chicago Press, 1999).

3. Jules Vallée Guérin (1866–1946) was born in St. Louis, Missouri, and began exhibiting his work at the Art Institute of Chicago in the 1890s. He moved to New York in 1900 and there made his name as the leading painter of architectural subjects and as an illustrator. His lithographs appeared in numerous articles in *Century, Scribner's,* and *Harper's.* As an architectural renderer he worked with leading architects of his day on major projects, including Charles McKim's winning plans for the National Mall in Washington, D.C. and Daniel Burnham and Edward Bennett's "Plan of Chicago," 1909.

4. Randall Blackshaw, "The New New York," *Century Magazine* 64 (August 1902): 492–513, quotation 493.

5. The literature on Paris as the capital of France is enormous; that on London, less so. For Paris, see David Pinkney, *Napoleon III and the Rebuilding of Paris* (Princeton: Princeton University Press, 1958); David Jordan, *Transforming Paris* (New York: Free Press, 1995); David Harvey, *Consciousness and the Urban Experience* (Baltimore: Johns Hopkins University Press, 1985). For London, see Donald Olsen, *The Growth of Victorian London* (New York: Holmes and Meier, 1976) and Ken Young and Patricia Garside, *Metropolitan London: Politics and Urban Change, 1837–1981* (New York: Holmes and Meier, 1982).

6. See Marguerite Shaffer, *See America First: Tourism and National Identity, 1880–1940* (Washington, DC: Smithsonian Institution Press, 2001).

7. Herbert Croly, "New York as the American Metropolis," *Architectural Record* 13 (March 1903): 199–200, 205. See also other articles by Croly, including "American Architecture of To-Day," *Architectural Record* 14 (December 1903): 413–435; "New World and the New Art," *Architectural Record* 12 (June 1902): 134–153; "What Is Indigenous Architecture?" *Architectural Record* 21 (June 1907): 434–442.

8. Hamilton Wright Mabie, "The Genius of the Cosmopolitan City," *Outlook* 76 (March 5, 1904): 577–593, quotation 578.

9. Mabie, 588, 593. As historian John Higham has noted, 1906–1907 marked "a new phase in the history of American nativism." Higham, *Strangers in the Land: Patterns in American Nativism, 1860–1925* (New York: Atheneum, 1977), 165. See also Stephen J. Diner, *A Very Different Age: Americans of the Progressive Era* (New York: Hill and Wang, 1998), 77.

10. The attraction of New York for the newly wealthy was not always popular with longer-established New Yorkers, despite the wealth such individuals or their corporations brought to the city. Like the character Dryfoos in *A Hazard of New Fortunes,* William Dean Howells's novel about class and money in late nineteenth-century New York, the new millionaires from the Midwest and West were frequently depicted as *arrivistes,* as flashy buffoons. Their new residences on Fifth Avenue were disparaged by the architectural press as "ridiculous" for their ostentation and poor taste. See Franz K. Winkler, "Architecture in the Billionaire District of New York City," *Architectural Record* 11 (October 1901): 679–699. This scathing article contains photographs of the new homes of such men as Andrew Carnegie and F. W. Woolworth. Howells's novel, although published in 1890, still provides a relevant description of the tensions between old money and new money as the two forces negotiated their respective places in the city's increasingly complicated social hierarchy.

11. Ibid., 590.

12. For a discussion of the growth of white-collar work in New York's financial sector during these years, see Angel Kwollek-Folland, *Engendering Business: Men and Women in the Corporate Office* (Baltimore: Johns Hopkins University Press, 1994), 15–40.

13. Carol Willis argues for an economic interpretation of New York's skyscrapers in *Form Follows Finance: Skyscrapers and Skylines in New York and Chicago* (New York: Princeton Architectural Press, 1995). Cultural geographer Mona Domosh offers a spatial and cultural argument for the significance of New York's skyscrapers in her *Invented Cities: The Creation of Landscape in Nineteenth-Century New York and Boston* (New Haven: Yale University Press, 1996).

14. See William Taylor, *In Pursuit of Gotham: Culture and Commerce in New York* (New York: Oxford University Press, 1992), 23–33 and 51–67.

15. Joseph B. Gilder, "The City of Dreadful Height," *Putnam's Monthly* 5 (November 1908): 131–143, quotation 132.

16. Barr Ferree, "The High Building and Its Art," *Scribner's Monthly* 15 (March 1894): 297–318, quotation 297.

17. Ibid. See the introduction to this book for a discussion of the contrasting national role and image of Chicago, the other American city associated with early skyscraper architecture.

18. English aesthetic theorists John Ruskin and William Morris initiated what became the Arts and Crafts movement in England. Their ideas underpinned the American version of that movement in the early twentieth century, the leading figure of which was Gustav Stickley. On the philosophy and cultural politics of the American movement, see Eileen Boris, *Art and Labor: Ruskin, Morris, and the Craftsman Ideal in America* (Philadelphia: Temple University Press, 1986) and Robert Judson Clark, ed., *The Arts and Crafts Movement in America, 1875–1920* (Boston: Museum of Fine Arts, 1987).

19. John Corbin, "The Twentieth Century City," *Scribner's Magazine* 33 (March 1903): 259–272, quotation 261.

20. Ibid., 262. Not all architectural critics agreed with the idea that American architects should break away from the building styles of Europe. The architect A. J. Bloor seemed to address Corbin directly when he wrote, "Who, of any taste in architecture, regrets that a beautiful tower in Seville should be virtually reproduced in Madison Square Garden?" See Bloor, "A Letter on Current American Architecture (Including the 'Skyscraper') and Architects," pamphlet (n.d., c. 1905). Footnote to title reads: "Suggested by an article of Mr. Montgomery Schuyler, in the 'Metropolitan Magazine' of July 1905." Bloor's pamphlet is in the NMAH Archives Center's Warshaw Collection, Box: "Architecture." A March 1907 editorial in *Scientific American,* entitled "A City of Towers," criticized the onset of tall buildings in New York. If, however, there were to be tall buildings in the city, the editors of the periodical suggested that architects work to accentuate the vertical rather than the horizontal lines of the buildings. They suggested taking "one of the beautiful cathedral towers of Europe as a model," to "reproduce something of the effect the great Gothic windows and other characteristic effects of these handsome structures." See "City of Towers," *Scientific American* 96 (March 30, 1907): 266. Six years later, Cass Gilbert, architect of the Woolworth Building, applied just such a Gothic treatment to the corporate offices of the "five and dime millionaire."

21. Ibid., 264, 266. The only European city to which Corbin ascribed a current modernity was Vienna, and he did so while arguing that the women of New York were more fashionable and more stylish than the women of Paris and London. Corbin noted that to find her European counterpart one would "have to go to the Kohlmarkt and the Ringstrasse. In Vienna the life is similarly shifting and cosmopolitan, there is a similar lack of indigenous style, and a similar willingness to take the best, wherever it is to be found."

22. George Ethelbert Walsh, "Modern Towers of Babel in New York," *Harper's Weekly* 151 (January 12, 1907): 68. See also other articles by Walsh, including "Potential Value of a City Roof," *World To-Day* 10 (June 1906): 646–647 and "Traffic Congestion in New York," *Cassier* 34 (June 1908): 151–155. The planning, building, and completion of the Singer Building, the world's

tallest building until the completion of the Metropolitan Life Tower in 1909, occasioned many articles on the merits and styles of tall buildings in New York. See, for example, "Office-building 612 feet tall," *Scientific American* 95 (September 8, 1906): 169, 174; C. M. Ripley, "Singer Building, New York, Forty-Seven Stories High," *World's Work* 14 (October 1907): 9459–9461; "Erection of the 612-foot Singer Building," *Scientific American* 97 (September 7, 1907): 168–169; and Gardner Richardson, "Great Towers of New York," *Independent* 65 (August 6, 1908): 301–305.

23. Herbert T. Wade, "Tall Buildings and Their Problems," *American Review of Reviews* 38 (November 1908): 577, 586. See also F. W. Fitzpatrick, "Building Against Fire," *Outlook* 88 (April 25, 1908): 936–945; J. K. Freitag, "Fire Prevention in High Buildings," *Engineering Magazine* 34 (February 1908): 735–740; and T. K. Thomson, "Caisson Foundations of Skyscrapers," *Scientific American* 65 (March 7, 1908): 152–154.

24. A. C. David, "The New Architecture: The First American Type of Real Value," *Architectural Record* 28 (December 1910): 388–403.

25. Stephen Daniels, *Fields of Vision: Landscape Imagery and National Identity in England and the United States* (Princeton: Princeton University Press, 1993), 5.

26. Angela Miller, *Empire of the Eye: Landscape Representation and American Cultural Politics, 1825–1875* (Ithaca, NY: Cornell University Press, 1993), 7.

27. Harriet Monroe, "Arizona," *Atlantic Monthly* 89 (June 1902): 780–789.

28. On the history of early twentieth-century U.S. imperialism, see Kristin Hoganson, *Fighting for American Manhood: How Gender Politics Provoked the Spanish-American and Philippine-American Wars* (New Haven: Yale University Press, 1998); Laura Wexler, *Tender Violence: Domestic Visions in an Age of U.S. Imperialism* (Chapel Hill: University of North Carolina Press, 2000); and Amy Kaplan and Donald E. Pease, *Cultures of United States Imperialism* (Durham, NC: Duke University Press, 1993).

29. For histories of the railroad system and its effects on national culture, see Sarah H. Gordon, *Passage to Union: How the Railroads Transformed American Life, 1829–1929* (Chicago: Ivan R. Dee, 1996); John F. Stover, *American Railroads* (Chicago: University of Chicago Press, 1976). For the West specifically, see the entry under "railroads" in Howard R. Lamar, ed., *The Reader's Encyclopedia of the American West* (New York: Thomas Y. Crowell, 1977).

30. For discussions of the role of the railroads in building western tourism and developing National Parks, see Ann Farrar Hyde, *An American Vision: Far Western Landscape and National Culture, 1890–1920* (New York: New York University Press, 1990); Marguerite Shaffer, *See America First,* esp. ch.

6; and Alfred Runte, *Trains of Discovery: Western Railroads and the National Parks* (Niwot, CO: Robert Rinehart, 1990).

31. Monroe, "Arizona," 780.

32. Robert T. Hill, "The Wonders of the American Desert," *World's Work* 3 (March 1902): 1821–1823.

33. Monroe, "Arizona," 781.

34. Ibid., 782.

35. Hyde, *American Vision.*

36. For an example of the metaphorical muddle brought on by efforts to describe the unfamiliar landscapes of the West, see Arthur Inkersly, "The Grand Canyon of Arizona," *Overland Monthly* 41 (June 1903): 423–432.

37. Hyde, *American Vision,* 208–209.

38. On the construction of national identities, see Benedict Anderson, *Imagined Communities* (New York: Verso, 1983); John Bodnar, ed., *Bonds of Affection* (Princeton: Princeton University Press, 1996); Eric Hobsbawm and Terence Ranger, eds., *The Invention of Tradition* (New York: Cambridge University Press, 1983).

39. Pierre Loti, "Impressions of New York," *Century Magazine* 85 (February 1913): 611. Pierre Loti was the pseudonym of Louis-Marie-Julien Viaud (1850–1923), a French naval officer, writer, photographer, and artist best known in the United States for his play *Madame Chrysanthemum,* the basis for David Belasco's better-known play *Madame Butterfly* (itself the basis for Puccini's opera). He adopted the name Pierre Loti in 1881, taking the last name from the followers of a Tahitian Monarch, Queen Pomaré IV. Loti's Orientalism, stemming from his travels in the South Pacific and the Far East, no doubt influenced his reaction to New York City.

40. Ibid., 609.

41. Idem, "Impressions of New York" (second article in two-part series), *Century* 85 (March 1913): 758–759.

42. Anonymous, "Confessions of a Westerner and What He Sees in New York," *Independent* 91 (September 15, 1917): 424, 431.

43. James Duncan, "Sites of Representation: Place, Time and the Discourse of the Other," in *Place, Culture, Representation,* ed. James Duncan and David Ley (New York: Routledge, 1993). For an eloquent and important discussion of the issue of the construction of time, space, and place, see Johannes Fabian, *Time and the Other: How Anthropology Makes Its Object* (New York: Columbia University Press, 1983).

44. After the Battle of Wounded Knee in 1890, representations of Native Americans shifted from "savage" to tragic. The classic primary source is the work of the American photographer Edward Curtis (1868–1952). For critical studies of Curtis, see Christopher M. Lyman, *The Vanishing Race and Other Illusions: Photographs of Indians by Edward S. Curtis* (Washington, DC:

Smithsonian Institution Press, 1982) and *The Plains Indians Photographs of Edward S. Curtis* (Lincoln: University of Nebraska Press, 2001), which includes essays by scholars of the photography of the American West such as Martha Sandweiss and Martha H. Kennedy.

45. See William H. Truettner, ed., *The West as America: Reinterpreting Images of the Frontier, 1820–1920* (Washington, DC: National Museum of American Art/Smithsonian Institution Press, 1991); Beaumont and Nancy Newhall, *T. H. O'Sullivan: Photographer* (Rochester, NY: George Eastman House/Amon Carter Museum of Western Art, 1966); David Margolis, *To Delight the Eye: The Original Photographic Book Illustrations of the American West* (Dallas: DeGolyer Library, 1994); and Alan Trachtenberg, *Reading American Photographs: Images as History—Mathew Brady to Walker Evans* (New York: Hill and Wang, 1990, reprint).

46. The most recent critical analysis of the role photography played in constructing the imagery and mythology of the American West is Martha Sandweiss, *Print the Legend: Photography and the American West* (New Haven: Yale University Press, 2002).

47. Henry Blake Fuller, *The Cliff-Dwellers: A Novel* (Ridgewood, NJ: Gregg Press, 1968). Originally published by Harper Brothers, 1893.

48. Ibid., 1–3.

49. Foster and Reynolds Company, *New York: The Metropolis of the Western World* (New York: Foster and Reynolds Company, 1902), 9.

50. Singer Manufacturing Company, *Singer Souvenirs of New York City* (New York: Singer Manufacturing Company, 1905). NMAH. Archives Center. Warshaw Collection. New York City Boxes, Box 21.

51. Taylor, *In Pursuit of Gotham,* 23.

52. Zoning ordinances, height restrictions, and the requirement of "set-backs" to stagger the mass of tall buildings were not introduced until 1916 and then more comprehensively in the early 1920s, following the Regional Plan for Greater New York. For more on the history of planning and building laws in New York City, see Richard Plunz, *History of Housing in New York City* (New York: Columbia University Press, 1990) and the essays by Keith Revell, Marc Weiss, and Robert Fishman in *The Landscape of Modernity: Essays on New York City,* ed. David Ward and Olivier Zunz (New York: Russell Sage, 1992).

53. Corbin, "Twentieth Century City."

54. Ibid., 260.

55. The publication reviewed was Frederick Keppel, *Mr. Pennell's Etchings of New York "Sky Scrapers"* (New York: Frederick Keppel and Co., 1905).

56. Giles Edgerton [Mary Fanton Roberts], "How New York has Redeemed herself from Ugliness—An Artist's Revelation of the Beauty of the Skyscraper," *Craftsman* 11 (January 1907): 458.

57. See also *Architectural Record* 22 (September 1907): 161 and Joseph B. Guilder, "The City of Dreadful Height," *Putnam's Monthly* 5 (November 1908): 131–143, esp. 131 and 136, for references to the seeming naturalness of the skyscraper landscape and the appearance from the bay of New York as a city "set on a hill," echoing much older constructions of the meaning and role of America.

4   NEW YORK IS NOT AMERICA

1. Ford Madox Ford, *New York Is Not America* (New York: Albert and Charles Boni, 1927), 107 and chs. 4 and 5. Ford Madox Hueffer (1873–1939), changed his last name to Ford after World War I. Perhaps best known for his novel *The Good Soldier* (1915), Ford was a novelist, essayist, and editor of a literary review; his circle of acquaintances included Gertrude Stein and others of the American expatriate circle in Paris in the war period and the 1920s as well as most of the leading younger writers in London both before and after the war. See Alan Judd, *Ford Madox Ford* (Cambridge, MA: Harvard University Press, 1991) and Bernard J. Poli, *Ford Madox Ford and the Transatlantic Review* (Syracuse, NY: Syracuse University Press, 1967).

2. John Higham, *Strangers in the Land: Patterns of American Nativism, 1865–1925* (New Brunswick, NJ: Rutgers University Press, 1955). On early twentieth-century immigration, see also Alan M. Kraut, *Silent Travelers: Germs, Genes, and the "Immigrant Menace"* (Baltimore: Johns Hopkins University Press, 1994).

3. For studies of post–World War I American culture and politics, see Michael E. Parrish, *Anxious Decades: America in Prosperity and Depression, 1920–1941* (New York: W. W. Norton, 1992); Lynn Dumenil, *The Modern Temper: American Culture and Society in the 1920s* (New York: Hill and Wang, 1995); Frederick Lewis Allen, *Only Yesterday: An Informal History of the 1920s* (New York: Harper and Brothers, 1931); Arthur M. Schlesinger Jr., *The Crisis of the Old Order, 1919–1933* (Boston: Houghton Mifflin, 1957); William E. Leuchtenburg, *The Perils of Prosperity, 1914–1932* (Chicago: University of Chicago Press, 1958); Lawrence Levine, "Progress and Nostalgia," in his *The Unpredictable Past: Explorations in American Cultural History* (New York: Oxford University Press, 1993); and T. J. Jackson Lears, *No Place of Grace: Antimodernism and the Transformation of American Culture, 1880–1920* (New York: Pantheon, 1981).

4. The exchange between the *Globe* and the *Saturday Evening Post* was reported in "New York Scolded for Its Moral and Other Shortcomings," *Current Opinion* 68 (April 1920): 523–524.

5. Ibid., 524.

6. Sinclair Lewis's novel *Babbitt* (New York: Harcourt, Brace and Company, 1922), satirized life in the fictional midwestern town of Zenith and

became both a bestseller and cultural shorthand for contemporary suburban consumerism and small-town social conformity. Sherwood Anderson wrote even harsher condemnations of small-town American life and values. See Anderson's *Winesburg, Ohio: A Group of Tales of Ohio Small Town Life* (New York: B. W. Huebsch, 1919).

7. George Ade, "Oh, Yes! We Will Visit New York—But We'll Pin a Return Ticket Inside Our Vest," *American Magazine* 91 (March 1921): 14–15. Other examples of this debate about New York are Mark Sullivan, "Why the West Dislikes New York: The Eternal Conflict between City and Country," *World's Work* 51 (February 1926): 406–411; "Why a Cartoonist Would Rather Live in Des Moines Than in New York," *Literary Digest* 62 (July 12, 1919): 86–90; and "New York City as the World's Prize 'Borough of Bunk,'" editorial, *Literary Digest* 70 (August 27, 1921): 37–38. Part of this debate about New York focused on especially contentious neighborhoods such as Greenwich Village. See, for example, "The Lure of Greenwich Village," *Literary Digest* 65 (May 8, 1920): 46–47 and "Greenwich Village Virus," *Saturday Evening Post* 194 (October 15, 1921): 14–15.

8. James Middleton, "New York the Stupendous," *World's Work* 31 (March 1916): 538–554. See also "One million six hundred and forty-three thousand Jews in New York City," editorial, *World's Work* 47 (November 1923): 20–22. For more on the geography of New York's Jews, see Deborah Dash Moore, *At Home in America: Second-Generation New York Jews* (New York: Columbia University Press, 1981) and her article "On the Fringes of the City: Jewish Neighborhoods in Three Boroughs," in *Landscape of Modernity,* ed. Ward and Zunz.

9. Middleton, "New York the Stupendous," 554.

10. M. Christine Boyer, *Dreaming the Rational City: The Myth of American City Planning* (Cambridge, MA: MIT Press, 1983), 91–95, 155–159, 178–185. See also Keith Revell, "Regulating the Landscape: Real Estate Values, City Planning, and the 1916 Zoning Ordinance," in *Landscape of Modernity,* ed. Ward and Zunz, 19–45 and Robert Fishman, "The Regional Plan and the Transformation of the Industrial Metropolis," in ibid., 106–125.

11. The original version of the map, as used by the Lusk Committee, is housed in the New York State Archives in Albany. A photograph of the map can be found in Paul E. Cohen and Robert T. Augustyn, eds., *Manhattan in Maps, 1527–1995* (New York: Rizzoli, 1997).

12. The Rand School was an adult education facility founded in 1905 and sponsored by the Socialist Party. Although many of its faculty and students were socialists, the faculty also included such nonsocialist luminaries as Charles Beard and John Dewey. For more on the Rand School, see Mari Jo Buhle, Paul Buhle, and Dan Georgakas, eds., *Encyclopedia of the American Left* (New York: Garland, 1990). The Rand School and other New York insti-

tutions and publications were named as the source of high school students' knowledge of Bolshevism, according to an article in the *Literary Digest* in July 1919. The article stated that a questionnaire given to high school students in the city that summer revealed publications such as *The New Republic, The Nation, The New York Call,* and *The Liberator,* as well as the Rand School, to be the main sources of Bolshevik information. See "Bolshevism in New York and Russian Schools," *Literary Digest* 62 (July 5, 1919): 40–41.

13. Madison Grant, *The Passing of the Great Race,* 4th ed. (New York: Scribner's, 1921); Lothrop Stoddard, *The Rising Tide of Color against White World-Supremacy* (New York: Charles Scribner's Sons, 1920); and Matthew Frye Jacobson, *Whiteness of a Different Color: European Immigrants and the Alchemy of Race* (Cambridge, MA: Harvard University Press, 1998), 75–90, 92–102, 176. See also David Roediger, *The Wages of Whiteness: Race and the Making of the American Working Class* (London: Verso, 1991).

14. James Weldon Johnson, "Harlem: The Cultural Capital," in *The New Negro: An Interpretation,* ed. Alain Locke (New York: A. and C. Boni, 1925), quoted in David Levering Lewis, *When Harlem Was In Vogue* (New York: Oxford University Press, 1989), 113.

15. John Bruce Mitchell, "'Reds' in New York Slums: How Insidious Doctrines are Propagated in New York's 'East Side,'" *Forum* 61 (April 1919): 442–455. See also Nicholas M. Butler, "Our Bolshevik Menace," *Forum* 63 (January 1920): 49–56; Franklin M. Giddings, "Bolsheviki Must Go," *Independent* 97 (January 18, 1919): 88; "Is Bolshevism in America Becoming a Real Peril?" editorial, *Current Opinion* 67 (July 1919): 4–6; "How the Russian Bolshevik Agent Does Business in New York City," editorial, *Literary Digest* 61 (May 17, 1919): 60–63; Clayton R. Lusk, "Hatching Revolution in America," *Current Opinion* 71 (September 1921): 290–294; and "Radicalism Under Inquiry," *Review of Reviews* 61 (February 1920): 167–171.

16. Frederic Cople Jaher, *The Urban Establishment: Upper Strata in Boston, New York, Charleston, Chicago, and Los Angeles* (Urbana: University of Illinois Press, 1982), 276.

17. The Immigration Restriction League, though founded in 1894 by a group of Boston Brahmins from Harvard, attracted members from other northeastern elites, especially old New Yorkers. On membership in the league, see Higham, *Strangers in the Land,* 102. See also Jaher, *Urban Establishment.*

18. Fundraising form letter, from Henry Fairfield Osborn. Henry Fairfield Osborn Papers; Correspondence: Organizations; Eugenics: Second International Congress, 1921. Archives, Department of Library Services—Special Collections, American Museum of Natural History.

19. Robert W. Rydell, *World of Fairs: The Century-of-Progress Expositions* (Chicago: University of Chicago Press, 1993), 47–48.

20. Details of Henry Fairfield Osborn's family background and career are from Ronald Rainger, *An Agenda for Antiquity: Henry Fairfield Osborn and Vertebrate Paleontology at the American Museum of Natural History, 1890–1935* (Tuscaloosa: University of Alabama Press, 1991). See Osborn's own works relevant to this chapter, such as Henry Fairfield Osborn, *Men of the Old Stone Age: Their Environment, Life, and Art* (New York: Scribners, 1915); "Our Ancestors Arrive in Scandinavia," *Natural History* 22 (1922): 116–134; and "The Approach to the Immigration Problem Through Science," *Proceedings of the National Immigration Conference* 26 (1924): 44–53. On Osborn's involvement in the evolution debates of the 1920s, see his *Evolution and Religion* (New York: Scribners, 1923). Some of the most significant criticism of Osborn's views came from Franz Boas, a colleague at the American Museum of Natural History, already one of America's most respected anthropologists by the second decade of the twentieth century. See, for example, Franz Boas, *The Mind of Primitive Man* (New York: The Macmillan Company, 1911). For Boas's views of Osborn and others' eugenical beliefs and "scientific racism," see Boas, "Question of Racial Purity," *American Mercury* 3 (October 1924): 163–169; "This Nordic Nonsense," *Forum* 74 (October 1925): 502–511; and "Fallacies of Racial Inferiority," *Current History* 25 (February 1927): 676–682. See also the very popular works of his pupils, Margaret Mead, *Coming of Age in Samoa* (New York: William Morrow, 1928) and Zora Neale Hurston, *Mules and Men* (Philadelphia and London: J. B. Lippincott Company, 1935).

21. Grant, *Passing.* Grant went on to write other books on the issue of race and immigration in the United States, such as *The Conquest of a Continent; or, The Expansion of Races in America* (New York: Scribners, 1933) and, with Charles Stewart Davison, *The Alien in Our Midst; or, "Selling Our Birthright for a Mess of Pottage"* (New York: The Galton Publishing Company, Inc., 1930).

22. Grant, *Passing,* 89–90.

23. Ibid., 91.

24. Ibid., 92.

25. In the New York *World,* see "Melting Pot Has Proved Failure in America as Vices of Mingled Races Are Perpetuated," September 23, 1921, 3; "Nature Leader of Man in Mechanics," September 24, 1921, 9; "Warns of Race Decline," September 25, 1921, 9; and "Eugenist Denies Bars To Marriage Can Improve Race," September 27, 1921, 7. In the New York *Sun,* see "Noted Scientists Here for Eugenics Conference," September 22, 1921, 2; "Questions Darwinian Theory," September 24, 1921, 2; "Decries Beauty in Picking Mate," September 27, 1921, 9; and "Race War Seen in Class Clash," September 28, 1921, 8. In the *New York Times,* see "Tracing Parentage by Eugenic Tests," September 23, 1921, 8; "Want More Babies in Best Families," September 25,

1921, 16; "Eugenists Uphold Control of Birth/Scientists Come Out for Limitation of Families Where Poverty and Disease Are Perils," September 27, 1921, 20; and "Sees American Man as Superior of Woman," September 28, 1921, 11. See also editorial in New York *World,* September 26, 1921, 10; see also "America and the Man," *Sun,* September 27, 1921, 16, and "Who Are The 'Fittest'?" *Sun,* September 28, 1921, 14.

26. See, for example, "Ku Klux Klan Used Army and Navy Club Address to Peddle Memberships in Campaign by Mail; The World Reproduces 'Grand Goblin' Documents," New York *World,* September 8, 1921, 1. The KKK remained on the *World*'s front page for the rest of the month.

27. See "Immigration Must Soon Cease From Some Countries," New York *World,* September 25, 1921, 24. This story was accompanied by a photograph of a crowd of people captioned, "Immigrants Awaiting a Ruling on Their Appeals" and another picture of two young women struggling with their luggage captioned, "Deported."

28. Books of nostalgic reminiscences published by this generation include James H. Callender, *Yesterdays in Little Old New York* (New York: Dorland Press, 1929) and Charles Townsend Harris, *Memories of Manhattan in the Sixties and Seventies* (New York: The Derrydale Press, 1928). See also "The Old Bowery Wouldn't Know Itself Now," editorial, *Literary Digest* 65 (May 8, 1920): 70–75; Robert and Elizabeth Shackleton, "Vanishing New York," *Century* 100 (June 1920): 150–164; Theodore Dreiser, *The Color of a Great City* (New York: Boni and Liverwright, 1923); Mrs. J. B. Harriman, "Hither and Yon," two-part series of articles on old New York, *Century* 106 (September 1923): 651–663 and (October 1923): 873–886; and Herbert Asbury's articles in the *American Mercury,* late 1920s, e.g., "Days of Wickedness," vol. 12 (November 1927): 359–369.

29. For more on both preservation activities in New York and the history of the preservation movement throughout the United States, see Charles B. Hosmer Jr., *Presence of the Past: A History of the Preservation Movement in the United States before Williamsburg* (New York: G. P. Putnam's Sons, 1965); Susan Porter Benson et al., *Presenting the Past: Essays on History and the Public* (Philadelphia: Temple University Press, 1986).

30. On "primitivism" in American art and culture in the early twentieth century, see Warren Susman's essay on concepts of "civilization" in the 1920s in his *Culture As History* (New York: Pantheon, 1984); for New York specifically, see Ann Douglas, *Terrible Honesty: Mongrel Manhattan in the 1920s* (New York: Farrar Straus Giroux, 1995); and W. Jackson Rushing, *Native American Art and the New York Avant-Garde: A History of Cultural Primitivism* (Austin: University of Texas Press, 1995). For a broader study, see Marianna Torgovnik, *Gone Primitive: Savage Intellects, Modern Lives* (Chicago: University of Chicago Press, 1990). For the theoretical background of primi-

tivism and early anthropology, see James Clifford, *The Predicament of Culture* (Cambridge, MA: Harvard University Press, 1988).

31. Lynn Dumenil, *The Modern Temper: American Culture and Society in the 1920s* (New York: Hill and Wang, 1995), 77. See also Boyer, *Dreaming*, 139–140, 183–184.

32. Magazine articles on the joys and perils of automobile touring rapidly increased in numbers in the 1920s. See, for example, George W. Sutton, "Rolling Vacations," *Colliers* 68 (August 6, 1921): 13; Alexander Johnston, "America: Touring Ground of the World," *Country Life* 37 (January 1920): 25–34; V. Gurney, "Auto-burro Honeymoon," *Sunset* 43 (July 1919): 40–42; Elon H. Jessup, "Flight of the Tin Can Tourists," *Outlook* 128 (May 25, 1921): 166–169; Myron J. Whitney, "Fording the Atlantic Coast," *Outing* 75 (January–February 1921): 231–234, 282–285; and Helen M. Mann, "May Day Motorists," *Overland* 75 (May 1920): 419–424. See also Warren Belasco, *Americans on the Road: From Autocamp to Motel, 1910–1945* (Cambridge, MA: MIT Press, 1979); John A. Jakle, *The Tourist: Travel in Twentieth-Century North America* (Lincoln: University of Nebraska Press, 1985); and Marguerite Shaffer, *See America First: Tourism and National Identity, 1905–1930* (Washington, DC: Smithsonian Institution Press, 2001).

33. See Edwin G. Conklin, "Some Biological Aspects of Immigration," *Scribner's Magazine* 69 (March 1921): 352–359; Henry H. Curran, U.S. Commissioner of Immigration at the Port of New York, "Fewer and Better, Or None," *Saturday Evening Post* 196 (April 26, 1924): 8–9, 189; Lothrop Stoddard, "Is America American?" *World's Work* 41 (December 1920): 201–203; Kenneth L. Roberts, "East is East," *Saturday Evening Post* 196 (February 23, 1924): 6–7, 138, 143, 145–146; "An Alien Antidumping Bill," editorial, *Literary Digest* 69 (May 7, 1921): 12–13; Calvin Coolidge, "Whose Country Is This?" *Good Housekeeping* 72 (February 1921): 13–14; George Creel, "Melting Pot or Dumping Ground?" *Collier's* 68 (September 3, 1921): 9–10; "Ellis Island Sob Stuff," editorial, *Saturday Evening Post* 194 (November 26, 1921): 20; Owen Wister, "Shall We Let the Cuckoos Crowd Us out of Our Nest?" *American Magazine* 91 (March 3, 1921): 47; and Willet M. Hays, "Immigration and Eugenics," *Review of Reviews* 69 (April 1924): 405–406.

34. See Louis Dodge, "The Sidewalks of New York," *Scribner's Magazine* 70 (July–December 1921): 584–592. On the relationship between American identities and New York's metropolitan status, see "New York's Big Foreign Population," editorial, *Literary Digest* 73 (April 29, 1922): 13; "Is New York American?" editorial, *Saturday Review of Literature* 2 (January 2, 1926): 457; Mary Agnes Hamilton, "Red-Haired City," *Atlantic Monthly* 139 (April 1927): 491–497; "Why Hate New York?" editorial, *Outlook* 142 (March 17, 1926): 404; Jacques LeClercq, "Why I Live in America," *American Mercury* 6 (September 1925): 25–31; and Chester T. Crowell, "'Welcome, Stranger!' Said Little Old New York," *Independent* 102 (April 24, 1920): 121–122.

35. Fremont Rider, *Rider's Guide to New York City* (New York: Henry Holt and Company, 1923). For more on the use of Baedeker guides by American tourists in Europe, see Harvey Levenstein, *Seductive Journey: American Tourists in France From Jefferson to the Jazz Age* (Chicago: University of Chicago Press, 1998), esp. 33, 158–159.

36. Rider, *Rider's Guide*, 122, 124.

37. In the first edition of his New York guide, Rider made only passing reference to the immigrant neighborhoods of the Lower East Side. See Fremont Rider, *Rider's New York City* (New York: Henry Holt and Company, 1916), 149–150.

38. On the ethnic and racial "mainstreaming" of white ethnics after the 1924 Act, see Jacobson, *Whiteness*, 91–135. See also Higham, *Strangers in the Land*.

39. Edward Corsi, "My Neighborhood," *Outlook* 141 (September 16, 1925): 90–92. See also the series of articles by Rollin Lynde Hartt that appeared in the summer of 1921, giving portraits of racially or ethnically distinct New York neighborhoods. Hartt's articles offer an excellent example of the type of popular discourse opposing negative views of immigrant, or "foreign," neighborhoods in the early 1920s. See Rollin Lynde Hartt, "New York and the Real Jew," *Independent* 105 (June 25, 1921): 658–660; "Made in Italy," *Independent* 106 (July 23, 1921): 19–20; and "More Irish Than Ireland," *Independent* 106 (August 20, 1921): 68–69. Hartt also wrote an article about Harlem, unusual not only because magazine articles about black Harlem were very rare, but also because of his laudatory tone: "I'd Like to Show You Harlem!" *Independent* 105 (April 2, 1921): 334–335.

40. Corsi, "My Neighborhood," 90.

41. On the history of "seeing" Jewishness in the face or body of a Jew, see Jacobson, *Whiteness*, 171–202.

42. Hutchins Hapgood, "Picturesque Ghetto," *Century Magazine* 94 (July 1917): 469–473; Corsi, "My Neighborhood." By 1917, Hapgood was familiar as the author of *The Spirit of the Ghetto,* published in 1902. Hapgood hired a then-unknown artist, Jacob Epstein, to illustrate the book with sketches of the Lower East Side's Jewish population. Epstein used the proceeds from this work to pay his way to France, where he trained as a sculptor. Epstein later moved to England, where he achieved great success and became one of the twentieth century's most acclaimed sculptors. See Hutchins Hapgood, *The Spirit of the Ghetto: Studies in the Jewish Quarter of New York* (New York: Funk and Wagnalls, 1902). For more on Epstein, see Jacob Epstein, *Let There Be Sculpture* (New York: G. P. Putnam's Sons, 1940). On racial typologies, see the earlier discussion on Osborn and Grant. See also W. Z. Ripley, *The Races of Europe: A Sociological Study* (New York: D. Appleton and Company, 1899).

43. Some examples of the work of these and other illustrators include Will Irwin, *Highlights of Manhattan,* illus. E. H. Suydam (New York: The Century Company, 1927); Vernon Howe Bailey, *Magical City: Intimate Sketches of New York* (New York: Scribners, 1935) and *Skyscrapers of New York* (New York: W. E. Rudge, 1928); Helen Josephy and Mary Margaret McBride, *New York is Everybody's Town,* illus. Margaret Freeman (New York: G. P. Putnam's Sons, 1931); Scudder Middleton, *Dining, Wining, and Dancing in New York,* illus. Loren Stout (New York: Dodge Publishing Company, 1938); J. George Frederick, *Adventuring in New York. With Ten Etchings* (New York: N. L. Brown, 1923); Joseph Pennell, *The Glory of New York* (New York: W. E. Rudge, 1926); Rian James, *All About New York: An Intimate Guide,* illus. "Jay" (New York: The John Day Company, 1931); and Charles G. Shaw, *Nightlife,* illus. Raymond Bret-Koch (New York: The John Day Company, 1931).

44. Caroline Singer, "An Italian Saturday," *Century* 101 (March 1921): 590–600. Caroline Singer and illustrator Cyrus LeRoy Baldridge frequently worked together. Subsequent publications, for both adults and children, on which they collaborated include *Turn to the East* (New York: Minton, Balch and Company, 1926); *White Africans and Black* (New York: W. E. Rudge, 1929); *Boomba Lives in Africa* (New York: Holiday House, 1935); *Ali Lives in Iran* (New York: Holiday House, 1937); *Half the World Is Isfahan* (New York: Oxford University Press, 1936); *Race? What the Scientists Say* (Camden, NJ: The Haddon Craftsmen, 1939); and *Santa Claus Comes to America* (New York: A. A. Knopf, 1942).

45. Helena Smith Dayton and Louise Bascom Barratt, *New York in Seven Days* (New York: Robert M. McBride and Company, 1925). See also Sarah M. Lockwood, *New York: Not So Little and Not So Old* (Garden City, NY: Doubleday, Page and Company, 1926). Journalist and illustrator Helen Worden wrote several guides to New York, some of which she illustrated herself: *The Real New York; A Guide for the Adventurous Shopper, the Exploratory Eater and the Know-It-All Sightseer Who Ain't Seen Nothin' Yet* (Indianapolis: The Bobbs-Merrill Company, 1932); *Round Manhattan's Rim* (Indianapolis: The Bobbs-Merrill Company, 1934); *Discover New York with Helen Worden* (New York: American Women's Voluntary Services, 1943); and *Here Is New York* (New York: Doubleday, Doran and Company, 1939). More guides by women include: Rosalie Slocum and Ann Todd, *A Key to New York* (New York: Modern Age Books, 1939); Marjorie Hillis Roulston, *New York, Fair or No Fair: A Guide for the Woman Vacationist* (Indianapolis: The Bobbs-Merrill Company, 1939); Gretta Palmer, *A Shopping Guide to New York* (New York: R. M. McBride and Company, 1930); Eva McAdoo, *How Do You Like New York? An Informal Guide* (New York: The Macmillan Company, 1936); Clara Laughlin, *So You're Visiting New York City!* (Boston: Houghton

Mifflin, 1939); and Elizabeth Hubbard Lansing, *Seeing New York* (New York: Thomas Y. Crowell Company, 1938).

46. Robert Shackleton, *The Book of New York* (Philadelphia: The Penn Publishing Company, 1920), 178. See also Elizabeth Frazer, "Our Foreign Cities: New York," *Saturday Evening Post* 195 (June 16, 1923): 6–7.

47. Mabel Osgood Wright, *My New York* (New York: The Macmillan Company, 1926), 264, 266.

48. Ibid., 275.

49. Konrad Bercovici, *Around the World in New York* (New York: The Century Company, 1924). Information on Bercovici's background is from his obituary, *New York Times,* December 28, 1961, 27.

50. The Map Division of the New York Public Library has an extensive collection of pictorial maps of New York. Some examples from the 1920s and 1930s in this collection include "The Heart of New York as Served by New York Central Railroad" (New York: Rand McNally, 1930); "A Pictorial Map of New York, Necessarily Incomplete, On Which are Displayed the Cultural Centers of the City," *New York Times Magazine,* July 31, 1927; "East Side, West Side, All Around the Town" (New York: Empire State Sightseeing Corporation, 1932); and "A Pictorial Map of that Portion of New York City Known as Manhattan" (Winchester, MA: Ernest Dudley Chase, 1939).

5   BRAND NEW YORK

1. James L. Ford, quoted in the editorial "Misrepresenting New York in Fiction," *Literary Digest* 72 (March 25 1922): 26–27.

2. On the relationship between business and government after World War I, see William Leach, *Land of Desire: Merchants, Power and the Rise of a New American Culture* (New York: Vintage, 1994), ch. 6; Ellis W. Hawley, *The Great War and the Search for a Modern Order: A History of the American People and Their Institutions, 1917–1933* (New York: St. Martin's Press, 1979); Morton Keller, *Regulating a New Society: Public Policy and Social Change in America, 1900–1933* (Cambridge, MA: Harvard University Press, 1994); Robert D. Cuff, *The War Industries Board: Business-Government Relations during World War One* (Baltimore: Johns Hopkins University Press, 1973).

3. Roland Marchand, *The Corporate Soul: The Rise of Public Relations and Corporate Imagery in American Big Business* (Berkeley: University of California Press, 1998), 166. See also Louis Galambos, *The Public Image of Big Business in America, 1880–1940* (Baltimore: Johns Hopkins University Press, 1975).

4. See, for example, Elizabeth Frazer, "Let's Go to a Cabaret," *Saturday Evening Post* 197 (July 19, 1924): 18–19; "New York's Crime Wave," *New Republic* 30 (April 19, 1922): 38; "New York, The Gunman's Paradise," *Literary Digest* 79 (December 1, 1923): 14–15; "New York Getting Its Gunmen,"

Literary Digest 79 (December 15, 1923): 10–11; "Chicago Stuff in New York," *Literary Digest* 98 (July 21, 1928): 10; and "Is New York a Modern Gomorrah?" *Literary Digest* 87 (November 7, 1925): 32. See also anti-immigration articles cited in previous chapter.

5. George M. Cohan, "The Flavor of the Cities: New York," *American Magazine* 84 (November 1917): 37. Known for his populist patriotism, Cohan (1878–1942) began his career in vaudeville and wrote such famous songs as "Give My Regards to Broadway" and "I'm a Yankee Doodle Dandy."

6. FPA [Franklin P. Adams], "It's a Fine Place to Visit, Yes—But I'd Hate To Live There," *Everybody's Magazine* 3 (December 1916): 181–189. The late 1910s and 1920s was the great era of newspaper and magazine columnists in the city. Probably the most famous and best paid in New York at the time was Franklin P. Adams, whose *New York Tribune* column, "The Conning Tower," ran for almost thirty years. The famous Algonquin Round Table group of writers and other literati began as a lunch date between Adams and two other well-known journalists, Heywood Broun and Alexander Woollcott. FPA remained its unofficial leader until its eventual demise in the early 1930s.

7. Harold Phillips, *Visiting New York City* (New York: Harold Phillips, 1920), 10.

8. Grover Whalen, *Mr. New York: The Autobiography of Grover Whalen* (New York: G. P. Putnam's Sons, 1955), 297–299.

9. Ibid., 25–33. For other accounts of Tammany's choice of Hylan and of the Hylan election and administration, see W. A. Swanberg, *Citizen Hearst* (New York: Charles Scribner's Sons, 1961). For the perhaps predictably unflattering portraits of Hylan, see Gene Fowler, *Beau James: The Life and Times of Jimmy Walker* (New York: Viking Press, 1949) and George Walsh, *Gentleman Jimmy Walker: Mayor of the Jazz Age* (New York: Praeger Publishers, 1974). More research may help clarify why the Wanamakers supported Whalen's public involvement in city politics yet opposed Preston Lynn's political ambitions.

10. Leach, *Land of Desire*, 361.

11. Wroe Alderson, "Advertising for Community Promotion," *Domestic Commerce* no. 21, Bureau of Foreign and Domestic Commerce, Department of Commerce (Washington, DC: U.S. Government Printing Office, 1928), 8.

12. Don E. Mowry, *Community Advertising: How to Advertise the Community Where You Live* (Madison, WI: Cantwell Press, 1924), 29.

13. Ibid., 1–7. See also William Ganson Rose, *Putting Marshville on the Map* (New York: Duffield and Company, 1912), a brief but rich fictional account of community advertising and boosting. Scholarly attention to the history of community advertising has been growing in recent years. See, for example, Stephen V. Ward, *Selling Places: The Marketing and Promotion of Towns and Cities, 1850–2000* (London: E. and F. N. Spon, 1998); C. Rutheiser,

Imagineering Atlanta (London: Verso, 1996); J. C. Cobb, *The Selling of the South: The Southern Crusade for Industrial Development* (Urbana: University of Illinois Press, 1993); John R. Gold and Stephen V. Ward, eds., *Place Promotion: The Use of Publicity and Marketing to Sell Towns and Regions* (Chichester, U.K.: Wiley, 1994); John R. Gold and Margaret M. Gold, *Imagining Scotland: Tradition, Representation, and Promotion in Scottish Tourism since 1750* (Aldershot, U.K.: Scolar Press, 1995); and Gerry Kearns and Chris Philo, eds., *Selling Places: The City as Cultural Capital, Past and Present* (Oxford: Pergamon Press, 1993). On the history of outdoor advertising, see Catherine M. Gudis, *Buyways: Automobility, Billboards, and the American Cultural Landscape* (New York: Routledge, 2004).

14. Merchants' Association of New York, "Fourteenth Annual Report of the President For the Year 1911," *Yearbook* (New York: Merchants' Association of New York, 1912).

15. See Merchants' Association annual reports, 1920–1930. Throughout this period Whalen maintained his position as vice chairman of the Mayor's Committee for the Reception of Distinguished Guests, continuing to organize the vast citywide celebrations welcoming such celebrities as Britain's Prince of Wales, cross-channel swimmer Gertrude Ederle, and pioneer transatlantic aviator Charles Lindbergh.

16. "Report of the Publicity Bureau" and "Report of the Convention Bureau," in MANY, *Yearbook* (New York: MANY, 1914): 30–33, 49–52.

17. "Twenty-First Annual Report of the President," "Report of the Publicity Bureau" and "Report of the Convention Bureau," in MANY, *Yearbook* (New York: MANY, 1918): 14, 38–41, 79–82.

18. "Report of the Convention Bureau," MANY, *Yearbook* (New York: MANY, 1930): 85.

19. See, for example, the listing of hotels and their addresses in *Rand McNally Guide to New York City and Environs* (New York: Rand McNally and Company, 1922), 47. On details of hotel facilities, see *Rider's Guide to New York City* (New York: Henry Holt and Company, 1923).

20. Robert H. Fuller, manager of the Publicity Bureau, proudly reported the involvement of the bureau on behalf of the Merchants' Association in opposing the longshoreman's strike of 1920. The association helped form the Citizens' Transportation Committee, a strikebreaking organization. "It was important," Fuller wrote, "that the public should have the right point of view with regard to the issues involved, and that its sympathy should be with the business men of the City rather than with the strikers. This object was successfully attained." "Report of the Publicity Bureau," MANY, *Yearbook* (New York: MANY, 1921), 22.

21. Typed manuscript, dated February 1921. From New York City Municipal Archives, Hylan Papers, Subject Files, 1919–1926, Box 174, Folder: Celebrations, Silver Jubilee; Exhibition Plan of the City Dept.

22. Brooks McNamara, *Day of Jubilee: The Great Age of Public Celebrations in New York, 1788–1909* (New Brunswick, NJ: Rutgers University Press, 1997); see also Leach, *Land of Desire,* 175–176, for a discussion of other boosting events on a smaller scale involving business-city government alliances in New York and St. Louis. On the uses of history and memory in America culture, see Michael Kammen, *Mystic Chords of Memory: The Transformation of Tradition in American Culture* (New York: Vintage Books, 1993) and Edward T. Linenthal, *Sacred Ground: Americans and Their Battlefields* (Urbana: University of Illinois Press, 1994).

23. For accounts of the MANY Silver Jubilee, including extracts of speeches made at the event by political and business leaders, see MANY, *Greater New York* 11, nos. 40, 41, and 42 (November 6, 13, and 20, 1922). President Harding was invited but was unable to attend due to Mrs. Harding's ill health. Speakers included Julius H. Barnes, president of the United States Chamber of Commerce; General John Pershing; and Governor-Elect Alfred Smith.

24. Minutes, Meeting of Advisory Committee, Mayor's Committee on Twenty-Fifth Anniversary of Greater New York, City Hall, Thursday, April 6, 1923, 4. From New York City Municipal Archives, Hylan Papers, Subject Files, 1919–1926; Box 174, Folder: Celebrations, Silver Jubilee, Part I, 1923. On the relationship between Hearst and Hylan, see Swanberg, *Citizen Hearst,* esp. chs. 10–13.

25. Ibid.

26. Ibid., 11.

27. Untitled typed manuscript, 4–5. From New York City Municipal Archives, Hylan Papers, Subject Files, 1919–1926; Box 174, Folder: Celebrations, Silver Jubilee, Part I, 1923.

28. "The First Official Announcement of New York's Silver Jubilee, April 27, 1923," printed pamphlet, Hylan Papers, Subject Files, 1919–1926; Box 174, Folder: Celebrations, Silver Jubilee, Part I, 1923.

29. Press clippings, Hylan Papers, Subject Files, 1919–1926; Box 174, Folder: Celebrations, Silver Jubilee, Part I, 1923. The clippings are filed without attribution and without dates, except for the last story mentioned, entitled "To Show This City as It Is," hand-dated, "April 7, 1923."

30. *World,* May 26, 1923, 1, 3; *World,* May 27, 1923, 1, 3; *New York Times,* May 26, 1923, 8; May 27, 1923, 1–2; May 29, 1923, 1–2. On the jubilee and the exposition, see also "New York to Celebrate Its Twenty-Fifth Anniversary," *American City* 28 (March 1923): 138 and John F. Hylan, "New York's Silver Jubilee Exposition," *American City* 29 (July 1923): 3–7.

31. Mayor's Committee on Celebration of the Twenty-Fifth Anniversary of the Greater City of New York, *Official Book of the Exposition. Silver Jubilee of Greater New York* (New York: Mayor's Committee on Celebration of the

Twenty-Fifth Anniversary of the Greater City of New York, 1923), 42. The authors of the book were perhaps referring to another famous jeweled fountain, the "Tower of Jewels" displayed at the 1915 Pan Pacific International Exposition in San Francisco.

32. Robert W. De Forest, *Art in Merchandise: Notes on the Relationships of Stores and Museums* (New York: Metropolitan Museum of Art, 1928). See Leach, *Land of Desire* and Evart G. Routzahn and Mary Swain Routzahn, *The ABC of Exhibit Planning* (New York: Russell Sage Foundation, 1918).

33. See William R. Taylor, ed., *Inventing Times Square: Commerce and Culture at the Crossroads of the World* (New York: Russell Sage Foundation, 1991).

34. Elizabeth Blackmar, "Uptown Real Estate and the Creation of Times Square," in *Inventing Times Square,* ed. Taylor, 51–65. For the classic theoretical discussion of the production of space and its commodification, see Henri Lefebvre, *The Production of Space,* trans. Donald Nicholson-Smith (Oxford: Blackwell, 1991). Other scholars have drawn on Lefebvre's work to inform their own studies of the spatial and economic development of cities. For example, see David Harvey, *Consciousness and the Urban Experience: Studies in the History and Theory of Capitalist Urbanization* (Baltimore: Johns Hopkins University Press, 1985); M. Christine Boyer, *The City of Collective Memory* (Cambridge, MA: MIT Press, 1996); Edward Soja, *Postmodern Geographies: The Reassertion of Space in Critical Social Theory* (London: Verso, 1990); and Sharon Zukin, *Landscapes of Power: From Detroit to Disney World* (Berkeley: University of California Press, 1991); and *The Cultures of Cities* (Oxford: Blackwell, 1995).

35. Van Wyck Brooks, "On Creating a Usable Past," *Dial* 64 (April 11, 1918): 337–341; Kammen, *Mystic Chords of Memory,* 281. For comparative work on Britain, see Eric Hobsbawm and Terence Ranger, eds., *The Invention of Tradition* (New York: Cambridge University Press, 1983).

36. Henry Collins Brown, *Fifth Avenue Old and New, 1824–1924* (New York: Fifth Avenue Association/Wynkoop Hallenbeck Crawford Co., 1924).

37. W. J. Pedrick, "Freeing the Streets from Protruding and Unsightly Signs," *American City* 32 (January 1925): 73–74 and "Story of Fifth Avenue," *Magazine of Business* 53 (February 1928): 153–155.

38. John H. Towne and Robert Grier Cooke, foreword to Brown, *Fifth Avenue Old and New,* 14. The campaign to remove pushcart vendors from Fifth Avenue and other "mainstream" shopping streets is discussed by Daniel Bluestone in his article "The Push Cart Evil," in *The Landscape of Modernity: New York City, 1900–1940,* ed. David Ward and Olivier Zunz (New York: Russell Sage Foundation, 1992). Traffic congestion in Manhattan was one of the key urban planning issues of the 1920s, as it was a problem that profoundly affected the everyday lives of New Yorkers. See John Day, "Experiences of a

Traffic Cop," *American Magazine* 94 (December 1922): 38–40; "New York's Traffic Towers," *American City* 26 (January 1922): 71; "Street Widenings an Important Factor, but Afford Feeble Traffic Relief," *American City* 38 (January 1928): 92; "Congested Traffic," *New Republic* 57 (November 28, 1928): 29–31; and Patrick D. Hoyt, "New Traffic Regulations Effective January 1, 1927, in New York City," *American City* 36 (January 1927): 101–109.

39. Adding to the familiar power of this perspective on the city was the likely awareness on the part of the viewer in 1924 of the innovative technology involved in making such a photograph. Aerial photography was developed during World War I. The fledgling flying corps of the United States and Great Britain employed the new technology to provide photographic surveillance and mapping information to commanders in the field. Soon after the war, the Long Island–based Fairchild Aerial Camera Corporation, the leader in aerial photography, published its *Aerial Survey of Manhattan* (1921), providing the first extensive use of the technology to depict the city. Over the next decade, aerial photography, in peacetime as in war, provided the basis for many new maps of New York and other cities. See L. J. Wilson, "Mapping New York City from the Air," *Illustrated World* 36 (February 1922): 839–840 and S. M. Fairchild, "Aerial Mapping of New York City," *American City* 30 (January 1924): 74–75.

40. Brown, *Fifth Avenue Old and New*, 101.

41. Ibid., 102.

42. Ibid., 104.

43. Ibid., 116.

44. Ibid., 124.

45. On the tercentenary, see also "New York City's Tercentenary," *Outlook* 136 (April 23, 1924): 675 and "Tercentenary Educational Celebration," *School and Society* 19 (April 12, 1924): 27–28.

46. Broadway Association, *Broadway, Grand Canyon of American Business* (New York: Broadway Association, 1926). Numerous articles in the periodical press during the 1920s referred to the debate over the relative morality of Broadway theatrical productions and the new efforts to censor such shows. See, for example, "Ash-barrel Talk Fills the Theaters," *Current Opinion* 78 (February 1925): 201–202; "Another stage purification campaign," *Literary Digest* 84 (March 7, 1925): 26–27; B. H. Clark, "Broadway Censorship and a Couple of New Plays," *Drama* 17 (March 1927): 171; "Censorship as Self-Control," *New Republic* 50 (February 23, 1927): 5–7; F. F. Van der Water, "Obscene Drama," *Ladies' Home Journal* 44 (April 1927): 8; and R. D. Skinner, "Drama, Tabloid and Otherwise," *Independent* 118 (April 23, 1927): 445.

47. Ibid., 7.

48. Susan Smulyan, *Selling Radio: The Commercialization of American Broadcasting, 1920–1934* (Washington, DC: Smithsonian Institution Press,

1996). For the next phase of radio and advertising, see William L. Bird, *"Better Living": Advertising, Media, and the New Vocabulary of Business Leadership, 1935–1955* (Chicago: Northwestern University Press, 1999) and Barbara Dianne Savage, *Broadcasting Freedom: Radio, War, and the Politics of Race, 1938–1948* (Chapel Hill: University of North Carolina Press, 1999).

49. William Barlow, *Voice Over: The Making of Black Radio* (Philadelphia: Temple University Press, 1999), 23–24.

50. See chapter 2 for the 1890s use of this descriptive language.

51. "How New York's Street Plan Came to Be Rectangular and Its Downtown Parks So Small," *American City* 29 (September 1923): 248 and "Economics of the Great White Way," *Literary Digest* 86 (September 12, 1925): 23.

52. On the spatial evolution of the Times Square/Midtown area, see Betsy Blackmar, "Uptown Real Estate and the Creation of Times Square," in *Inventing Times Square,* ed. Taylor. To compare the use of public space by consuming and nonconsuming strollers in New York, Paris, and London, see Vanessa R. Schwartz, *Spectacular Realities: Early Mass Culture in Fin-de-siècle Paris* (Berkeley: University of California Press, 1998); Erika Rappoport, "'A New Era of Shopping': The Promotion of Women's Pleasure in London's West End, 1909–1914," in *Cinema and the Invention of Modern Life,* ed. Leo Charney and Vanessa Schwartz (Berkeley: University of California Press, 1995); and Rachel Bowlby, *Just Looking: Consumer Culture in Dreiser, Gissing, and Zola* (New York and London: Methuen, 1985).

53. Martin Clary, *Mid-Manhattan, the Multimillionarea* (New York: Forty-Second Street Property Owners and Merchants Association, Inc., 1929).

54. Arthur Williams in foreword to ibid.

55. See "Where is the World Metropolis?" *Review of Reviews* 60 (September 1919): 317–318; William Joseph Showalter, "New York: The Metropolis of Mankind," *National Geographic* 34 (July 1918): 1–49; Rollin Lynde Hartt, "New York, the National Stepmother," *Century* 93 (January 1917): 351–363; and Charles Beard, "New York, The Metropolis of To-Day," *Review of Reviews* 69 (June 1924): 608–624.

CONCLUSION

1. Recent scholarly interpretations of the effect of "9/11" on New York's people, architecture, and urban culture can be found in Michael Sorkin and Sharon Zukin, eds., *After the World Trade Center: Rethinking New York City* (Routledge, 2002). For equally useful journalistic responses, see the entire issue of the *New York Times Magazine,* November 11, 2001. For urban vignettes by a range of New Yorkers, known and unknown, on New York City before and after September 11, 2001, see Thomas Beller, *Before and After Stories from New York* (New York: W. W. Norton, 2002).

ESSAY ON PRIMARY SOURCES

Writing about New York can be a daunting task. Luckily, as a young graduate student, I did not quite understand that truth and so approached my research more with excitement than with the dread of the better informed. As an interdisciplinary cultural historian, my research took me to a vast number and array of sources, some of which never made it into the final text but all of which informed the writing. I offer this essay, then, as a guide to fellow future historians of New York and of urban cultural history. For selected references to the secondary literature, see my notes to the introduction and chapters.

Cultural historians ask questions about *meaning*, not just about when, where, and how. If you want to examine the meaning of cultural change over time, then you must consult sources that offer a range of representations and interpretations. When I began my research, my broad goal was to examine changing representations of New York City in the early twentieth century; in particular I wanted to know how and why the meanings of Manhattan for the broad middle class of Americans (both New Yorkers and non–New Yorkers) changed over time. So I went in search of archival sources that would indicate changing public discourses about the city at the local and national levels—a shifting textual and visual narrative about New York.

Map collections offer some of the richest sources for city history and for the representation of place. I spent the first three months of my archival research in the Map Division of the New York Public Library. Guided by Curator Alice Hudson and her staff, I pieced together the basic narrative of my project by examining, in chronological order, almost every map listed under the New York City entries in the division's printed catalogue up through the 1930s. From nineteenth-century bird's eye views to transit maps to cartoon maps for tourists, from thematic maps of disease and alcohol consumption to maps of the New York World's Fair of 1939–40, these cartographic representations suggested the conflicting meanings and public images of New York produced for various audiences over half a century. At a slightly more mundane level, they also familiarized me with the city and region's geography and the locations of the city's major institutions and landmarks.

Primary sources related to tourism are more plentiful than one might imagine. A potentially rich and varied source is the postcard. Postcards show the images selected by card publishers to represent a place at a particular time, particularly how the representation of that place (for example, Times Square) did or did not change over time. Postcards that have been sent through the mails allow the historian to indulge in the otherwise frowned-upon pleasure of reading other people's mail. By looking at the addresses on the cards, the postmark, and the message written on the card, we can learn where and when the cards were sent and, most tellingly, what visitors thought worthwhile to tell the folks back home about the place they were visiting. Postcards can thus sometimes offer material as rich as letters or diaries. The Smithsonian's National Museum of American History has a postcard collection contained within the Warshaw Collection of Business Americana in addition to the large Victor A. Blenkle Postcard Collection. Other institutions with postcard collections include the Museum of the City of New York, the National Building Museum, and the New-York Historical Society, whose postcard collection is housed in the Division of Prints and Photographs.

Stereographs, a popular pre-cinematic form of home visual entertainment, offer some of the same research value as postcards. Stereographs were often sold in sets or series by door-to-door salesmen or through printed advertisements. Stereographs tell the historian which places, people, or predicaments their publishers and consumers found educational, entertaining, or amusing. For an historian of tourism and travel, they are excellent sources for examining such issues as the rising popularity of images of the American West and other national landscapes. The dated catalogues of stereograph companies similarly offer stories of the relative importance of domestic over international travel images or the rise and fall of "risqué" images of women or of humorous images of domestic life. Major stereograph collections can be found at the Smithsonian in the National Museum of American History's Archives Center's Underwood and Underwood Glass Stereograph Collection and in the collection housed in the NMAH's Division of Photographic History. Another stereograph collection useful to the historian of New York can be found at the New-York Historical Society's Division of Prints and Photographs.

Guidebooks offer the urban historian a textually and often visually rich set of sources. The dates that the first guidebooks to a city were published suggest the beginnings of business and pleasure travel to that place and thus contribute to the history of consumer culture and business; like city directories, one can use guidebooks to trace the location and numbers of types of businesses, such as hotels and restaurants; the images in guidebooks provide a visual account of the place and also indicate what impression the publisher sought to convey by emphasizing, for example, grand buildings over street scenes. For the historian of tourism, guidebooks represent a vital source for questions about changing itineraries and representations of places, their key sites and inhabitants. Guidebooks from the late nineteenth and early twentieth centuries are in wide circulation in secondhand bookstores in North America at varying prices and in varying conditions. They are commonly found in university libraries housed alongside secondary source volumes. City and regional museums and historical societies have routinely collected guidebooks along with other descriptive literature about their subject area. For example, the New-York Historical Society has a modest New York City Guidebook Collection. Since guidebooks are often classified as ephemera, they may be incorporated within larger general place-oriented collections, so researchers should not presume to find guidebook collections per se but should instead cast their nets widely over each library's general holdings as well as archival collections.

For many historians of New York, the Municipal Archives are their major archival source. For this particular project, since I was pursuing the more nefarious issue of the city's public image and its changing meanings, I came to the Municipal Archives in the later stages of my research to find information about the Hylan Administration in the early 1920s. The Archives houses the papers of the city's mayors as well as its major departments, agencies, and committees. It is therefore best approached with specific research questions rather than initial general questions about New York City's history. One can also consult the institution's library to find newspaper clippings, photographs, and other ephemera about particular events, such as the Greater New York Silver Jubilee.

Lastly, the beginning historian of New York should not assume that New York–based archives and libraries are the only starting point. Given the varied collections housed at the Smithsonian Institution's museums as described above and the location of the Library of Congress, Washington, D.C., could well be the place to start. Particularly if you have questions concerning the place of New York in the national imagination or some other national or international context, the collections of the Library of Congress are invaluable and sometimes more easily accessible than duplicate collections in the New York libraries. The Library of Congress's collections of periodicals and newspapers, as well as its vast general book stacks and reference resources, are unsurpassed and offer the cultural and social historian possibly their major primary source archive.

Listing of Books and Articles

Adams, Dr. I. Howe. "Photography; or The Munchausen of the Arts." *Outing* 16, no. 6 (September 1890): 476–480.

Addams, Jane. *Hull House Maps and Papers.* New York and Boston: T. Y. Crowell and Company, 1895.

Ade, George. "Oh, Yes! We Will Visit New York—But We'll Pin a Return Ticket Inside Our Vest." *American Magazine* 91, no. 3 (March 1921): 14–15.

Alderson, Wroe. "Advertising for Community Promotion." *Domestic Commerce* no. 21. Bureau of Foreign and Domestic Commerce. Department of Commerce. Washington, DC: U.S. Government Printing Office, 1928.

"Alien Antidumping Bill," *Literary Digest* 69 (May 7, 1921): 12–13.

"Alleyne Ireland Favors Microscope Upon Voters/He Tells Cult's Congress Politics Is So Bad It Should Be Scientifically Investigated." *The World,* September 27, 1921, 7.

"America and the Man." *The Sun,* September 27, 1921, 16.

"Another Stage Purification Campaign." *Literary Digest* 84 (March 7, 1925): 26–27.

Asbury, Herbert. "Days of Wickedness." *American Mercury* 12 (November 1927): 359–369.

"Ash-barrel Talk Fills the Theaters." *Current Opinion* 78 (February 1925): 201–202.

Bailey, Vernon Howe. *Magical City: Intimate Sketches of New York.* New York: Scribners, 1935.

Beard, Charles. "New York, The Metropolis of To-Day." *Review of Reviews* 69 (June 1924): 608–624.

———. *Skyscrapers of New York.* New York: W. E. Rudge, 1928

Beebe, Lucius. *The Ritz Idea: The Story of a Great Hotel.* New York: privately printed, 1936.

Bercovici, Konrad. *Around the World in New York.* New York: The Century Company, 1924.

———. *Crimes of Charity.* New York: Alfred A. Knopf, 1917.

Betts, Lillian W. "The Tenement-House Exhibit." *Outlook* 64 (March 1900): 589–592.

Blackshaw, Randall. "The New New York." *Century Illustrated Monthly Magazine* 64, no. 4 (August 1902): 492–513.

Boas, Franz. "Fallacies of Racial Inferiority." *Current History* 25 (February 1927): 676–682.

———. *The Mind of Primitive Man.* New York: The Macmillan Company, 1911.

———. "Question of Racial Purity." *American Mercury* 3 (October 1924): 163–169.

———. "This Nordic Nonsense." *Forum* 74 (October 1925): 502–511.

"Bolshevism in New York and Russian Schools." *Literary Digest* 62, no. 1 (July 5, 1919): 40–41.

Booth, Charles. *Life and Labour of the People in London.* 17 volumes. London: Williams and Northgate, 1889–1903.

Broadway Association. *Broadway, Grand Canyon of American Business.* New York: Broadway Association, 1926.

Brooks, Van Wyck. "On Creating a Usable Past." *Dial* 64 (April 11, 1918): 337–341.

Brown, Henry Collins. *Fifth Avenue Old and New, 1824–1924* (New York: Fifth Avenue Association/Wynkoop Hallenbeck Crawford Co., 1924.

Butler, Nicholas M. "Our Bolshevik Menace." *Forum* 63 (January 1920): 49–56.

Byington, Margaret. "Fifty Annual Reports." *Survey* 23, no. 26 (March 26, 1910): 970–977.

Callender, James H. *Yesterdays in Little Old New York.* New York: Dorland Press, 1929.

"Censorship as Self-Control." *New Republic* 50 (February 23, 1927): 5–7.

"Chicago Stuff in New York." *Literary Digest* 98 (July 21, 1928): 10.

"City of Towers." *Scientific American* 93 (July 1, 1905): 4.

Clark, B. H. "Broadway Censorship and a Couple of New Plays." *Drama* 17 (March 1927): 171.

Clary, Martin. *Mid-Manhattan, the Multimillionarea.* New York: Forty-Second Street Property Owners and Merchants Association, Inc., 1929.

Cobb, Irvin S. *"Who's Who" plus "Here's How!"* New York: Hotel Waldorf-Astoria Corporation, 1934.

Cohan, George M. "The Flavor of the Cities: New York." *American Magazine* 84 (November 1917): 37.

"Confessions of a Westerner and What He Sees in New York." *Independent* 91, no. 3589 (September 15, 1917): 424.

"Congested Traffic." *New Republic* 57 (November 28, 1928): 29–31.

Conklin, Edwin G. "Some Biological Aspects of Immigration." *Scribner's Magazine* 69 (March 1921): 352–359.

Coolidge, Calvin. "Whose Country Is This?" *Good Housekeeping* 72 (February 1921): 13–14.

Corbin, John. "The Twentieth Century City." *Scribner's Magazine* 33, no. 3 (March 1903): 259–272.

Corsi, Edward. "My Neighborhood." *Outlook* 141 (September 16, 1925): 90–92.

Creel, George. "Melting Pot or Dumping Ground?" *Collier's* 68 (September 3, 1921): 9–10.

Crowell, Chester T. "'Welcome, Stranger!' Said Little Old New York." *Independent* 102 (April 24, 1940): 121–122.

Curran, Henry H. "Fewer and Better, Or None." *Saturday Evening Post* 196 (April 26, 1924): 8–9.

David, A. C. "The New Architecture: The First American Type of Real Value." *Architectural Record* 28, no. 6 (December 1910): 388–403.

Davison, George. "Impressionism in Photography." *Journal of the Society of the Arts* 39, no. 1987 (December 19, 1890): 65–74.

Day, John. "Experiences of a Traffic Cop." *American Magazine* 94 (December 1922): 38–40.

Dayton, Helena Smith, and Louise Bascom Barratt. *New York in Seven Days.* New York: Robert M. McBride and Company, 1925.

"Decries Beauty in Picking Mate." *The Sun,* September 27, 1921, 9.

De Forest, Robert W. *Art in Merchandise: Notes on the Relationships of Stores and Museums.* New York: Metropolitan Museum of Art, 1928.

De Forest, Robert W., and Lawrence Veiller. *The Tenement House Problem.* 2 vols. New York: The Macmillan Company, 1903.

De Leeuw, Rudolph M. *Both Sides of Broadway.* New York: The De Leeuw Riehl Publishing Company, 1910.

Dodge, Louis. "The Sidewalks of New York." *Scribner's Magazine* 70 (July–December 1921): 584–592.

Dreiser, Theodore. *The Color of a Great City.* New York: Boni and Liverwright, 1923.

"Economics of the Great White Way." *Literary Digest* 86 (September 12, 1925): 23.

Edgerton, Giles [Mary Fanton Roberts]. "How New York has Redeemed herself from Ugliness—An Artist's Revelation of the Beauty of the Skyscraper." *Craftsman* 11 (January 1907): 458–471.

"Ellis Island Sob Stuff," *Saturday Evening Post* 194 (November 26, 1921): 20.

Engels, Friedrich. *The Condition of the Working Class in England.* New York: Penguin Books, 1987. Originally published in 1845.

"Eugenist Denies Bars To Marriage Can Improve Race." *World,* September 27, 1921, 7.

"Eugenists Uphold Control of Birth." *New York Times,* September 27, 1921, 20.

"Eviction in the Tenement District of the City of New York." *Harper's Weekly* 34 (February 1, 1890): 83.

Fairchild, S. M. "Aerial Mapping of New York City." *American City* 30 (January 1924): 74–75.

Fitzpatrick, F. W. "Building Against Fire." *Outlook* 88 (April 25, 1908): 936–945.

"For Systematic Charity." *New York Times,* December 10, 1897, 5.

Ford, Ford Madox. *New York Is Not America.* New York: Albert and Charles Boni, 1927.

Foster, George. *New York by Gas-Light.* New York: W. F. Burgess, 1850.

———. *New York in Slices: By an Experienced Carver.* New York: W. F. Burgess, 1849.

Foster and Reynolds Company. *New York: The Metropolis of the Western World.* New York: Foster and Reynolds, 1902.

FPA [Adams, Franklin P.]. "It's a Fine Place to Visit, Yes—But I'd Hate To Live There." *Everybody's Magazine* 3 (December 1916): 181–189.

Frazer, Elizabeth. "Chicago Stuff in New York," *Literary Digest* 98 (July 21, 1928): 10.

———. "Let's Go To A Cabaret." *Saturday Evening Post* 197 (July 19, 1924): 18–19.

———. "Our Foreign Cities: New York." *Saturday Evening Post* 195 (June 16, 1923): 6–7.

Frederick, J. George. *Adventuring in New York. With Ten Etchings.* New York: N. L. Brown, 1923.

Freitag, J. K. "Fire Prevention in High Buildings." *Engineering Magazine* 34 (February 1908): 735–740.

Fuller, Henry Blake. *The Cliff-Dwellers: A Novel.* Ridgewood, NJ: The Gregg Press, 1968. Originally published by Harper Brothers, 1893.

The Gate to the Sea. Brooklyn, NY: Eagle Press, c. 1897.

Giddings, Franklin M. "Bolsheviki Must Go." *Independent* 97 (January 18, 1919): 88.

Godey's Illustrated Souvenir Guide to Chicago, World's Fair and New York. Chicago: E. Lockwood and Co., 1893.

Godkin, E. L. "A Key to Municipal Reform." *North American Review* 151, no. 4 (October 1890): 422–431.

Gould, E. R. L. "The Housing Problem." *Municipal Affairs* 3, no.1 (March 1899): 108–131.

Grant, Madison. *The Conquest of a Continent; or, The Expansion of Races in America.* New York: Scribners, 1933.

———. *The Passing of the Great Race.* 4th edition. New York: Scribners, 1921.

Grant, Madison, and Charles Stewart Davison. *The Alien in Our Midst; or, "Selling Our Birthright for a Mess of Pottage."* New York: The Galton Publishing Company, Inc., 1930.

"Greenwich Village Virus." *Saturday Evening Post* 194 (October 15, 1921): 14–15.

The Guest's Handy Book and Guide to Points of Interest in New York City. New York: Hotel Publishing and Advertising Company, 1886.

The Guide of Guides. New York: Davis and Hopp Bros., 1896.

Guilder, Joseph B. "The City of Dreadful Height." *Putnam's Monthly* 5, no. 2 (November 1908): 131–143.

Gunnison, Herbert Foster. *A Visitor's Guide to the Greater New York.* Brooklyn, NY: Eagle Press, 1896.

Gurney, V. "Auto-burro Honeymoon." *Sunset* 43 (July 1919): 40–42.

Hamilton, Mary Agnes. "Red-Haired City." *Atlantic Monthly* 139 (April 1927): 491–497.

Hapgood, Hutchins. "Picturesque Ghetto." *Century Magazine* 94 (July 1917): 469–473.

———. *The Spirit of the Ghetto.* New York: Funk and Wagnalls, 1902.

Harriman, Mrs. J. B. "Hither and Yon." *Century* 106 (September 1923): 651–663.

———. "Hither and Yon." *Century* 106 (October 1923): 873–886.

Harris, Charles Townsend. *Memories of Manhattan in the Sixties and Seventies.* New York: The Derrydale Press, 1928.

Hartt, Rollin Lynde. "I'd Like to Show You Harlem!" *Independent* 105 (April 2, 1921): 334–335.

———. "Made in Italy." *Independent* 106 (July 23, 1921): 19–20.

———. "More Irish Than Ireland." *Independent* 106 (August 20, 1921): 68–69.

———. "New York and the Real Jew." *Independent* 105 (June 25, 1921): 658–660.

———. "New York, the National Stepmother." *Century* 93 (January 1917): 351–363.

Haupt, Lewis M. "On the Graphical Presentation of Statistics." *Journal of the Franklin Institute* 148 (1899): 384–390.

Hays, Willet M. "Immigration and Eugenics." *Review of Reviews* 69 (April 1924): 405–406.

Hill, Robert T. "The Wonders of the American Desert." *World's Work* 3 (March 1902): 1818–1832.

"How New York's Street Plan Came to Be Rectangular and Its Down-town Parks So Small." *American City* 29 (September 1923): 248.

"How the Russian Bolshevik Agent Docs Business in New York City." *Literary Digest* 61 (May 17, 1919): 60–63.

"How To Get There" in New York. New York: Hall Publishing Company, 1897.

How to Know New York. Boston: Rand Avery Company, 1887.

Howells, William Dean. *A Hazard of New Fortunes.* New York: Harper and Brothers, 1890.

Hoyt, Patrick D. "New Traffic Regulations Effective January 1, 1927, in New York City." *American City* 36 (January 1927): 101–109.

Hudnut, James M. *New-York Almanac for 1880.* New York: Francis Hart and Company, 1880.

Hurston, Zora Neale. *Mules and Men.* Philadelphia: J. B. Lippincott Company, 1935.

Hylan, John F. "New York's Silver Jubilee Exposition." *American City* 29 (July 1923): 3–7.

"Immigration Must Soon Cease from Some Countries." *World,* September 25, 1921, 24.

Ingersoll, Ernest. *A Week in New York.* New York: Rand, McNally and Co., 1892.

Inkersly, Arthur. "The Grand Canyon of Arizona." *Overland Monthly* 41 (June 1903): 423–432.

Irwin, Will. *Highlights of Manhattan.* New York: The Century Company, 1927.

"Is Bolshevism in America Becoming a Real Peril?" *Current Opinion* 67 (July 1919): 4–6.

"Is New York American?" *Saturday Review of Literature* 2 (January 2, 1926): 457.

"Is New York a Modern Gomorrah?" *Literary Digest* 87 (November 7, 1925): 32.

"Is the Camera the Friend or Foe of Art?" *Studio* 1, no. 1 (April 1893): 96–102.

James, Rian. *All About New York: An Intimate Guide.* New York: The John Day Company, 1931.

Jelf, E. A. "Photography as Evidence." *Idler* 4 (December 1893): 519–525.

Jenkins, Stephen. *The Greatest Street in the World: The Story of Broadway, Old and New, from Bowling Green to Albany.* New York: Putnam, 1911.

Jessup, Elon H. "Flight of the Tin Can Tourists." *Outlook* 128 (May 25, 1921): 166–169.

Johnston, Alexander. "America: Touring Ground of the World." *Country Life* 37 (January 1920): 25–34.

Josephy, Helen, and Mary Margaret McBride. *New York is Everybody's Town.* New York: G. P. Putnam's Sons, 1931.

Keppel, Frederick. *Mr. Pennell's Etchings of New York "Sky Scrapers."* New York: Frederick Keppel and Co., 1905.

King, Moses. *King's Handbook of New York City.* Boston: Moses King, 1893.

———. *King's Photographic Views of New York.* Boston: Moses King, 1895.

———. *New York: The Metropolis of the American Continent.* Boston: Moses King, 1893.

Kobbe, Gustav. *New York and Its Environs.* New York: Harper and Brothers, 1891.

"Ku Klux Klan Used Army and Navy Club Address to Peddle Memberships in Campaign by Mail; The World Reproduces 'Grand Goblin' Documents." *World,* September 8, 1921, 1.

"Language of the Tenement Folk." *Harper's Weekly* 41, no. 2092 (January 23, 1897): 90.

Lansing, Elizabeth Hubbard. *Seeing New York.* New York: Thomas Y. Crowell Company, 1938.

Laughlin, Clara Laughlin. *So You're Visiting New York City!* Boston: Houghton Mifflin, 1939.

Laut, Agnes. "Why Go Abroad?" *Sunset Magazine* 29 (June 1912): 667–671.

Le Clercq, Jacques. "Why I Live in America." *American Mercury* 6 (September 1925): 25–31.

Lewis, Sinclair. *Babbitt.* New York: Harcourt, Brace and Company, 1922.

"Life among the Tenements." *Harper's Weekly* 31, no. 1596 (July 23, 1887): 529.

Lockwood, Sarah M. *New York: Not So Little and Not So Old.* Garden City, NY: Doubleday, Page and Company, 1926.

Loti, Pierre. "Impressions of New York." *Century* 85, no. 4 (February 1913): 609–613.

———. "Impressions of New York." *Century* 85, no. 5 (March 1913): 758–762.

"Lure of Greenwich Village." *Literary Digest* 65 (May 8, 1920): 46–47.

Lusk, Clayton R. "Hatching Revolution in America." *Current Opinion* 71 (September 1921): 290–294.

———. "Radicalism Under Inquiry." *Review of Reviews* 61 (February 1920): 167–171.

Macoy, Robert. *History of and How to See New York and Its Environs.* New York: Robert Macoy, 1876.

Mann, Helen M. "May Day Motorists." *Overland* 75 (May 1920): 419–424.

Mayhew, Henry. *London Labor and the London Poor.* New York: Penguin Books, 1985. Originally published in 1862.

"Mayor and the Tenements." *Harper's Weekly* 25, no. 1295 (October 15, 1881): 699.

Mayor's Committee on Celebration of the Twenty-Fifth Anniversary of the Greater City of New York. *Official Book of the Exposition. Silver Jubilee of Greater New York.* New York: Mayor's Committee on Celebration of the Twenty-Fifth Anniversary of the Greater City of New York, 1923.

McAdoo, Eva. *How Do You Like New York? An Informal Guide.* New York: The Macmillan Company, 1936.

McCabe, James D. *Lights and Shadows of New York Life.* Philadelphia: National Publishing Company, 1872.

———. *New York by Sunlight and Gaslight.* Philadelphia: Douglass Brothers, 1882.

Mead, Margaret. *Coming of Age in Samoa.* New York: William Morrow, 1928.

"Melting Pot Has Proved Failure in America as Vices of Mingled Races Are Perpetuated." *World,* September 23, 1921, 3.

Merchants' Association of New York. *Yearbook.* New York: Merchants' Association of New York, 1900–1930.

Middleton, James. "New York the Stupendous." *World's Work* 31 (March 1916): 538–554.

Middleton, Scudder. *Dining, Wining, and Dancing in New York.* New York: Dodge Publishing Company, 1938.

"Midsummer Night among City Tenements." *Harper's Weekly* 27, no. 1384 (June 30, 1883): 410.

"Misrepresenting New York in Fiction." *Literary Digest* 72 (March 25, 1922): 26–27.

Mitchell, John Bruce. "'Reds' in New York Slums: How Insidious Doctrines are Propagated in New York's 'East Side.'" *Forum* 61 (April 1919): 442–455.

"Model Tenements." *Harper's Weekly* 32, no. 1621 (January 14, 1888): 31.

Monroe, Harriet. "Arizona." *Atlantic Monthly* 89 (June 1902): 780–789.

Mowry, Don E. *Community Advertising: How to Advertise the Community Where You Live.* Madison, Wisconsin: Cantwell Press, 1924.

"Nature Leader of Man in Mechanics." *World,* September 24, 1921, 9.

Nelsons' Guide to the City of New York and Its Neighbourhood. London: T. Nelson and Sons, 1858.

"New York City as the World's Prize 'Borough of Bunk.'" *Literary Digest* 70, no. 9 (August 27, 1921): 37–38.

"New York City's Tercentenary." *Outlook* 136 (April 23, 1924): 675.

New-York Compliments of Joseph Biechele Soap Company, Canton, Ohio. Canton, OH: Joseph Biechele Soap Company, c. 1884.

[New York] From Recent Photographs. New York: Rand, McNally and Company, 1895.

"New York Getting Its Gunmen," *Literary Digest* 79 (December 15, 1923): 10–11.

New York Illustrated. New York: D. Appleton and Co., 1869.

New York Information Agency. *Hints for Strangers, Shoppers and Sight Seers in the Metropolis.* New York: c. 1891. Uncorrected proof.

"New York's Big Foreign Population." *Literary Digest* 73 (April 29, 1922): 13.

"New York Scolded for Its Moral and Other Shortcomings." *Current Opinion* 68 (April 1920): 523–524.

"New York's Crime Wave." *New Republic* 30 (April 19, 1922): 38.

"New York's Traffic Towers." *American City* 26 (January 1922): 71.

"New York Tenements and Slums." *London Quarterly Review* 78, no. 155 (April 1892): 48–67.

"New York, The Gunman's Paradise." *Literary Digest* 79 (December 1, 1923): 14–15.

New York: The Metropolis of the American Continent. Boston: Moses King, 1893.

"New York to Celebrate Its Twenty-Fifth Anniversary." *American City* 28 (March 1923): 138.

"New York 'World.'" *Harper's Weekly* 134, no. 1726 (January 18, 1890): 43–44.

"Noted Scientists Here for Eugenics Conference." *Sun,* September 22, 1921, 2.

"The Old Bowery Wouldn't Know Itself Now." *Literary Digest* 65 (May 8, 1920): 70–75.

Osborn, Henry Fairfield. "The Approach to the Immigration Problem through Science." *Proceedings of the National Immigration Conference* 26 (1924): 44–53.

———. *Evolution and Religion.* New York: Scribners, 1923.

———. *Men of the Old Stone Age: Their Environment, Life, and Art.* New York: Scribners, 1915.

———. "Our Ancestors Arrive in Scandinavia." *Natural History* 22 (1922): 116–134.

Palmer, Gretta. *A Shopping Guide to New York.* New York: R. M. McBride and Company, 1930.

Peabody, Francis G. "The Modern Charity Worker." *Charities Review* 6, no. 1 (March 1897): 17–26.

Pedrick, W. J. "Freeing the Streets from Protruding and Unsightly Signs." *American City* 32 (January 1925): 73–74.

———. "Story of Fifth Avenue." *Magazine of Business* 53 (February 1928): 153–155.

Pennell, Joseph. *The Glory of New York.* New York: W. E. Rudge, 1926.

"Photography in Travel." *Around the World* 1, no.1 (December 1893): 7–9.

Pictorial New York and Brooklyn. New York: Smith, Bleakley and Co., 1892.

Pidgin, Charles F. "How to Make Statistics Popular." *Publications of the American Statistical Association* 2, nos. 11, 12 (September, December 1890): 107–115.

Pierce, Frederick E. "The Tenement House Committee Maps." *Harper's Weekly* 39, no. 1987 (January 19, 1895): 60–62.

"Questions Darwinian Theory." *Sun,* September 24, 1921, 2.

"Race War Seen in Class Clash." *Sun,* September 28, 1921, 8.

Rand McNally and Company. *Rand McNally Guide to New York City and Environs.* New York: Rand McNally and Company, 1922.

Richardson, Gardner. "Great Towers of New York." *Independent* 65 (August 6, 1908): 301–305.

Rider, Fremont. *Rider's Guide to New York City.* New York: Henry Holt and Company, 1923.

Riis, Jacob. *How the Other Half Lives: Studies among the Tenements of New York.* New York: Charles Scribner's Sons, 1890.

———. *The Making of An American.* New York: Grosset and Dunlap, 1901.

Ripley, C. M. "Singer Building, New York, Forty-Seven Stories High." *World's Work* 14 (October 1907): 9459–9461.

Ripley, W. Z. "Notes on Map Making and Graphic Representation." *Publications of the American Statistical Association* 6, no. 47 (September 1899): 313–327.

————. *The Races of Europe: A Sociological Study.* New York: D. Appleton, 1899.

Roberts, Kenneth L. "East is East." *Saturday Evening Post* 196 (February 23, 1924): 6–7.

Rose, William Ganson. *Putting Marshville on the Map.* New York: Duffield and Company, 1912.

Roulston, Marjorie Hillis. *New York, Fair or No Fair: A Guide for the Woman Vacationist.* Indianapolis: The Bobbs-Merrill Company, 1939.

Routzahn, Evart G., and Mary Swain Routzahn. *The ABC of Exhibit Planning.* New York: Russell Sage Foundation, 1918.

"Sees American Man as Superior of Woman." *New York Times,* September 28, 1921, 11.

Select New York. New York: A. Wittemann, 1889.

Shackleton, Robert and Elizabeth Shackleton. "Vanishing New York." *Century* 100 (June 1920): 150–164.

Shaw, Charles G. *Nightlife.* New York: The John Day Company, 1931.

Showalter, William Joseph. "New York: The Metropolis of Mankind." *National Geographic* 34 (July 1918): 1–49.

Singer, Caroline. "An Italian Saturday." *Century* 101 (March 1921): 590–600.

Singer Manufacturing Company. *Singer Souvenirs of New York City.* New York: Singer Manufacturing Company, 1905.

Skinner, R. D. "Drama, Tabloid and Otherwise." *Independent* 118 (April 23, 1927): 445.

Slocum, Rosalie, and Ann Todd. *A Key to New York.* New York: Modern Age Books, 1939.

Small, Albion W. "Methods of Studying Society." *Chautauquan* 21 (April–September 1895): 52–56.

Spearman, Edmund R. "French Police Photography." *Nature* 42, no. 1096 (October 30, 1890): 642–644.

Stoddard, Lothrop. "Is America American?" *World's Work* 41 (December 1920): 201–203.

————. *The Rising Tide of Color against White World-Supremacy.* New York: Charles Scribner's Sons, 1920.

Street, Julian. "Abroad At Home: Chapter One—Stepping Westward." *Collier's* 53, no. 10 (May 23, 1914): 5–7.

"Street Widenings an Important Factor, but Afford Feeble Traffic Relief." *American City* 38 (January 1928): 92.

Sullivan, Mark. "Why the West Dislikes New York: The Eternal Conflict between City and Country." *World's Work* 51 (February 1926): 406–411.

The Sun's Guide to New York. New York: R. Wayne Wilson and Company, 1892.

Sutton, George W. "Rolling Vacations." *Colliers* 68 (August 6, 1921): 13.

"Tenement-House Calamity." *Harper's Weekly* 25, no. 1300 (November 19, 1881): 775.

"Tenement House Problem." *Harper's Weekly* 39, no. 1986 (January 12, 1895): 423.

"Tercentenary Educational Celebration." *School and Society* 19 (April 12, 1924): 27–28.

Thomson, T. K. "Caisson Foundations in Skyscrapers." *Scientific American* 65 (March 7, 1908): 152–154.

"Tracing Parentage by Eugenic Tests." *New York Times,* September 23, 1921, 8.

Van der Water, F. F. "Obscene Drama." *Ladies' Home Journal* 44 (April 1927): 8.

Van der Weyde, H. "The Pictorial Modification of Photographic Perspective." *Journal of the Society of Arts* 41, no. 2110 (April 28, 1893): 591–596.

Van Dyke, John C. *The New New York.* New York: Macmillan, 1909.

Veiller, Lawrence. "The Tenement-House Exhibition of 1899." *Charities Review* 10, no. 1 (March 1900): 19–27.

A Visitor's Guide to the City of New York. Brooklyn, NY: Brooklyn Daily Eagle, 1899.

Wade, Herbert T. "Tall Buildings and Their Problems." *American Review of Reviews* 38 (November 1908): 577–586.

Walsh, George Ethelbert. "Modern Towers of Babel in New York." *Harper's Weekly* 51 (January 12, 1907): 68–69.

"Want More Babies in Best Families." *New York Times,* September 25, 1921, 16

"Warns of Race Decline." *World,* September 25, 1921, 9.

"Wash Day in the Tenements." *Harper's Weekly* 33, no. 1722 (December 21, 1889): 1014.

Whalen, Grover. *Mr. New York: The Autobiography of Grover Whalen.* New York: G. P. Putnam's Sons, 1955.

"What the West Means to the Nation." *Craftsman* 22 (August 1912): 569–571.

"Where is the World Metropolis?" *Review of Reviews* 60 (September 1919): 317–318.

Whitney, Myron J. "Fording the Atlantic Coast." *Outing* 75 (January–February 1921): 231–234, 282–285.

"Who Are the 'Fittest'?" *Sun,* September 28, 1921, 14.

"Why a Cartoonist Would Rather Live in Des Moines Than in New York." *Literary Digest* 62, no. 2 (July 12, 1919): 86–90.

"Why Hate New York?" *Outlook* 142 (March 17, 1926): 404.

Williamson, Jefferson. *The American Hotel.* New York: Knopf, 1930.

Wilson, L. J. "Mapping New York City from the Air." *Illustrated World* 36 (February 1922): 839–840.

Winkler, Franz K. "Architecture in the Billionaire District of New York City." *Architectural Record* 11, no. 2 (October 1901): 679–699.

Wister, Owen. "Shall We Let the Cuckoos Crowd Us out of Our Nest?" *American Magazine* 91 (March 3, 1921): 47.

Wittemann, A. *East River Bridge.* New York: Wittemann Brothers, c. 1884.

———. *New-York.* New York: Wittemann Brothers, n.d.

Worden, Helen. *Discover New York with Helen Worden.* New York: American Women's Voluntary Services, 1943.

———. *Here Is New York.* New York: Doubleday, Doran and Company, 1939.

———. *The Real New York; A Guide for the Adventurous Shopper, the Exploratory Eater and the Know-It-All Sightseer Who Ain't Seen Nothin' Yet.* Indianapolis: The Bobbs-Merrill Company, 1932.

———. *Round Manhattan's Rim.* Indianapolis: The Bobbs-Merrill Company, 1934.

Wright, Mabel Osgood. *My New York.* New York: The Macmillan Company, 1926.

INDEX

Italic page numbers indicate illustrations.

DATE			